The Roman Army, 31 BC–AD 337

The Roman imperial army was unrivalled until recent times in its professional structure, efficient training, detailed organization, and ordnance support. It was remarkable in an age of poor communications and limited technological advance. The army sustained a great empire militarily and politically. First, its skill and success ensured Rome's domination, and second the loyalty of the troops ensured the political survival of the emperors, who sought to preserve the fabric of government and make it work. The army was therefore a vital element in the subsequent development of Western Civilization.

The large number of soldiers and their associated dependants meant that they had significant impact socially, economically, and culturally on the settlements that grew up round the camps and on some of the communitites where they settled after discharge. The privileges of the soldiers set them apart from other men of their social class, and the enhanced position of veterans established them as a very important group in their own right, an integral part of the whole phenomenon of Roman 'government'. The study of the Roman army therefore embraces not only military but also political, social and economic history.

This source book collects literary and epigraphic material, and papyri and coins which illustrate the varied aspects of army life both at war and at peace, and it takes account of evidence made available by recent archaeological investigations in many parts of the empire. Subjects covered include training, officers, the role of the emperor, fighting, community life, politics, and veterans. The introductions to each section and the linking passages provide a narrative structure and explain difficulties of the source material.

This book will appeal to a wide audience: students of the army and the Roman empire, and all those interested in the ancient world and military studies.

Brian Campbell is Lecturer in Ancient History at the Queen's University of Belfast. He is the author of *The Emperor and the Roman Army, 31 BC–AD 235* (1984).

The Roman Army, 31 BC–AD 337

A Sourcebook

Brian Campbell

London and New York

First published 1994
by Routledge
2 Park Square, Milton Park, Abingdon, Oxon, OX14 4RN

Simultaneously published in the USA and Canada
by Routledge
270 Madison Ave, New York NY 10016

Reprinted 1996, 2000

Transferred to Digital Printing 2005

Routledge is an imprint of the Taylor & Francis Group

Typeset in 10/12pt Times by
Ponting-Green Publishing Services, Chesham, Bucks

British Library Cataloguing in Publication Data
A catalogue record for this book is available from the British Library

Library of Congress Cataloguing in Publication Data
Campbell, J. B.
  The Roman Army, 31 BC-AD 337: A sourcebook /
  Brian Campbell
    p. cm.
  Includes bibliographical references and index.
  1. Roman –Army   I. Title.
  U35.C35   1994
  335´00937–dc20   93–9032

ISBN 0–415–07172–0 (hbk)   0–415–07173–9 (pbk)

For Karen

Contents

Plates

Figures and tables

FIGURES

TABLE

Preface and acknowledgements

The Roman army inspires wide interest, yet the sources are multifarious and often difficult of access, especially for those with no Greek or Latin. In choosing material for this collection I have tried to illustrate not only military organization and practice but also something of the role of the soldiers in the social, political, and economic life of the empire. I have confined my attention to the imperial period since only then can we speak of 'the' Roman army; before, there were transient legions and then the various armies of military dynasts. Nevertheless, since the army of Augustus and his successors owed so much to the military practices of the Republic, I have included a brief introductory survey of the army before 31 BC. The changes made in the army by Diocletian and Constantine are a convenient stopping point, although there is a large body of evidence for post-Constantinian military developments.

In presenting material I have used introductions and short commentaries to establish a narrative framework, primarily in cases where the sources are difficult or inadequate. In citing literary sources, I have given once in each section the dates of the author's activity. In the case of inscriptions and papyri, I have included the find spot, the modern place-name where appropriate, the Roman province, and a precise date if possible, or an indication of the century, where this is pretty certainly known from internal evidence. In citing collections of inscriptions and papyri I have used the most accessible rather than the most recent, unless there are important new interpretations, and have sometimes included an alternative collection in addition to a basic work. As far as possible, papyri have been set out as the original editor transcribed the documents.

John Curran, Raymond Davis, and Lawrence Keppie read parts of the text and made many useful suggestions; Walter Cockle patiently kept me informed about material from the Mons Claudianus excavations;

Margaret Roxan and Valerie Maxfield generously supplied photographs for some of the illustrations. I should like to thank all these scholars and exculpate them from responsibility for the author's decisions and errors. I also thank my editor Richard Stoneman for so readily accepting this venture and for his subsequent guidance.

Acknowledgements

Acknowledgements for plates (apart from those contributed by Richard Stoneman):

Plate 1, Ch. Koukouli-Chrysanthuki, Kavalla Museum.
Plates 3 and 4, Lepper and Frere 1988, by courtesy of Mr. F. Lepper.
Plate 5, 6 and 12, The British Museum.
Plates 13–18, Dr. M. Roxan.

Acknowledgements for figures:

Figure 1, *Tacitus: Agricola*, edited by R.M. Ogilvie and Sir Ian Richmond (Oxford, 1967), p. 72, figure 9, by permission of Oxford Univeristy Press.

Figure 2, *The Making of the Roman Army: From Republic to Empire*, Lawrence Keppie (London, 1984), p. 183, figure 48, by permission of B. T. Batsford Ltd.

Figure 5, *Rapidum: Le camp de la cohort des Sardes en Maurétanie Césarienne*, J.-P Laporte (Università degli Studi di Sassari, 1989), p. 26, figure 4, by permission of the author.

Abbreviations

AE	*L'Année épigraphique* (Paris, 1893–).
AJ	F. F. Abbott and A. C. Johnson, *Municipal Administration in the Roman Empire* (Princeton, 1926; reprint, New York, 1968).
ANRW	H. Temporini *et al.* (eds), *Aufstieg und Niedergang der römischen Welt* (Berlin, 1972–).
BGU	*Berliner griechische Urkunden (Ägyptische Urkunden aus den königlichen Museen zu Berlin* (Berlin, 1895–)).
BJ	*Bonner Jahrbücher des Rheinisches Landesmuseum*, Bonn.
BMC	H. Mattingly (ed.), *Coins of the Roman Empire in the British Museum* (vol. 1, 1923; vol. 3, 1966).
CIL	Th. Mommsen *et al.* (eds), *Corpus Inscriptionum Latinarum* (Berlin, 1863–).
CJ	P. Krueger (ed.), *Codex Iustinianus; Corpus Iuris Civilis* vol. II (Berlin, 1877).
Cohen	H. Cohen (ed.), *Description historique des monnaies frappées sous L'Empire romaine* (Paris, 2nd edn., 1880–92).
CPL	R. Cavenaile (ed.), *Corpus Papyrorum Latinarum* (Wiesbaden, 1958).
CTh	Th. Mommsen (ed.), *Codex Theodosianus* (Berlin, 1905).
D	Th. Mommsen (ed.), *Digesta; Corpus Iuris Civilis* vol. I (Berlin, 1872).
Daris, *Documenti*	S. Daris (ed.), *Documenti per la storia dell'esercito romano in Egitto* (Milan, 1964).
Diz. epig.	E. De Ruggiero (ed.), *Dizionario epigrafico di antichità romane* (Rome, 1895–).
EJ	V. Ehrenberg and A. H. M. Jones, *Documents*

	illustrating the Reigns of Augustus and Tiberius, ed. by D. L. Stockton (Oxford, 1976).
Fink *RMR*	R. O. Fink, *Roman Military Records on Papyrus* (Case Western Reserve University, 1971).
FIRA	S. Riccobono *et al.* (eds), *Fontes iuris Romani anteiustiniani* (2nd edn, 3 vols, Florence, 1940–3).
IGR	R. Cagnat *et al.* (eds), *Inscriptiones Graecae ad res Romanas pertinentes* (Paris, 1906–27).
ILA	S. Gsell *et al.* (eds), *Inscriptions Latines de l'Algérie* (Alger, 1922–76).
ILS	H. Dessau (ed.), *Inscriptiones Latinae Selectae* (Berlin, 1892–1916).
IRT	J.M. Reynolds and J.B. Ward Perkins (eds), *The Inscriptions of Roman Tripolitania* (British School at Rome, 1952).
JRS	*Journal of Roman Studies*
MW	M. McCrum and A. G. Woodhead (eds), *Select Documents of the Principates of the Flavian Emperors including the Year of Revolution, A.D. 68–96* (Cambridge, 1961).
OGIS	W. Dittenberger (ed.), *Orientis Graeci Inscriptiones Selectae* (1903–5).
P.Amh.	B. P. Grenfell and A.S. Hunt, *The Amherst Papyri* (2 vols London, 1900–1901).
P. Fayum	B. P. Grenfell, A. S. Hunt, D. G. Hogarth, *Fayum Towns and their Papyri* (London, 1900).
Pflaum, *Carrières*	H.-G. Pflaum, *Les Carrières procuratoriennes équestres sous le haut-empire romain* (4 vols., Paris 1960–1; *Supplément*, Paris, 1982).
P. Hamb.	P. M. Meyer (ed.), *Griechische Papyrusurkunden der Hamburger Staats und Universitäts-bibliothek* (Leipzig-Berlin 1911–24).
P. Lond.	F. G. Kenyon and H. I. Bell (eds), *Greek Papyri in the British Museum* (London, 1893–1917).
P. Mich.	*Papyri in the University of Michigan Collection*, vol. III (J. G. Winter (ed.), 1936); vol. VIII (H. C. Youtie and J. G. Winter (eds), 1951).
P. Oxy.	B. P. Grenfell, A. S. Hunt *et al.* (eds), *The Oxyrhynchus Papyri* (London, 1898–).
P. Ryl.	M. Johnson, V. Martin, A. S. Hunt, C. H. Roberts, E. G. Turner (eds), *Catalogue of the Greek Papyri in the*

	John Rylands Library at Manchester (Manchester, 1911–52).
P. S. I.	*Pubblicazioni della società italiana per la ricerca dei papiri greci e latini in Egitto: Papiri greci e latini* (1912–57).
RIB	R. G. Collingwood and R. P. Wright (eds), *The Roman Inscriptions of Britain*, I *Inscriptions on Stone* (Oxford, 1965).
SB	F. Preisigke, F. Bilabel, E. Kiessling, (eds), *Sammelbuch griechischer Urkunden aus Ägypten* (Strassburg, Heidelberg, Wiesbaden, 1915–).
SCI	*Scripta Classica Israelica*
SEG	J. J. E. Hondius *et al.* (eds), *Supplementum Epigraphicum Graecum* (1923–).
Smallwood, GN	E. M. Smallwood (ed.), *Documents illustrating the Principates of Gaius Claudius and Nero* (Cambridge, 1967).
Smallwood, NH	E. M. Smallwood (ed.), *Documents illustrating the Principates of Nerva Trajan and Hadrian* (Cambridge, 1966).
SP	A. S. Hunt and C. C. Edgar (eds), *Select Papyri: Non-Literary Papyri* (2 vols., Cambridge, Mass., 1932–4).
ZPE	*Zeitschrift für Papyrologie und Epigraphik.*

NOTES

Passages from collections of documents are cited by number.

[ ] enclose letters or words that no longer exist in the surviving text, but have been restored by modern scholars.

[_ _ _] indicate a lacuna where no restoration has been attempted but where the approximate number of letters or words can be estimated.

{ } are used to surround passages where an alternative interpretation exists.

= indicates an alternative collection/source.

. . . indicate passages omitted by this editor.

( ) indicate explanatory supplements by this editor.

Emperors from Augustus to Constantine

The names by which emperors are commonly known are italicized.

27 BC–AD 14   Imperator Caesar *Augustus*
AD 14–37   *Tiberius* Caesar Augustus (thereafter 'Augustus' used to designate emperors)
37–41   *Gaius* Caesar Germanicus (*Caligula*)
41–54   Tiberius *Claudius* Caesar Germanicus
54–68   *Nero* Claudius Caesar Germanicus
68–69   Ser. Sulpicius *Galba* Caesar
69   M. Salvius *Otho* Caesar
69   A. *Vitellius* Germanicus
69–79   (T. Flavius) Imperator Caesar *Vespasian* (thereafter 'Imperator Caesar' became usual prefix to imperial names and titles)
79–81   *Titus* (Flavius) Vespasian
81–96   (T. Flavius) *Domitian*
96–98   (M. Cocceius) *Nerva*
98–117   (M. Ulpius) Nerva *Trajan*
117–38   (P. Aelius) Trajan *Hadrian*
138–61   (T. Aelius Hadrian Aurelius Fulvus Boionius Arrius) *Antoninus Pius*
161–9   *Marcus Aurelius* Antoninus and *Lucius* Aurelius *Verus*
169–76   *Marcus Aurelius* Antoninus
176–80   *Marcus Aurelius* Antoninus and (L.) Aurelius *Commodus*
180–92   (L.) Aurelius *Commodus*
193   P. Helvius *Pertinax*
  M. *Didius* Severus *Julianus*
193–8   L. *Septimius Severus* Pertinax
198–208   L. *Septimius Severus* and M. Aurelius Antoninus (*Caracalla*)

208–11	L. *Septimius Severus*, M. Aurelius Antoninus (*Caracalla*), and P. Septimius *Geta*
211–12	M. Aurelius Antoninus (*Caracalla*) and P. Septimius *Geta*
212–17	M. Aurelius Antoninus (*Caracalla*)
217–18	M. Opellius *Macrinus*
218	M. Opellius *Macrinus* and M. Opellius Antoninus *Diadumenianus*
218–22	M. Aurelius Antoninus (*Elagabalus*)
222–35	M. Aurelius *Severus Alexander*
235–8	D. Julius Verus *Maximinus*
238	D. Caelius Calvinus *Balbinus* and M. Clodius *Pupienus*
238–44	M. Antonius Gordianus (*Gordian III*)
244–8	M. Julius Philippus (*Philip*)
248–9	M. Julius Philippus and his similarly named son
249–51	C. Messius Quintus *Trajan Decius*
251–3	C. Vibius *Trebonianus Gallus* and C. Vibius Afinius Gallus Veldumnianus *Volusian*
253	M. Aemilius *Aemilian*
253–60	P. Licinius *Valerian* and P. Licinius *Gallienus*
260–8	P. Licinius *Gallienus*
268–70	M. Aurelius *Claudius* (*II, Gothicus*)
270	M. Aurelius *Claudius Quintillus*
270–5	L. Domitius *Aurelian*
275–6	M. Claudius *Tacitus*
276	M. Annius *Florian*
276–82	M. Aurelius *Probus*
282–3	M. Aurelius *Carus*
283–5	M. Aurelius *Carinus*
283–4	M. Aurelius Numerius *Numerianus*
284–305	C. Aurelius Valerius *Diocletian*
286–305	M. Aurelius Valerius *Maximian*
305–306	Flavius Valerius *Constantius*
305–11	C. *Galerius* Valerius Maximianus
306–7	Flavius Valerius *Severus*
306–12	M. Aurelius Valerius *Maxentius*
307–37	Flavius Valerius *Constantine*
308–24	Valerius Licinianus *Licinius*
308/9–313	C. Valerius Galerius *Maximin*

Weights, measures, and money

GREEK

Money

Attic talent	= 60 *minae* (26.196 kg = 57.8 lb)
mina	= 100 *drachmae* (436.6 gr = 15.5 oz)
stater	= 2 *drachmae*
drachma	= 6 obols
obol	= 12 *chalcia*
Egyptian drachma	= ¼ Attic drachma
1 Attic drachma	= 1 Roman denarius

Weights and measures

artabe (Persian)	= *c*.1 *medimnos* (*c*. 52 litres; dry measure equivalent to Roman *medimnus*)
pechus (cubit)	= 1½ *podes* (44.4 cm = 17.48 inches)
pous (foot)	= 16 *daktuloi* (29.6 cm = 11.6 inches)
daktulos (finger breadth)	= 18.5mm = 0.728 inches
aroura (used in Egypt)	= *c*. 1 Roman *iugerum*

ROMAN

Money

libra (pound)	= 12 *unciae* (*c*. 327.5 gr = 11.5 oz)
aureus (gold piece)	= 25 *denarii*

denarius ('ten *as*-piece') = 4 sesterces
sestertius (HS) = 4 *asses* (originally 2½ *asses*)

Weights and measures

modius = ⅙ *medimnus*
(*c.* 8.6 litres = 15.17 pints)
pes (foot) = 29.57 cm (11.6 inches)
mille passus (mile) = *c.* 1500 m (1,618 yards)
iugerum = 28,800 sq Roman ft (0.252 ha)

Introduction

The sources

There is no history of the Roman imperial army by any ancient author and little detailed examination of military practices. It is indeed curious that one of the best descriptions of the army in war and peace was written by Josephus, a Jewish leader of the revolt against Rome in AD 66. Roman writers were in the main men of property and settled respectability who feared the army as a threat to public order and private wealth and looked down upon the ordinary soldier, who generally came from the lower classes. So the traditional respect accorded in Roman society to proficiency in the military arts was concentrated on the person of emperors and senatorial commanders, to the neglect of the working of the army itself. Consequently evidence from our literary sources is deficient in scope and chronological span, emphasizing the conduct of the army in civil wars and individual battles. But here too ancient writers often fail to provide a reliable account of army life, or the development of military tactics, or the capabilities of Rome's enemies. They may have found these topics too dull or difficult, and a wish to provide an exciting story has in many cases overlaid the real features of a battle. A problem often associated with sourcebooks is that extracts from literary sources illustrate an isolated opinion without establishing the context of the work. But in the history of the army this accurately reflects the often brief and allusive nature of the comments of ancient authors. I have tried to explain difficulties where appropriate in the text.

Roman army studies are well served by inscriptions, which illuminate the careers of officers, soldiers, and veterans, the location and movements of army units, recruiting and settlement patterns, the role of the legions in road and bridge building, and life in military communities. In particular, bronze tablets (diplomata) listing soldiers' benefits are still being found, with invaluable and often precisely dated evidence about discharge procedure, the identification and location of auxiliary units, and their commanders. Inscriptions are also useful in that many are repetitive, and by their cumulative effect confirm aspects of army life. In a sense it is the routine not the dramatic that we need to hear about. The number of inscriptions available varies greatly, however, according to area and period, and this type of evidence often has limited relevance in that inscriptions may, for example, suggest the importance of centurions in the army but tell us little about their system of promotion or their duties. They can show what military posts a man held, but rarely the qualities he displayed in the execution of his duties or the reasons for his appointment or what was exceptional in his career.

Papyri provide uniquely detailed evidence of the life and administration of army units in Syria and Egypt; the discovery of the Vindolanda tablets in Britain suggests that much of the bureaucratic procedure was typical wherever the army was stationed. Duty rosters, personnel lists, and accounts offer a valuable if limited and rather repetitious view of military bureaucracy, while other papyri illustrate the relationship between individuals, local communities, and the army.

Archaeology (including aerial photography) is playing an increasing role in the history of the Roman army's presence in frontier zones, illustrating the location, layout, and construction of forts, the disposition of troops, the development of legionary bases, the course of military campaigns, military equipment, medical provision, hospitals, and even the soldiers' diet. This type of evidence cannot be properly expounded in a sourcebook though I have tried to draw attention to relevant works of reference. However, the significance of certain archaeological discoveries has sometimes been pressed too far. The evidence is uneven, since some areas have been particularly conducive to the survival of ancient sites, and some have been more systematically investigated than others. Indeed the layout of a fort cannot in the absence of other evidence tell us its original purpose or how conceptions of that purpose changed even though the structure remained unaltered. So, the existence of a large fort does not prove that an entire unit was permanently stationed there, since it is possible that only part of it was present, in a structure built to a larger scale in the expectation that it might be needed at some stage. Similarly, the precise function of smaller installations is often difficult to establish.

Coins played an important part in ancient society and those issued by the imperial authorities certainly expressed ideas acceptable to the emperor and his advisers. The army, however, was rarely celebrated on the coinage except in ceremonial aspects of military victories and imperial speeches to the troops, since emperors sought to conceal their political dependence on the military. Coins bearing the legend 'concord of the armies' provide double-edged evidence, perhaps declaring the reality of political loyalty among the soldiers, or hoping to instill it. Some issues, like those of Hadrian celebrating the army stationed in its provincial billets, or of Septimius Severus in honour of the legions that supported his bid for power in AD 193, give a tantalizing glimpse of the importance attached by emperors to influencing the army by pictures and slogans. The evaluation of this kind of evidence is notoriously difficult not least because so little is known of the process from initial decision to the end product of a coin. How far did coin types and legends take into account the views and prejudices of soldiers, who probably received in pay and donatives a substantial proportion of coins issued? In what ways were emperors personally involved in deciding how to influence public opinion through coin types? How successful were they? How was the presentation of ideas afffected by the degree of artistic licence to be expected in ceremonial or memorial art?

Students of the Roman army face two main problems. First, although there is a large amount of evidence, it forms a mosaic made from pieces covering a span of more than three centuries. It is therefore difficult to trace developments in the army of the imperial period, and we may indeed underestimate the degree of change precisely because of the uneven nature of the sources and the lack of a firm chronological context. Second, we remain strikingly ill-informed in certain key areas, for example, the size of a legion and its detailed organization, promotion procedures for centurions and junior officers, the appointment of senior commanders, strategy and battle tactics. We would like to know how often legions and other units were up to full strength and had the approved number of artillery pieces, and to what extent Trajan's column, which shows the army at its very best like a recruiting poster of a modern army, differs from reality. In fact the wealth of evidence available is often not of the right kind to answer some of the most important questions. We need the reminiscences of a centurion, the personal diaries of a commander, and memoranda of meetings between an emperor and his advisers discussing a military crisis and planning the logistics of a campaign.

The Army of the Republic

According to tradition, king Servius Tullius (*c.* 580–30 BC) divided the citizen body into classes on the basis of wealth, an action which had military as well as political significance in that a man's wealth determined the standard of weaponry he could provide for himself; in reality, this is more likely to have been a gradual development. The richest group, the *equites*, were divided into eighteen centuries and served as cavalry; then came five classes of ordinary citizens, equipped as their resources permitted, who served as infantry. Below these classes was another group, the *capite censi* (literally 'registered by a head count'), who had no property, could afford no weapons, and were excluded from military service. From the early period then, military service was an obligation and duty upon Roman citizens, but also a kind of privilege. The soldiers recruited in this way, probably numbering about 4,000, will have fought in a legion as heavy infantry in the style of the Greek phalanx; 600 cavalry made up the fighting strength.

This was the army of the early republic after the expulsion of the kings towards the end of the sixth century BC, and in sporadic fighting Rome won control of Latium and captured its rival, Veii, in 396 BC. Soon after, however, the invading Gauls defeated all opposition and almost captured Rome in 387 BC. Perhaps as a result of these setbacks, the inflexible phalanx formation was modified by the creation of smaller tactical units (maniples) which could be drawn up and manoeuvred independently. There were also changes in equipment; the legionaries now adopted an oval shield and some were armed with a throwing spear (*pilum*) instead of the usual thrusting spear (*hasta*). By 311 BC Rome controlled much of Italy and normally had a military force of four legions commanded by the two consuls, supported by troops supplied by allied or subject Italian communities, serving under their own commanders. Specialist military units, like archers, were recruited from foreign mercenaries. This army was the basis of the Romans' conquest of the Mediterranean world against the Hellenistic kings who were still using the old phalanx method of fighting.

The first two Punic wars (264–241 and 218–201 BC) and their aftermath brought important developments in the Roman military establishment. There was a tremendous strain on manpower as losses had to be replenished, since at Cannae alone over 50,000 Romans and their allies were killed, and new legions had to be raised to counter the Carthaginian threat. By 201 BC sixteen legions were in service. So, men were required to serve for longer, and the number of potential recruits was increased by a reduction in the property qualification, which seems to be associated with the creation of a group of lightly-armed soldiers (*velites*) who could not afford body armour. The Greek writer Polybius, who himself had served as a cavalry commander in his native country, gives us one of the best descriptions of the army of the Republic, and it is likely that he is referring to the army in the period after the war with Hannibal. Each year men were selected from those of military age (17–46), and were required to spend up to six years in service (i.e. fighting when needed on campaign), and to be available for up to sixteen years; the maximum length of service for a cavalryman was ten years. Although compulsion was an important part of this procedure, there will always have been some volunteers. As before, all troops received an allowance to offset the cost of sustenance and equipment. Each legion contained between 4,200 and 5,000 men, with the support of 300 cavalry, and in battle the manipular formation was still in use; the *velites* served as a protective screen of light assault troops, who could then retreat through three ranks of legionaries behind them. The *hastati* and *principes* carried an oval shield, two throwing-spears of different weights, and the two-edged Spanish sword; the most experienced soldiers, the *triarii*, formed the third rank armed with thrusting-spears. All the legionaries were equipped with helmet, bronze corslet, and greaves. Each of the three battle lines contained ten maniples of 120 men, or sixty in the case of the *triarii*, drawn up with gaps between them, though these may have been closed before the moment of impact. The first two ranks threw their javelins, then tried to settle the battle with their swords at close range. If they were repulsed the third rank remained as a last defence and a source of counterattack. Cavalry and other troops from Rome's Italian allies were placed on the wings. The manipular arrangement ensured that the legion could be regrouped as the conditions of the battle required and may have made commanders more aware of the potential of the deployment of reserves, a factor that required the commander-in-chief to stay out of the battle in a position from which he could see the whole field. Armies were still commanded by the chief magistrates, the consuls, or occasionally by praetors. Sometimes, however, the power a man possessed while in his magistracy was extended so that he could take on a further command as proconsul or propraetor. This was in part an intelligent response to the problem of annual magistrates as generals. The commander was assisted by six senior officers, the military tribunes, who were mainly of equestrian rank, though some were the sons of senators, and all were supposed to have served for at least five years in the army. It seems that pairs of tribunes in rotation were responsible for individual legions. In the early second century BC, the post of *legatus*, generally held by an experienced senator appointed by the senate on the recommendation of the commander, came to have greater significance, and these officers could be given responsibility for a body of troops in a semi-independent command.

The defeat of Carthage was of crucial importance in the consolidation of Rome's control in Italy and the advance of her armed might in the Mediterranean. Thereafter there was no power who could seriously threaten Rome's domination. One consequence of this was the acquisition of more provinces with attendant military responsibilities and the need to keep legions in service for a long time. Although the army was well trained and disciplined, with a determined, semi-professional approach which can be seen in the routine for building camps, military organization had not kept pace with imperial expansion, and dissension arose over the levy since men of military experience were valued and tended to be called up repeatedly or kept in service longer, to the detriment of their business or farming interests. Consequently there was a decline in the property qualification required for military service. In the midst of another lengthy war against the African prince Jugurtha, Gaius Marius rose to prominence partly by exploiting popular discontent at the incompetent conduct of some commanders. Marius having been elected consul and given the command in Africa (107 BC), immediately called for volunteers, enlisting men who lacked the property qualification, whom he arranged to have equipped at the state's expense. This was an evolutionary not revolutionary move, but Marius' success in Africa and subsequently against the German tribes invading Italy, strengthened his influence and set the Roman army on a new course of development that confirmed it as the dominant military force in the Mediterranean. Since conscription was still employed when necessary, the old recruiting system was not abolished, but more men now preferred to serve for longer, probably for sixteen years, and the essential basis was created for a long-service army with a more professional and single-minded attitude. It may have been at this time that the eagle was adopted as the symbol of each legion, signifying its permanent existence.

Marius is usually credited with the tactical innovation which replaced the maniple with the cohort. A legion now consisted of ten cohorts, subdivided into six centuries of eighty men commanded by a centurion. The first cohort may have been larger, and including legionary cavalry, a legion will have contained over 5,000 men. It is possible that this change was not directly the work of Marius and that the two formations existed simultaneously for a time. The cohort, however, offered greater strength and cohesion than the maniple, while retaining much of its flexibility, and soon became the basic fighting formation of the Roman army. All legionaries were now equipped with the *pilum* and two-edged sword, and the design of the former was altered by Marius so that a wooden pin replaced the two iron bolts attaching the iron tip to the wooden shaft. The *pilum* would now bend more easily on impact and make it impossible for the enemy to utilize in turn.

From 91 to 87 BC Rome fought her former Italian allies in the Social War and although victorious conceded Roman citizenship to most of them, which made available a large number of potential recruits. By the end of the Republic almost a quarter of a million Italians were under arms. However, one of the unforeseen consequences of Marius' changes was that the army became much more of a political instrument. Men who served for a long time virtually as professional soldiers expected a substantial reward in money or land on their retirement, but since the state did not assume responsibility for this, individual commanders tended to seek benefits for their men, whose political support they could therefore subsequently expect. Moreover, men recruited by a military commander or his agents often formed a bond of affection and loyalty with their leader rather than the senate or Roman state, especially since certain generals held protracted or repeated commands and must have seemed like a permanent fixture to their troops. And since the Roman ideal of office-holding made no clear distinction between civil and military functions, any political leader was potentially an army commander. After Sulla had used his army to march on Rome in 88 BC and seize power for himself, political life increasingly centred on a quest for important commands, which then could be used to extort further political advancement from the senate. In this era of military dynasts, constitutional politics took second place to contests between ambitious generals who, while not spurning popular support, estimated their political strength by the size of their personally loyal mercenary armies which provided access to wealth and power. During his ten-year proconsulship of Gaul, Caesar increased his army from four to twelve legions and in 49 BC doubled his men's pay in preparation for war against Pompey and the senate, which led to his dictatorship. After Caesar's murder in 44 BC, the empire was split in a struggle between warring factions which ended only in 31 BC when Octavian (or Augustus, as he was to be called from 27 BC) defeated Marcus Antonius, his last rival for supreme power. Although by this time Rome controlled most of the lands round the Mediterranean, in many cases there had been no complete pacification and a large-scale, permanent military presence was required. Furthermore, Augustus could not dismantle the army which had been the source of his political triumph. So, the force he reorganized to suit his own purposes was substantially the army of the Republic – the body of Roman citizens fighting in legions as heavy infantry, supported by auxiliary troops who supplied cavalry and other specialist requirements. Augustus' achievement was to fit the army smoothly into his political domination and the senatorial tradition of army command, in a way that ensured a remarkably stable system that was to be the basis of Roman power for over three hundred years.

1 The soldiers

RECRUITMENT

From 49 to 32 BC about 420,000 Italians were recruited, and this could not have been achieved without widespread conscription, which was generally unpopular. Augustus desired to bring peace and stability, but it seems that there were not enough volunteers to meet the manpower requirements of his standing army (probably about 5–6,000 men were needed every year to keep the legions up to strength), and he was unable to dispense with conscription. However he limited its incidence in Italy, though here too special levies were held in times of military crisis, as in AD 6 and 9. So, the number of Italians enlisting declined steadily and by Hadrian's reign they formed a negligible proportion of the legions, presumably because they did not wish to enter a period of lengthy service far from their homes. Legionaries were recruited from provincial Roman citizens, or men to whom citizenship was given on enlistment. In the first century AD many recruits in the west came from Spain, Narbonensis, and Noricum, and in the east from the Greek cities of Asia and Macedonia. But a disinclination to serve away from home must also have influenced provincials, and references to the levy (*dilectus*) held in the provinces in the first and second centuries AD, which show that it was often accompanied by oppression, suggest that it must have involved conscription. Now, the government presumably preferred willing soldiers, who might be expected to fight enthusiastically in defence of their homeland and families, and this was probably a factor in the gradual movement towards local recruitment, which came to predominate after Hadrian. There will also have been fewer administrative problems in the transport and assignment of recruits. The likelihood that a soldier had a reasonable chance of serving near his home will have made military life more acceptable and may have encouraged the flow of volunteers. It is precisely in the late second and early third century, when a military career seemed most attractive, that the evidence suggests a predominance of volunteers. These considerations will also have applied to the recruitment of *auxilia*. However, Italians continued to enlist in the praetorian guard, which remained attractive with its superior service conditions and usual location in Rome, and newly-created legions tended to be recruited in Italy.

Special officers were appointed to collect recruits in certain areas, while elsewhere commanding officers were normally responsible for recruiting men to the units under their charge. In the absence of sufficient volunteers, Roman officials would have to rely on the local authorities of the cities to produce men from the territory under their jurisdiction. An examination (*probatio* or *inquisitio*) was held to ensure that recruits were physically fit and legally eligible to serve. There is no clear evidence that recruits were expected to have a letter of recommendation on enlistment (Forni 1953; 1974; Gilliam 1957a; Mann 1963; Davies 1969a; Brunt 1971: 509–12; 1974a).

1 *CPL* 102, papyrus, Fayum, Egypt, AD 92

Titus Flavius Longus, orderly (*optio*) of Legion III Cyrenaica, in the century of Arellius (?), made a declaration [and gave as guarantors _ _ _] Fronto, in the century of Pompeius Reg[_ _ _, and Lucius Longinus] Celer in the century of Cre[_ _ _], and Lucius Herennius Fuscus, veteran, and stated on oath that he was freeborn and a Roman citizen, and had the right of serving in a legion.

Whereupon his guarantors, [_ _ _ Fronto, and Lucius Longinus Celer, and Lucius Herennius Fuscus, declared on oath by Jupiter] Best and Greatest and the spirit of Emperor Caesar Domitian Augustus, Conqueror of the Germans that [the aforementioned Titus Flavius Longus] was freeborn and a Roman citizen and had the right of serving in a legion.

Transacted in the Augustan camp in the winter-quarters of Legion III [_ _ _], year 17 of Emperor Caesar Domitian Augustus, Conqueror of the Germans, in the consulship of Quintus Volusius Saturninus and Lucius Venuleius Montanus Apronianus.

2 *D* 49. 16. 2. 1

(Arrius Menander (late 2nd C.AD), **Bk. I On Military Affairs**)

It is considered a serious crime for someone to enlist as a soldier if he is not permitted to do so, and the gravity is increased, as in other offences, by the dignity, rank, and type of military service.

Cf. *D* 49. 16. 4. 1–9; 16. 11; 16 – people considered unsuitable for military service: slaves, those convicted and condemned to the beasts or deported, those who had been exiled, those convicted of adultery or another crime in the public jury courts, those actually involved in litigation, and deserters who enlisted in another arm of the service.

3 Pliny (1st–2nd C.AD), *Letters* 10. 29–30

Pliny to Emperor Trajan. Sempronius Caelianus, an excellent young man, sent to me two slaves who were discovered among the recruits; I postponed their punishment so that I could consult you, as founder and guarantor of military discipline, about the type of penalty. The fact about which I am particularly doubtful is that although they had already taken the oath of allegiance, they had not yet been enrolled in a unit. Therefore, Sir, I request that you write and inform me what course of action I should follow, especially since the decision may provide a precedent.

Trajan to Pliny. Sempronius Caelianus acted in accordance with my instructions in sending to you these men in respect of whom it will be necessary to conduct an investigation to see if they merit capital punishment. It is relevant if they offered themselves as volunteers or were conscripted or indeed were presented as substitutes. If they were conscripted, the examination was at fault; if they were presented as substitutes, the blame lies with those who presented them; if they enlisted of their own free will although they were fully aware of their own status, they will have to be executed. It is not of great significance that they have not yet been enrolled in a unit. For on that very day on which they were approved for service in the army, they ought to have given a true account of their origins.

Pliny was governor of Bithynia probably 109–11.

4 Vegetius (4th C.AD), *Epitome of Military Matters* 1. 6

The recruiting officer should diligently ensure that through a careful examination of their face, eyes, and physical constitution, he chooses men who are likely to prove good soldiers. For the qualities not only of a man but also of horses and dogs are revealed by many indications. . . The potential young recruit therefore ought to have alert eyes, should carry his head erect, have a broad chest, muscular shoulders, strong arms, long fingers, a small waist, slim buttocks, and legs and feet which are not fleshy but sinewy and strong. When you find all these indications in a recruit, you need not pay too much attention to his height, for brave soldiers are more valuable that tall ones.

Vegetius was writing after AD 383, but he collected material from many sources and periods and much of his work relates to an earlier age, though it is difficult to identify his source for this passage (see Barnes 1979).

5 Acts of Maximilianus 1. 1–5 (Musurillo 1972: 17), AD 295

On 12 March at Tebessa in the consulship of Tuscus and Anullinus, Fabius Victor was brought into the forum along with Maximilianus; Pompeianus was allowed to act as their advocate. He said: 'Fabius Victor, agent responsible for the recruiting tax (*temonarius*), is present along with Valerianus Quintianus, imperial officer (*praepositus Caesariensis*), and Victor's son Maximilianus, an excellent recruit. Since he has the necessary qualities, I request that he be measured'.

Dion the proconsul said: 'What is your name?'.

Maximilianus replied: 'Why do you want to know my name? I am not permitted to serve in the army since I am a Christian'.

Dion the proconsul said: 'Get him ready'.

While he was being made ready Maximilianus replied: 'I cannot serve in the army; I cannot do evil; I am a Christian'.

Dion the proconsul said: 'Let him be measured'.

When he had been measured, one of his staff said: 'He is five feet ten inches tall' (about 5 feet 8 inches in English measurements).

Dion said to his staff: 'Give him the military seal'.

Maximilianus, continuing to resist, replied: 'I am not going to do it; I cannot serve as a soldier'.

This is one of the more reliable of the Christian Martyr Acts, and may have been based on an official report of the trial. If so, it serves as a good example of the examination of a potential recruit in the first two centuries of the imperial period since it is unlikely that the general procedures had changed significantly. The military seal was a piece of lead containing a seal and the recruit's name, which he wore round his neck. For minimum height requirements, see Vegetius, 1. 5.

6 *P. Oxy.* 39, papyrus, Oxyrhynchus, Egypt, AD 52

Copy of a release, signed in year twelve of Emperor Tiberius Claudius Caesar Augustus Germanicus, 29 Pharmuthi. Released from service by Gnaeus Vergilius Capito, prefect of both (Upper and Lower Egypt): Tryphon son of Dionysius, a weaver of the metropolis of Oxyrhynchus, suffering from cataract and impaired vision. The examination was conducted in Alexandria.

7 *D* 49. 16. 4. pr.

(Arrius Menander, **Bk. I On Military Affairs**)

A man born with one testicle or a man who has lost one, can legitimately serve in the army, according to a rescript of the divine Trajan. Indeed both the commanders Sulla and Cotta are said to have had that condition.

8 Suetonius (1st–2nd C.AD), *Augustus*, 24. 1

He (Augustus) sold off a Roman *eques* and his property at public auction because he had cut off the thumbs of his two young sons to make them unfit for military service.

Cf. *D* 49. 16. 4. 10–12. It was a serious offence to evade military service.

9 *P. Oxy.* 1022 = Fink *RMR* 87, papyrus, Oxyrhynchus, Egypt, AD 103

Copy

Gaius Minicius Italus sends greetings to his own Celsianus. Give orders that the six recruits approved by me should be included in the roster of the cohort which you command, to take effect from February 19. I have appended their names and distinguishing marks to this letter. Farewell dearest brother.

Gaius Veturius Gemellus, age 21, no distinguishing mark
Gaius Longinus Priscus, age 22, a scar on left eyebrow
Gaius Julius Maximus, age 25, no distinguishing mark
[_ _ _] Julius? Secundus, age 20, no distinguishing mark
Gaius Julius Saturninus, age 23, a scar on left hand
Marcus Antonius Valens, age 22, a scar on right side of forehead.

Received February 24, year six of our Emperor Trajan by means of Priscus, aide. I, Avidius Arrianus senior clerk (*cornicularius*) of the third (or second) cohort of Ituraeans declare that the original letter is in the archives of the cohort.

10 *BGU* 423 = *SP* 112, papyrus, Fayum, Egypt, 2nd C.AD

Apion to Epimachus his father and lord, very many greetings. First of all I pray for your good health and that you may always be strong and fortunate, along with my sister, her daughter, and my brother. I give thanks to the lord Serapis because when I was in danger at sea he immediately saved me. When I got to Misenum I received three gold pieces from Caesar as my travelling expenses (*viaticum*). Everything is going well for me. So, I ask you, my lord and father, to write me a letter, first about your welfare, secondly about that of my brother and sister, and thirdly so that I can do reverence to your handwriting, since you educated me well and as a result of that I hope to be advanced quickly, if the gods so wish. Give all my best wishes to Capiton and my brother and sister and Serenilla and my friends. I have sent you through Euctemon a portrait of myself. My name is now Antonius Maximus. . .

Apion was enlisted as a sailor and examined in Egypt, after which he travelled by sea to Misenum where he received his *viaticum*; since he was not a Roman citizen he was given an official Roman name. The *viaticum* of seventy-five *denarii* is the equivalent of one instalment of a legionary's annual wage of 300 *denarii* after Domitian. For the *viaticum*, see also Fink *RMR* 70 (late second century AD).

11 *SP* 368 = Fink *RMR* 74, papyrus, Egypt, AD 117

Longinus Longus, standard-bearer of the first cohort of Lusitanians, of the century of Tituleius, sends greetings to Longinus Tituleius, doctor [?], centurion. I have received from you 423 *denarii* 20 obols to be retained on deposit for the recruits from Asia who have been distributed in the century, to the number of 20 men. Year twenty-one of Trajan Optimus Caesar, our lord, Thoth 6 (3 September).

This is an extract from a papyrus containing six receipts, written by the standard-bearers of the cohort's six constituent centuries, to the senior centurion of the cohort. The money involved was probably the residue of the *viaticum* granted to the new recruits from Asia. Fink notes the large numbers of these recruits, in one case 40 per cent of the strength of the century, and suggests that the cohort had suffered heavy casualties in the Jewish revolt of 115–16. The receipts were written in Greek, perhaps indicating the daily speech of the soldiers in Egypt. For 'doctor' see p. 103.

12 *EJ* 368, inscription, Alexander Troas, Asia, early 1st C.AD

To Gaius Fabricius Tuscus, son of Gaius, of the Aniensis tribe, Member of the Board of Two (*duovir* – chief magistrates in a colony or municipality), augur, prefect of the Apulan cohort and of the works which were carried out in the colony (Alexander Troas) on the orders of Augustus, military tribune of Legion III Cyrenaica for eight years, tribune in charge of the levy of freeborn men which Augustus and Tiberius Caesar held in Rome, prefect of engineers for four years, prefect of cavalry of a praetorian *ala* for four years, granted an Untipped Spear and Gold Crown by Germanicus Caesar Imperator in the German war, by decree of the town councillors.

Brunt (1974b) has argued persuasively that this exceptional levy occurred in AD 6 in response to the Pannonian revolt. Suetonius (*Aug.* 25. 2) and Dio (55. 31; 56. 23) assert that conscription was used in AD 6, and in AD 9 after the destruction by the Germans of the three legions of Quinctilius Varus, and that freedmen were also enlisted. Indeed the inscription's precise definition of a levy of freeborn men implies that other levies were taking place. We may surmise that certain cohorts of *cives Romani ingenui* which are not described as volunteers and which were probably raised by conscription in AD 6 or 9, were so designated to differentiate them from freedmen. Finally, we must also distinguish the *cohortes voluntariae* of Roman citizens, which had existed before and of which the cohort of Apulians was one; on Augustus' death these troops received the same donative as legionaries, and probably had similar pay and conditions (Kraft 1951: 82). For other special levies in Italy note, for example, Memmius Macrinus sent by Hadrian 'to conduct a levy of the young men in the Transpadana region' (*ILS* 1068), and Claudius Fronto, 'sent to levy the young men throughout Italy' during the Parthian war of Lucius Verus (*ILS* 1098).

TRAINING

For an account of basic and field-service training, see Watson 1969: 54–72.

13 Vegetius (4th C.AD), 1. 1, 9, 10, 19; 2. 23

(Section 1) We see that the Roman people conquered the world by no other means than training in the military arts, discipline in the camp, and practice in warfare. . . But against all these (peoples) we triumphed by selecting recruits carefully, by teaching them, as I have pointed out, the principles of war, by toughening them by daily exercise, by teaching them in advance through manoeuvres in the field everything which can happen on the march and in battle, and by punishing severely the lazy. For knowledge of military science fosters courage in battle. No one is afraid to perform what he is confident he has learned well. . .

(Section 9) Right at the start of their training, therefore, recruits should be taught the military step. For on the march and in the battle line nothing should be safeguarded more carefully than that all the troops should keep in step. This can be achieved only if through repeated practice they learn to march quickly and in formation. An army which is split up and in disorder is always in grave danger from the enemy. So, 20 miles should be completed with the military step in five hours, but only in summer. With the fuller step, which is quicker, 24 miles should be completed in the same time. . . The soldiers should also be trained in jumping so that they can leap over ditches and surmount any height blocking the way, and consequently when difficulties of this kind appear, they can cross them without trouble. . .

(Section 10) All recruits without exception should during the summer months learn how to swim. For they cannot always cross rivers on bridges, but during a retreat or pursuit an army is frequently forced to swim. . .

(Section 19) Recruits should be compelled frequently to carry a burden of up to sixty pounds and to march with the military step, since on tough campaigns they face the necessity of carrying their provisions as well as their weapons. . .

(Book 2. Section 23) The younger soldiers and recruits normally were trained in the morning and afternoon with every kind of weapon. Veterans and experienced troops had one uninterrupted arms drill session every day. . . It is excellent to train them at a fencing post using wooden sticks, since they learn how to attack the sides or legs or head with the point and edge (of the sword). They should also learn how to strike a blow while simultaneously leaping up, to spring up with a bound and crouch down behind the shield again, to charge forward with one rush and then give way and charge back to the rear. They should also practise hurling their javelins at the posts from a distance in order to develop their accuracy and the strength of their throwing arm.

14 Vegetius 1. 27

An ancient practice has survived, for which provision has also been made in the enactments of the divine Augustus and Hadrian, that three times each month both the cavalry and infantry should be led out for marching exercise; for this word is used to describe this type of drill (*ambulatura*). The infantry wearing their armour and equipped with all their weapons were commanded to march for 10 miles and then return to the camp at the military pace, although they had to complete part of the route at a quicker speed. The cavalry, drawn up in squadrons and equipped in the same way, completed the same distance and practised cavalry drill, sometimes pursuing, then giving way, and then renewing the attack vigorously. . .

15 Arrian (2nd C.AD), *Tactica* **40**

(The Cantabrian manoeuvre) works as follows. A cavalry formation, fully equipped, is drawn up in the usual way on the left of the platform, except for the two cavalrymen who are to receive the direct barrage of javelins. They charge from the right as before (?) and wheel to the right. But while they are charging another charge begins on the left of the platform and wheels in a circle. These cavalrymen use not light javelins but full-size spears though with no iron tip; but their weight makes them awkward for the throwers and not without danger to the men who are the targets. They have orders, therefore, not to aim at the heads of the cavalrymen riding past or to throw a spear at the horse, but before the cavalryman wheels his horse and exposes any part of his flank, or his back becomes exposed while he is turning, to aim at the shield and strike it as hard as possible with the spear. The skill of this manoeuvre lies in the fact that the man in position in the Cantabrian formation should get as close as possible to those riding past and hit the centre of the shield with his spear, either striking a resounding blow or piercing it right through; then the second man attacks the second in the other formation, the third man the third, and so on in the same way.

Cavalry training: see Dixon and Southern 1992: 113–34; for Arrian see text no. 153.

16 Josephus (1st C.AD), *Jewish War* **3. 72–6**

Indeed, as if they had been born fully armed they never take a holiday from training and do not wait for crises to appear. Their training manoeuvres lack none of the vigour of genuine warfare and each soldier practises battle drill every day with great enthusiasm just as if he were in battle. Therefore they sustain the shock of combat very easily. For their usual well-ordered ranks are not disrupted by any confusion, or numbed by fear, or exhausted by toil; so, certain victory inevitably follows since the enemy cannot match this. Indeed one would not be wrong in saying that their training manoeuvres are battles without bloodshed, and their battles manoeuvres with bloodshed.

Josephus was a Jewish priest from an aristocratic background who was chosen by the Sanhedrin to defend Galilee in the Jewish revolt of AD 66. He was captured and then befriended by the Roman commander Vespasian, and when Vespasian became emperor in AD 69, Josephus remained in imperial favour and wrote a history of the revolt which provides much useful material on the organization, fighting qualities, and siege techniques of the Roman army, all of which Josephus had experienced at first hand. We should expect him to be more impartial than a Roman author, and although he was doubtless eager to please the Flavians, he achieved this by emphasizing the prowess of Vespasian and Titus as generals, not by distorting the achievements of the Roman army.

17 *ILS* 2487; 9133–5, inscription, Lambaesis, Africa, AD 128

Emperor Caesar Trajan Hadrian Augustus addressed his very own Legion III Augusta after inspecting their manoeuvres, in the words recorded below, in the consulship of Torquatus for the second time and Libo, 1 July.

To the chief centurions

[_ _ _] your commander has himself told me on your behalf of numerous factors which would have excused you in my judgement, namely, that one cohort is absent which every year is sent in rotation to the office of the proconsul (of Africa), that two years ago you contributed a cohort and four men from each century to supplement your colleagues in the third legion (III Cyrenaica or Gallica), that many outposts in different locations keep you far apart, that in my own memory you have not only changed camp twice but also built new ones. For these reasons I would have excused you if the legion had been dilatory in its manoeuvres for any length of time. But you have not been dilatory in any respect at all [_ _ _] The chief centurions and the centurions were fit and strong as usual.

To the cavalry of the legion

Military manoeuvres have their own rules so to speak and if anything is added or taken away from them the drill is made either less effective or more difficult. Indeed the more complications are added, the less impressive it appears. Of the difficult manoeuvres you have completed the most difficult of all, throwing the javelin while wearing metal corslets [_ _ _]. Furthermore, I commend your morale [_ _ _

[To a cavalry cohort]

[Defences which] others build in several days, you have completed in one; you have constructed a wall which requires considerable work and which is normally built for permanent winter quarters in a time not much longer than is usually needed to build a turf wall. For this type of wall the turf is cut to a regulation size, is easily carried and manoeuvred, and is erected without trouble, for it is naturally pliable and level. But you used large, heavy, and uneven stones which no one can carry, lift, or fit in position without the stones catching on each other because of their uneven surface. You dug a ditch straight through hard and rough gravel and made it smooth by levelling it. When your work had been approved you entered the camp quickly and got your rations and weapons, and when you had followed the cavalry which had been sent out, with a great shout as it returned [_ _ _

I commend [my legate] since he introduced you to this manoeuvre which has the appearance of real warfare and trains you in such a way that I can congratulate you. Cornelianus your prefect has performed his duties satisfactorily. However, the riding manoeuvres do not win my approval [_ _ _] The cavalryman should ride out from cover and engage in pursuit [cautiously, for if he cannot] see where he is going or if he cannot rein in his horse when he wishes, he will surely be exposed to hidden traps [_ _ _]

[_ _ _] July, to the first *ala* of Pannonians

You did everything in order. You filled the plain with your exercises, you threw your javelins with a certain degree of style, although you were using rather short and stiff javelins; several of you hurled your lances with equal skill. Just now you mounted your horses agilely and yesterday you did it swiftly. If anything had been lacking in your performance I should have noted it, if anything had been obviously bad I should have mentioned it, but throughout the entire manoeuvre you satisfied me uniformly. Catullinus my legate, distinguished man, shows equal concern for all the units of which he is in command. [_ _ _] your prefect apparently looks after you conscientiously. I grant you a donative [as travelling expenses (?) _ _ _

To the cavalry of the sixth cohort of Commagenians

It is difficult for cavalry attached to a cohort to win approval even on their own, and more difficult still for them not to incur criticism after a manoeuvre by auxiliary cavalry; they cover a greater area of the plain, there are more men throwing javelins, they wheel right in close formation, they perform the Cantabrian manoeuvre in close array, the beauty of their horses and the splendour of their weapons are in keeping with their pay. But, despite the heat, you avoided any boredom by doing energetically what had to be done; in addition you fired stones from slings and fought with javelins; on every occasion you mounted speedily. The remarkable care taken by my legate Catullinus, distinguished man, is obvious from the fact that he has men like you under [his command _ _ _

Quintus Fabius Catullinus became ordinary consul in AD 130. Hadrian was unique in the extent of his travels round the empire during which he carefully inspected the military establishments and the training of the soldiers, so that methods established by him remained the norm of Roman military practice down to Dio's day (Dio, 69. 9). This speech is the only surviving example of an imperial address to soldiers, and is remarkable for the emperor's knowledge and his forceful, direct style of language, likely to be comprehensible to the troops; notably he refers to 'his very own legion' (Campbell 1984: 77–80; see also, p. 74).

CONDITIONS OF SERVICE

Augustus decided to meet all the military needs of the empire from a standing, professional army, so that there was no need to raise any special levies. Military service was a career, and pay and service conditions were established which took account of the categories of soldier in the army: the praetorians, Augustus' personal bodyguard; the citizen legionary troops; the non-citizen auxiliaries. In 13 BC a term of 12 years' service was set for praetorians, and sixteen for legionaries, followed by four in reserve. In AD 5 legionary service was set at 20 years with probably five years in reserve, while praetorians served for 16 years (Dio, 54. 25; 55. 23). It is not clear how long auxiliaries were expected to serve. However, by the mid-first century legionaries and auxiliaries served for 25 years. On discharge a legionary received 12,000 sesterces under Augustus, and a praetorian 20,000, though this superannuation could be commuted to a plot of land. For rates of pay see Table 1. It is based on M. A. Speidel 1992; see also Brunt 1950; Breeze 1971; Jahn 1983.

Table 1 Rates of pay in sesterces

Date	Legionary infantryman	Auxiliary infantryman (*Miles cohortis*)	Auxiliary cavalryman of cohort (*Eques cohortis*)	Cavalryman of legion (*Eques legionis*) Auxiliary cavalryman of *ala*
Augustus	900*	750*	900*	1,050
Domitian	1,200*	1,000	1,200	1,400
Septimius Severus	2,400	2,000	2,400	2,800
Caracalla	3,600	3,000*	3,600	4,200
Maximinus	7,200*	6,000*	7,200	8,400*

Note: * Securely attested by literary or documentary evidence.

The annual cost of the legions, auxilia, and navy in the early first century AD may have amounted to more than 400 million sesterces, a large proportion of the empire's disposable income; a pay rise will have had serious financial implications (Hopkins *JRS* 1980: 124–5; Campbell 1984: 161–5, 171–6).

18 Augustus, *Res Gestae*, 17

In the consulship of Marcus Lepidus and Lucius Arruntius (AD 6) I transferred 170,000,000 sesterces from my own property to the military treasury, which had been set up on my advice in order to pay discharge benefits to soldiers who had served for twenty years or more.

Dio (55. 25) mistakenly believed that soldiers' wages were paid from the military treasury. The new treasury (administered by three prefects of praetorian rank) was to be financed by a 5 per cent tax on the estates of Roman citizens, except those of the very poor and those left to near relatives, and a 1 per cent tax on the sale of goods by auction. The introduction of the first direct tax on property in Italy since 167 BC shows the importance that Augustus attached to military superannuation. By contributing such a large sum personally (which would have provided benefits for about 14,000 men) he emphasized his personal connection with the army. But he was clearly finding it difficult to sustain the cost of discharge payments from his own funds; hence men were retained long after the official service period (see text no. 20). Tiberius was to protest that the resources of the state were inadequate to pay *praemia* unless soldiers were not discharged until after twenty years' service (Tacitus, *Annals* 1. 78).

19 Augustus, *Res Gestae*, 15. 3–16

In my fifth consulship (29 BC) I gave 1,000 sesterces out of booty to every one of the colonists settled from my soldiers; about 120,000 men in the colonies received this benefaction in celebration of my triumph.

I paid money to the towns for the lands which I granted to soldiers in my fourth consulship (30 BC) and subsequently in the consulship of Marcus Crassus and Gnaeus Lentulus Augur (14 BC). The sum which I paid out for lands in Italy amounted to about 600,000,000 sesterces, and that expended for provincial lands to about 260,000,000. In the recollection of contemporaries I was the first and only person to have done this of all those who founded colonies of soldiers in Italy or the provinces. Subsequently, in the consulships of Tiberius Nero and Gnaeus Piso (7 BC), of Gaius Antistius and Decimus Laelius (6 BC), of Gaius Calvisius and Lucius Pasienus (4 BC), of Lucius Lentulus and Marcus Messalla (3 BC), and of Lucius Caninius and Quintus Fabricius

(2 BC), I paid monetary rewards to soldiers whom I settled in their home towns after they had completed their service, and for this purpose I spent about 400,000,000 sesterces.

See also chapter 8.

20 Tacitus (1st–2nd C.AD), *Annals*, 1. 17

He (Percennius, leader of the mutineers in Pannonia) said that enough harm had been caused over the years by their passivity; old men, several of them with their bodies disfigured by wounds, were serving their thirtieth or fortieth year. There was no end to military service even when they were discharged, since they remained under the standards and performed the same toil under another name. And, if anyone survived all these perils, he was dragged off to a distant country where he received under the name of a plot of land waterlogged swamps or uncultivated mountainsides. Indeed military service was relentless and unprofitable; body and spirit were valued at two and a half sesterces a day, and out of this they had to pay for their clothing, weapons, and tents, and bribe vicious centurions to escape routine drudgery.

Serious mutinies broke out in Pannonia and Germany in AD 14 partly because the soldiers were worried about their conditions of service after the death of Augustus, so closely had he become associated with their emoluments. But there was obviously significant disquiet at low rates of pay, especially in contrast to the praetorians, long service, and unsuitable land allocations. For deductions from pay, see texts nos 24–5.

21 Kraay 1960: 114–16, *sestertius* of Domitian, AD 84

Obverse. Head of Domitian, laureate, with aegis.

EMPEROR CAESAR DOMITIAN AUGUSTUS, SON OF THE DIVINE VESPASIAN, CONQUEROR OF THE GERMANS, CONSUL FOR THE TENTH TIME.

Reverse. Domitian in military dress stands on a dais, extending his right arm; behind him stands another figure; at the foot of the dais stands a lictor. Three soldiers stand in front of the dais, two holding standards, the other raising both arms to meet Domitian's outstretched hand.

PAY OF EMPEROR AUGUSTUS DOMITIAN. BY DECREE OF THE SENATE.

Before Domitian, soldiers' salaries were paid in three annual instalments. His pay-rise perhaps added a fourth instalment – possibly signified on this coin if *Stip.* can be expanded to *stipendium*; however *stip.* may stand for *stipendia*, i.e. the emperor's general interest in military pay.

22 Cohen, vol. 4, p. 157. no. 126, bronze *as* of Septimius Severus and Caracalla, AD 205–8

Obverse. Head of Caracalla.

ANTONINUS PIUS AUGUSTUS

Reverse. Severus and Caracalla seated on a platform; an official stands behind, a legionary in front.

THE GENEROSITY OF THE EMPERORS. CONSUL FOR THE SECOND TIME. BY DECREE OF THE SENATE.

Severus had demonstrated his generosity by possibly doubling military pay around AD 195 (Herodian (see text no. 314), 3. 8), the first rise since Domitian.

23 Dio (2nd–3rd C.AD), 77. 3

Antoninus (Caracalla), although it was evening, secured the legions, shouting out all along the way that he had been plotted against and that his life was in danger. When he entered the camp he said, 'Rejoice fellow-soldiers, now I can indulge you. . . For I am one of you; it is for you alone that I want to live so that I can grant you all kind of favours; all the treasuries are yours'.

Dio is hostile to Caracalla whose extravagant treatment of the troops had in his view led to excessive expenditure and financial demands on the upper classes. His estimate that the emperor's pay-rise had cost in total 280 million sesterces (78. 36; cf. Herodian, 4. 4) may be exaggerated but is not out of the question. It would represent a rise of about 50 per cent (Speidel 1992).

24 Fink *RMR* 68, papyrus, Egypt, AD 81

In the consulship of Lucius Asinius
QUINTUS JULIUS PROCULUS from DAMASCUS
received the first salary instalment of the third year of the Emperor, $247^{1/2}$ drachmas, out of which

hay	10 drachmas
for food	80 drachmas
boots, socks	12 drachmas
Saturnalia of the camp	20 drachmas
?	60 drachmas
expenditure	182 drachmas
balance deposited to his account	$65^{1/2}$ drachmas
and had from before	136 drachmas
makes a total of	$201^{1/2}$ drachmas

received the second instalment of the same year $247^{1/2}$ drachmas, out of which

hay	10 drachmas
for food	80 drachmas
boots, socks	12 drachmas
to the standards	4 drachmas
expenditure	106 drachmas
balance deposited to his account	$141^{1/2}$ drachmas
and had from before	$201^{1/2}$ drachmas
makes a complete total of	343 drachmas

received the third instalment of the same year $247^{1/2}$ drachmas, out of which

hay	[10] drachmas
for food	80 drachmas
boots, socks	12 drachmas
for clothes	$145^{1/2}$ drachmas
expenditure	$247^{1/2}$ drachmas
balance deposited to his account	343 drachmas
Rennius Innocens	

GAIUS VALERIUS GERMANUS, from TYRE
received the first salary instalment of the third year of the Emperor, $247^{1/2}$ drachmas, out of which

hay	10 drachmas
for food	80 drachmas
boots, socks	12 drachmas
Saturnalia of the camp	20 drachmas
for clothes	100 drachmas
expenditure	222 drachmas
balance deposited to his account	$25^{1/2}$ drachmas
and had	21 drachmas
makes a complete total of	$46^{1/2}$ drachmas

received the second instalment of the same year, 247$^{1/2}$ drachmas, out of which

hay	10 drachmas
for food	80 drachmas
boots, socks	12 drachmas
to the standards	4 drachmas
expenditure	106 drachmas
balance deposited to his account	141$^{1/2}$ drachmas
and had from before	46$^{1/2}$ drachmas
makes a complete total of	188 drachmas

received the third instalment of the same year, 247$^{1/2}$ drachmas, out of which

hay	10 drachmas
for food	80 drachmas
boots, socks	12 drachmas
for clothes	145$^{1/2}$ drachmas
has on deposit	188 drachmas

The view of M. P. Speidel (1973) that this papyrus is a pay record of auxiliary infantry soldiers, with the sum of 247$^{1/2}$ drachmas representing a pay instalment of 250 drachmas (= sesterces), has now been confirmed by M. A. Speidel (1992). The discrepancy of 2$^{1/2}$ drachmas (= 1 per cent) may be explained on the hypothesis that the government charged a fee for conversion into Egyptian drachmas; or perhaps it was a deduction for some common fund. It is notable that auxiliary infantrymen received five-sixths of legionary pay and that *alares* were paid more than legionaries, but this may reflect the vital role of the auxilia in the army and the added expense of serving in the cavalry.

25 Cotton and Geiger 1989: 722, papyrus, Masada, AD 72 or 75

In the fourth consulship of Emperor [Ves]pas[ian] Augustus (?)

Pay Account (?)

Gaius Messius, son of Gaius, of the Fabia tribe, from Berytus

I have received as my salary	50 *denarii*
out of this I have paid:	
barley	
[_ _ _]rnius	[_ _ _]
food	20 *denarii*
boots	5 *denarii*
leather straps (?)	2 *denarii*
linen tunic	7 *denarii*

I have received as my salary	60 *denarii*
out of this I have paid:	
barley	? *denarii*
food	20 *denarii*
Gaius Antonius	
overall cloak	? *denarii*
Puplius Valerius	
white tunic	? *denarii*

This papyrus seems to contain an account of two pay periods of a soldier (probably a legionary cavalryman) serving in the Legion X Fretensis at Masada. It lists his expenses throughout the year paid out of his salary and is not a complete financial account like text no. 24. Speidel (1992: 92–6) suggests that the sums of 50 and 60 *denarii* represent his salary remaining after some unspecified transactions; on the other hand, Cotton and Geiger think that these sums represent the total of the deductions listed from the soldier's pay.

There is evidence in Tacitus (text no. 20), in text no. 24, and in this papyrus (cf. also *CPL* 124) for several statutory deductions from soldiers' pay for food, clothing, and weapons (Watson 1969: 102–4). That for food may have been at a standard rate; the 20 *denarii* in this papyrus corresponds with the 80 drachmas in text no. 24. Deductions in respect of clothing and weapons were probably irregular since it is likely that a recruit was provided with his basic uniform and weapons which he was expected to keep in reasonable order. Soldiers will have had to pay for periodic refurbishment or for replacement in cases of carelessness, misuse, or dishonesty.

26 Dio, 71, 3

Although a fierce battle (against the Germans) had taken place and a glorious victory had been won, the emperor (Marcus Aurelius) nevertheless did not grant a donative, which had been requested by the soldiers, saying that whatever they received in excess of their regular pay would be extracted from the blood of their families and kinsmen.

Donatives – irregular cash disbursements in the name of the emperor – became an important supplement to military pay and an additional burden on state expenditure, as this passage suggests. In the Republic donatives were granted to celebrate the end of a campaign, or to individuals for acts of valour. However the military dynasts used these cash handouts to instil personal loyalty among their troops, and it soon became the practice for an emperor to distribute a donative on politically sensitive occasions (see pp. 184–5). In his will Augustus left 1,000 sesterces per man to the praetorians, 500 to the urban cohorts, and 300 to the legionaries (Suetonius, *Aug.* 101. 2), and this proportion was retained though donatives bore no direct relation to rates of pay. Some were enormous, for example, that paid at the accession of

Marcus Aurelius and Lucius amounted to 20,000 sesterces for each praetorian; the total cost for the urban troops will have been about 240 million sesterces, with an additional 1,000 million if it was extended to the legionaries on a proportional basis. Furthermore, although donatives were initially confined to citizen troops, it seems unlikely that the *auxilia* can long have been excluded from this additional benefit of military service (Campbell 1984: 165–71; text no. 17).

27 *CJ* 4. 51. 1 (AD 224)

Emperor Alexander Augustus to Cattianus, soldier. If it is proved before the governor of the province that Julianus sold without legal authority your slaves to buyers who were aware of this fact, he will instruct the purchasers to restore the slaves to you. If, however, they were ignorant of this and have taken possession of the slaves, he will instruct Julianus to pay you the price of the slaves.

Given on 7 July in the consulship of Julianus and Crispinus.

28 *CJ* 3. 37. 2 (AD 222)

Emperor Alexander Augustus to Avitus, soldier. If it is proved before the governor of the province that your brother made over as a pledge vines held in common, since he was not entitled to make legally liable to a creditor your share which you have in the vines, the governor of the province will instruct that share to be returned to you along with any crops which the creditor has harvested from your share. . .

Published on 12 September in the consulship of Alexander Augustus.

29 *CJ* 4. 32. 6 (AD 212)

Emperor Antoninus Augustus to Antigonus, soldier. If in the presence of witnesses you gave money you owed along with the interest to a creditor, who through the pledge you gave her holds a security, and if when she did not accept it, you deposited the money with a seal on it, then you cannot be compelled to pay interest from the time when you made this deposit. However in the absence of the creditor you ought to approach the governor of the province about this.

Published on 11 February in the consulship of the two Aspri.

The evidence of the legal texts shows that some soldiers owned property and engaged in financial transactions. This may be explained partly in terms of inheritance or enrichment through illegal exactions. But equally it is possible that soldiers were able to save substantial sums; Domitian had prohibited soldiers from having more than 250 *denarii* in the camp bank, after Saturninus had seized these funds to finance his rebellion in AD 89; but this ban probably fell into desuetude and anyway did not prevent soldiers from lodging money with other agents. A papyrus from Egypt (Fink *RMR* 73; cf. 70; see also text no. 24) shows that in a squadron of auxiliary cavalry *c.* AD 120–150 twenty-five men had money on account, and the average amount for the last twelve, whose deposits are clearly known, was 387 *denarii*. It is possible that one soldier had 2,000 *denarii* on deposit (col. iii. 14). Although a soldier's salary was not large, he enjoyed the advantages of regular payments, supplementary donatives, a guaranteed discharge bonus, and a well-ordered existence in hygienic conditions with good medical attention. In general a soldier's lot was better than anything that could be expected by the lower classes (Campbell 1984: 176–81; 280–1; see also below, chap. 6).

CAREERS

Legionaries

Each Roman legion consisted of nine cohorts of 480 men, and a leading cohort which is thought to have been at least double in size; there were also about 120 legionary cavalry, making a complement of around 5,400, although a precise figure is not reliably recorded by any ancient source. Many soldiers served their entire military career in the ranks, but there were opportunities for secondment to specialized tasks and for promotion. Soldiers in the legions who performed special functions were excused from routine duties, and probably from the mid-second century AD were officially classed as *immunes*, although they did not receive any extra pay. During the period between Hadrian and the Severan dynasty, a clear distinction emerged between *immunes* and *principales*, who received either pay and a half or double pay for the special duties they carried out in the century, as *tesserarius* (password officer), *optio* (orderly), and *signifer* (standard-bearer), or on the staff at headquarters, as *aquilifer* (bearer of the eagle standard), *imaginifer* (bearer of the emperor's portrait), *speculator* (scout, later executioner), *beneficiarius* (clerk), *commentariensis* (clerk attached to an officer with judicial responsibilities). Among the *principales* posts had a relative seniority, but few clear patterns in promotion towards the centurionate (most commonly between thirteen and twenty years' service) can be discerned, because of the limitations of inscriptional evidence, and it is difficult to say if there was a deliberate attempt to give men experience of purely military functions and also of administration, or if a well-educated man who acquitted himself satisfactorily in a post was sent where necessary to another vacancy. Clerks derived their status from the rank of the officer they served. The senior clerk (*cornicularius*) on the staff of the provincial governor was next in rank to a centurion (see Watson 1969: 75–86; Breeze 1971; 1974; for the *frumentarii*, who had headquarters in Rome but were often sent to the provinces as imperial agents and attached to legions, see Mann 1988).

30 *RIB* 292, inscription, Viroconium Cornoviorum (Wroxeter), Britain, 1st C. AD

[Titus F]laminius, son of Titus, of the Pollia tribe, from Fa[ventia], 45 years old, with twenty-two years' service, soldier of Legion XIV Gemina. I served as a soldier and now here I am. Read this and be more or less lucky in your life. The gods keep you from the wine-grape and water when you enter Tartarus. Live decently while your star grants you time for life.

31 *RIB* 363, inscription, Isca (Caerleon), Britain

To the spirits of the departed. Julius Valens, veteran of Legion II Augusta, lived 100 years. Julia Secundina, his wife, and Julius Martinus, his son, had this constructed.

32 *ILS* 2259 = *EJ* 258, inscription, near Burnum, Dalmatia, 1st C. AD

Aulus Sentius, son of Aulus, of the Pomptina tribe, from Arretium, veteran of the eleventh legion, lies here; in his will he ordered that this should be constructed. This man was killed in the territory of the Varvarini in a small field by the river Titus at Long Rock. His heir had this constructed, Quintus Calventius Vitalis, son of Lucius.

33 *EJ* 260 = Smallwood *GN* 279, inscription, Simitthu (Chemtou), Africa, 1st C.AD

Lucius Flaminius son of Decimus, of the Arniensis tribe, soldier of Legion III Augusta, century of Julius Longus, chosen in a levy by Marcus Silanus, served nineteen years on garrison duty only to be killed in battle by the enemy in the Philomusian area. He lived dutifully for forty years. He lies here.

34 Speidel 1980: 739–40, inscription, Sebaste (Sivasli), Asia, late 2nd 3rd C.AD

In accordance with the frequent decisions of the council and the people, his native country (honours) its benefactor Aurelius Atticus, veteran of Legion X Gemina, like his ancestors an ex-magistrate and city councillor.

It is noteworthy that the family of this legionary soldier came from the local aristocracy in Sebaste. X Gemina was based at Vindobona in Upper Pannonia.

35 *D* 50. 6. 7

(Tarruntenus Paternus (2nd C.AD), **Bk. I On Military Affairs**).

The status of certain people grants them an exemption from more onerous duties; in this category are surveyors, the hospital orderly, medical personnel, dressers, ditchers, farriers, architects, helmsmen, shipwrights, artillerymen, glass-makers, smiths, arrow-makers, copper-smiths, helmet-makers, cartwrights, roof-makers, sword-makers, water pipe-makers, trumpet-makers, horn-makers, bow-makers, plumbers, metal-workers, stone-cutters, men who burn lime, men who cut wood, and men who chop and burn charcoal. In the same category are normally placed butchers, hunters, men who look after animals for sacrifice, the orderly in charge of the workshop, men who attend the sick, clerks who can act as teachers, clerks of the grain store, clerks of money left on deposit, clerks of property left without heirs, assistants of the chief clerks, grooms, horse-trainers (?), armourers, the herald, and the trumpeter. All these men therefore are classed as *immunes*.

Publius Taruttienus Paternus (the correct form of his name as it appears in *AE* 1971: 534) was a jurist who wrote on military law and became praetorian prefect at the end of Marcus Aurelius' reign.

Texts nos. 36–42 illustrate the careers of soldiers who gained promotion.

36 *P. Mich.* 466, papyrus, Karanis, Egypt, AD 107

Julius Apollinarius to Julius Sabinus his dearest father, very many greetings. Before everything else I pray for your good health, which is my wish because I revere you next to the gods. . . Things are [fine with me]. After Serapis escorted me here safely [_ _ _], while others were breaking stones all day and doing other things, up until today I have suffered none of this. In fact I asked Claudius Severus, the governor, to appoint me as a clerk on his staff, and he said, 'There is no vacancy; nevertheless in the meantime I shall appoint you as a clerk of the legion with expectation of advancement'. With this appointment I went from the governor and commander of the legion to the senior clerk (*cornicularius*). So, if you love me make every effort to write to me immediately about your health, and if you are concerned about me, send some linen clothing through Sempronius; for merchants come to us every day from Pelusium. I shall endeavour as soon as the commander begins to grant leave, to come to you at once. . .

You will pass on the message to those with Aphrodas, the son of the condiment dealer, that they enrolled me in the cohort at Bostra. It is situated eight days' journey from Petra and [_ _ _

In another letter (*P. Mich.* 465) Apollinarius describes himself as a *principalis*, but at a time before the distinction between *immunes* and *principales* had been formalized, this was presumably a casual arrogation to himself of a title generally indicating any superior status.

Gaius Claudius Severus (*PIR*² C 1023, consul in 112, probably in absence) was commander of the legion in Arabia and also the first governor of this province, which had been annexed in 106. Speidel suggests that Apollinarius belonged to III Cyrenaica, which may briefly have garrisoned Arabia after annexation, before returning for a time to Egypt. In the early stages apparently only one cohort was stationed at Bostra, which later became the legionary base (Speidel 1977: 691–7).

37 Speidel 1976b: 126–8, inscription, Byzantium, Bithynia, 3rd C.AD

To the spirits of the departed, in honour of Aurelius Surus, ex-trumpeter of Legion I Adiutrix Loyal and Faithful, served eighteen years, lived forty years. From Syria Phoenice (?). Septimius Vibianus his heir and colleague had this constructed for an estimable man.

38 Speidel 1976b: 124–6, inscription, Byzantium, 3rd C. AD

To the spirits of the departed, in honour of Titus Flavius Surillio, eagle-bearer of Legion II Adiutrix Loyal and Faithful, served eighteen years, lived forty years. Aurelius Zanax, eagle-bearer of the same legion, erected this in honour of his estimable colleague.

39 *ILS* 2344, inscription, Lambaesis, Africa, 3rd C.AD

Sacred to the spirits of the departed, in honour of Lucius Tullius Felix, lived twenty-five years, two months, seventeen days, learning the duties of the eagle-bearer, Legion III Augusta. Lucius Boncius Secundus erected this in his memory, to his uncle.

40 *ILS* 2442, inscription, Aquincum (Budapest), Lower Pannonia, AD 218

To Jupiter Best and Greatest, for the welfare of our lord Marcus Aurelius Antoninus Pius Fortunate Augustus, Lucius Septimius Constantinus, orderly (*optio*) with the expectation of promotion to centurion, of Legion II Adiutrix Loyal and Faithful, Antoniniana, willingly and deservedly fulfilled his vow, in the consulship of Emperor Antoninus and Adventus.

41 *CIL* 3. 11135 = *ILS* 4311, inscription, Carnuntum (Petronell), Upper Pannonia, AD 235–8

To Jupiter Best and Greatest of Doliche, for the safety of Emperor Caesar Gaius [Julius Verus Maximinus Pius Fortunate Invincible Augustus _ _ _ Ulpi]us Amandianus, soldier of Legion XIV Gemina, clerk of the above mentioned unit, armourer, standard-bearer, orderly (*optio*) of the second centurion in the e[ighth] cohort and candidate (for promotion to centurion), along with Ulpius Amandus, veteran of the above-mentioned le[gion], dedicated this to the deity.

The translation follows the interpretation of this inscription by M. P. Speidel (1982a). The *optio* normally took charge of the century in the absence of the centurion, and it is possible that those who specifically indicate their candidature for promotion to the centurionate were more senior, here ranking above a *signifer*.

42 Speidel 1970, inscription, Philippi, Macedonia, AD 106 (see Plate 1)

Tiberius Claudius Maximus, veteran, undertook the construction of this monument while he was still alive. He served as a cavalryman in Legion VII Claudia Loyal and Faithful, was appointed treasurer of the cavalry, guard of the commander of the same legion, standard-bearer of the cavalry, and in the Dacian war was awarded military decorations for bravery by Emperor Domitian. He was promoted to 'double pay' soldier (*duplicarius*) in the second *ala* of Pannonians by the divine Trajan, by whom he was also appointed to the position of scout in the Dacian war, and twice awarded military decorations for bravery in the Dacian and Parthian wars, and was promoted decurion in the same cavalry *ala* by the same emperor because he had captured Decebalus and brought his head back to him at Ranisstorum. After voluntarily serving beyond his time, he was honourably discharged by Terentius Scaurianus, commander with consular rank of the army in the new (?) province of [Mesopotamia (?)_ _ _]

Given Maximus' distinguished war record, his advancement was not rapid since some soldiers were promoted straight from the position of legionary cavalryman to the decurionate and progressed to a legionary centurionate. See further below, p. 46. Decebalus in fact committed suicide to avoid capture (Dio 68. 14).

43 *P. Mich.* 468, lines 31–41, papyrus, Karanis, Egypt, 2nd C.AD

I beg you, father, to write to me at once about your health, that you are well (?). I am anxious about things at home unless you write to me. God willing, I hope that I shall live frugally and be transferred to a cohort. However nothing gets done here without money, and letters of recommendation are no use unless a man helps himself.

This letter is part of an archive (*P. Mich.* VIII. 467–81) including correspondence in both Greek and Latin from a soldier, Claudius Terentianus, to his father Claudius Tiberianus, who was himself a soldier (a *speculator*) though at some stage he had become a veteran (*P. Mich.* 475). Terentianus was serving in the fleet at Alexandria but was eager for a transfer to an auxiliary cohort. His efforts were amply rewarded, since he later describes himself as a legionary soldier (*P. Mich.* 476). Promotions, and transfers to different parts of the army, could be subject to the operation of personal patronage, often expressed in a letter of recommendation written by an influential person to the officer or commander who could smooth the way. For example, in a fragmentary letter from the Vindolanda collection, a man writes to Crispinus, possibly a member of the governor's staff: '... so provide me with friends so that through your kindness I may be able to enjoy a pleasant period of military service' (Bowman and Thomas 1983: no. 37; also below, text no. 48).

Auxiliaries

Auxiliary troops were recruited from peoples within or on the periphery of Roman control and who in the main did not yet possess Roman citizenship. They provided cavalry, light infantry, and specialist requirements often supplied, in the Republic, by mercenaries. Originally the auxiliaries were recruited into ethnic units commanded by their own chieftains, or by Roman officers when they were incorporated into the formal structure of the army. At least from the middle of the first century AD there was a tendency to dilute the ethnic character of some units by using recruits from areas with plentiful manpower, notably Gallia Belgica, Lugdunensis, and Pannonia. By the late first century local recruiting had become common and units were kept up to strength by supplements from the province where they were serving, or areas adjacent to it. There were two reasons for this: firstly, the spread of Roman citizenship had restricted some of the traditional recruiting areas;

secondly, auxiliary units were now being stationed more permanently in established bases in the frontier provinces. In the early imperial period auxiliaries were probably conscripted through a levy imposed on conquered peoples, and some conscription will always have been needed, though in the later period, with improved service conditions, the number of volunteers is likely to have made up a larger proportion.

By the end of Augustus' reign auxiliaries may have been as numerous as legionaries, being organized in cavalry *alae* containing about 500 men (subdivided into *turmae*), part-mounted cohorts containing about 120 cavalry and 480 infantry, and infantry cohorts containing about 480 men (subdivided into centuries). A development perhaps dating from the reign of Vespasian saw the creation of some larger (milliary) units containing between 800 and 1,000 men. Many of the special posts available in the legions were also available in the cohorts and *alae* of the *auxilia*. Eventually the distinction between legions and auxilia became blurred and citizens are found serving in the auxilia in greater numbers (Cheesman 1914; Kraft 1951; Holder 1980; Saddington 1975; 1982; Eck and Wolff 1986; Dixon and Southern 1992; text no. 182).

Units of infantry and cavalry (*pedites singulares* and *equites singulares*) served as special guards in attendance upon officers and magistrates such as legionary legates, procurators, and most importantly, proconsuls and imperial legates. In the Republic commanders had traditionally taken some of their military guards from Italian allies or foreign troops. In the imperial period, although unit commanders recruited their guards from the soldiers under their direct command, soldiers who formed the guard of the provincial governor were chosen on temporary assignment from the auxilia stationed in the province. In the major consular provinces, units of *pedites singulares* and *equites singulares* were probably equal in strength to individual regular auxiliary *alae* and cohorts, and were commanded by men with the rank of legionary centurion. These units served to confer honour and prestige on men in authority; they acted as a bodyguard, assisted in ceremonial occasions, and performed police duties; in battle they attended upon the person of the commander, although there is no evidence that they formed a kind of strategic reserve.

44 *ILS* 2500, inscription, near Moguntiacum (Mainz), Upper Germany, early 1st C.AD

Adbogius, son of Coinagus, of the Petrocorian people (in Gaul), cavalryman of the *ala* of Ruso, 28 years old, ten years' service, lies here. His freedman set this up in accordance with his will.

45 *RIB* **201 = Smallwood *GN* 284 (a), inscription, Camulodunum (Colchester), Britain, 1st C.**AD

(Relief of cavalryman spearing a fallen enemy) Longinus, son of Sdapezematygus, soldier on double pay in the first *ala* of Thracians, from the district of Serdica, 40 years old, fifteen years' service. His heirs had this constructed in accordance with his will. He lies here.

46 *CIL* **8. 2094 = *ILS* 2518, inscription, Africa, 2nd C.**AD

To the spirits of the departed, Gaius Julius Dexter, veteran, soldier in a cavalry *ala*, clerk (*curator*) of a troop, armourer, standard-bearer of a troop, served twenty-six years, honourably and duly discharged, was a member of the Board of Two in his own colony of Thelepte, lived eighty-five years, was cremated here. Tutia Tertia, wife of Julius Dexter, lived seventy years, was cremated here.

Thelepte was a settlement in Africa (Medinet-el-Kedima in Tunisia), at a strategic point on the road from Ammaedara to Capsa. It was probably founded by veterans and was raised to the rank of colony in the reign of Trajan.

47 *ILS* **2558 = Smallwood *NH* 336, inscription, Danube area, 2nd C.**AD

I am the man who once was famous on the Pannonian shore and foremost in bravery among a thousand Batavians; with Hadrian watching I succeeded in swimming in full armour across the vast waters of the mighty Danube, and with a second arrow I transfixed and broke the arrow which I had shot from my bow, while it was still suspended in the air and falling back (to earth). No Roman or foreign soldier was ever able to outdo me in throwing the javelin, no Parthian in firing an arrow. Here I lie and here I have sanctified my achievements on this memorial stone. Let people see if anyone can emulate my feats after me. By my own example, I am the first person to have done such deeds.

Batavian cavalry units impressed Hadrian by swimming the Danube fully armed (Dio, 69. 9).

48 *P. Oxy.* **1666 = Daris, *Documenti* 8, papyrus, Oxyrhynchus, Egypt, 3rd C.**AD

Pausanias to his brother Heraclides, greetings. I think that our brother Sarapammon has told you the reason why I went down to Alexandria, and I have already written to you about young Pausanias enlisting in a legion. As he no longer wished to serve in a legion but in an *ala*, on learning this I was obliged however reluctantly to go to see him. So, after many appeals from his mother and sister to get him transferred to Coptos, I went down to Alexandria and used many approaches until he was transferred to the *ala* at Coptos. Although I wanted to pay you a visit on the voyage up, we were limited by the leave granted to the lad by the most distinguished Prefect, and for this reason I was unable to visit you. . .

49 *CIL* 8. 2251 = *ILS* 2578, inscription, Mascula (Khenchela), Numidia, late 1st/early 2nd C.AD

Titus Flavius Bitus, cavalryman of second twin cohort of Thracians, lived fifty-five years, served twenty-seven years, Julia Marcella, his sister, and Bitus [his son set this up].

50 *ILS* 2585, inscription, Strassheim, Upper Germany, 1st/2nd (?) C.AD

To Mars and Victory, Soemus Severus, chief clerk (*cornicularius*) of the first Flavian milliary cohort of Damascene mounted archers, willingly, happily, and deservedly fulfilled his vow.

51 *ILS* 2590, inscription, Asia

To the spirits of the departed, Lucius Calpurnius Valens, orderly (*optio*) of the first Lepidian part-mounted cohort of Roman Citizens, century of Ponticus, lived forty years, served eighteen years. Calpurnia Leda, his wife, erected this.

It is obscure how this cohort (first recorded in Syria *c.* AD 69) acquired its title 'Lepidiana' derived from a personal name (Holder 1980: 21–2; Speidel 1982b). The title 'Roman Citizens' indicates that at some point all members of the unit had received the citizenship before discharge.

52 *ILS* 2566, inscription, Aquae Mattiacae (Wiesbaden), Upper Germany

Quintus Vibius Agustus, Raetian, soldier of the second cohort of Raetians, 30 years of age, thirteen years' service. His heir had this set up.

53 *ILS* **2569, inscription, Colonia Agrippinensis (Cologne), Lower Germany**

Gaius Julius Baccus, son of Gaius, of the tribe Galeria, from Lugdunum, soldier of the first cohort of Thracians, 38 years old, fifteen years' service. Antistius Atticus and Bassius Communis, his heirs, had this erected.

Baccus was a Roman citizen serving in an auxiliary unit, unusually recording his tribe; cf. text no. 54, he was probably granted citizenship by Tiberius.

54 *ILS* **2571, inscription, near Bingium (Bingen), Upper Germany, 1st C.**AD

(Sculpture of a soldier) Tiberius Julius Abdes Pantera, from Sidon, 62 years old, forty years' service, soldier from the cohort of archers, is buried here.

55 *ILS* **2416, with Speidel 1978b: 71–2, inscription, Tarraco (Tarragona), Spain,** AD **182**

Sacred to Mars of the Parade and Training Ground for the welfare of Emperor Marcus Aurelius Commodus Augustus and the mounted guards, Titus Aurelius Decimus, centurion of Legion VII Gemina Fortunate, commander and also drill-instructor, dedicated this on 1 March, in the consulship of Mamertinus and Rufus.

56 *AE* **1923. 33, with Speidel 1978b: 75–6, inscription, Brohltal, Upper Germany, late 1st C.**AD

Sacred to Hercules Saxsanus. Celsus, centurion of the infantry guards, and his fellow-soldiers who are guards of Licinius Sura, legate, willingly, freely and deservedly fulfilled their vow.

This inscription from the stone quarries at Brohltal relates to units of the army of Lower Germany. It is not clear, however, if Sura is legate of Lower Germany or merely a legionary legate, since this officer also had *singulares*.

57 *ILS* **2588, with Speidel 1978b: 77, inscription, Alsheim, Upper Germany, 3rd C.**AD

In honour of Faustinius Faustinus, son of Sennaucus Florio, soldier of the first Flavian cohort of Damascenes, footguard of the governor, Gemellinia Faustina, his mother, and Faustinia Potentina, his sister, heirs, set this up in accordance with the wishes expressed in his will; he lived [twenty]-five years and died in the flower of his youth. They had this erected.

The Urban Soldiers

During the Republic a guard was set at the commander's headquarters (*praetorium*), but during the civil wars this had become a personal bodyguard in attendance upon the military leaders. Augustus transformed this practice by establishing in 27 BC an élite unit with superior emoluments, shorter service, and more elaborate uniform than the legionaries, to act as his permanent bodyguard. The praetorian guard consisted of nine cohorts with 1,000 or possibly 500 men in each, and was stationed in Italian towns in the vicinity of Rome, although three cohorts always attended upon the person of the emperor. These soldiers, though armed, did not appear in dress uniform. This was a political ploy designed to allay the fears of senators who were unaccustomed to the presence of soldiers in Rome or indeed in Italy. The guard remained largely Italian even when few Italians served in the legions.

When in 2 BC Augustus appointed two men of equestrian rank as praetorian prefects, they served as deputy commanders, since the emperor commanded the guard personally. By AD 23 Sejanus, the powerful praetorian prefect, had persuaded Tiberius to concentrate all the praetorians in a camp on the outskirts of Rome, and the guard remained central to Roman political life until disbanded by Constantine in AD 312. Sejanus may also have been responsible for increasing the number of cohorts to twelve (see text no. 96); Vitellius added another four, but Domitian settled the guard's strength at ten cohorts, each with 1,000 men. Septimius Severus further increased the complement of troops in Italy by stationing a legion at Albanum, fifteen miles south east of Rome. Part of the guard normally accompanied an emperor on campaign and under the Flavians a special mounted bodyguard was created (*equites singulares Augusti*).

Augustus also provided for a kind of police force – recruited from Italians, serving for twenty years in three urban cohorts, each 500 strong, commanded by a tribune, and under the overall direction of the prefect of the city. By Flavian times the number of cohorts had been increased to four, each of which contained 1,000 men. Additional cohorts were stationed at Puteoli, Ostia, and Carthage (all important for the shipment of corn to Rome), and at Lugdunum where there was a mint. Augustus instituted a fire brigade (*Vigiles*) possibly 3,920 strong, rising to 7,840 by AD 205, recruited from freedmen who served for six

years, and organized in seven cohorts commanded by tribunes, under
the general direction of the *praefectus Vigilum* (Baillie Reynolds 1926;
Durry 1938; Passerini 1939; Speidel 1965; Freis 1967; Rainbird 1986).

58 *CIL* 5. 2837 = *ILS* 2022, inscription, Patavium (Padua), 1st C.AD

Gaius Remmius Rufus, son of Publius, was discharged from the
praetorian guard of the divine Augustus, supervisor and [_ _ _

59 *CIL* 6. 2421 = *ILS* 2024, inscription, Rome

Titus Antistius Sabinus, of the tribe Stellatina, from Augusta Taurin-
orum (Turin), soldier for ten years in the first praetorian cohort, in the
century of Romulus.

60 *CIL* 6. 2489 = *ILS* 2028, inscription, Rome

To the spirits of the departed. Quintus Caetronius Passer, son of
Quintus, of the tribe Poblilia, soldier in the third praetorian cohort for
eighteen years, discharged under the two Gemini, (set this up) for
himself and for Masuria Marcella, daughter of Marcus.
  I lived as I wished, properly, in poverty, and honourably. I cheated no
one, and may that assist my shade.
Frontage 11$^{1/3}$ feet, 13$^{1/3}$ feet back (area attached to the tomb).

The meaning of 'Gemini' is obscure; it may refer to the consuls of AD 29, but it
has been suggested that the inscription dates from the late first century.

61 *ILS* 9494 = *EJ* 252, inscription, Ostia, early 1st C.AD

[_ _ _], soldier of the sixth praetorian cohort. The people of Ostia
granted a place for his burial and decreed that he should be buried with
a public funeral because he was killed while extinguishing a fire.
Frontage 12 feet, 25 feet back (area attached to the tomb).

62 *CIL* 6. 2558 = *ILS* 2036, inscription, Rome, 1st C. AD

Gaius Atilius Crescens, son of Gaius, of the tribe Romilia, served in
Legion IV for nine years, transferred to the praetorian guard, fifth
praetorian cohort, served three years.

Crescens probably served in the IV Macedonica, which supported Vitellius in
AD 69.

63 *CIL* 6. 2725 = *ILS* 2034, inscription, Rome, late 1st C.AD

Gaius Vedennius Moderatus, son of Gaius, of the tribe Quirina, from Antium, soldier in Legion XVI Gallica for ten years, transferred to the ninth praetorian cohort, in which he served for eight years, honourably discharged, recalled by the emperor and appointed imperial reservist (*evocatus Augusti*), builder (?) of the imperial armoury, reservist for twenty-three years, awarded military decorations on two occasions, by the divine Vespasian, and by Emperor Domitian Augustus, Conqueror of the Germans [_ _ _

The Legion XVI Gallica based in Lower Germany had sent detachments to Italy in AD 69 in support of Vitellius. Moderatus may have been one of the legionaries who, according to Tacitus, (*Histories* 2. 94), were rewarded by the new emperor with transfer to the praetorian guard.

64 *CIL* 6. 2437 = *ILS* 2037, inscription, Rome, 3rd C.AD

(Sculpture of a soldier) To the spirits of the departed, in honour of Gaius Maccenius Vibius, soldier of the first praetorian cohort, century of Primitivus, lived fifty-five years, soldier in Legion X Gemina for nine years, transferred from there to the praetorian guard, served for fourteen years; Ulpia Valentina set this up for her dearly-beloved, estimable husband, under the charge of Maccenius Crispinus, reservist of our Emperor, in accordance with the wishes expressed by his brother in his will.

65 *CIL* 6. 2758, inscription, Rome, late 2nd C.AD

Sacred to the spirits of the departed. Valerius Martinus, soldier of the tenth praetorian cohort, century of Martialis, who served in Legion XIV Gemina, was transferred to the praetorian guard for three years, of Pannonian nationality, lived twenty-five years, three months, fifteen days. Valerius Januarinus, orderly (*optio*) of the century, set this up for an estimable citizen.

In 193 Septimius Severus, governor of Upper Pannonia, marched on Rome and captured it. One of his first decisions was to disband the old praetorian guard which had connived at the overthrow of two emperors, and replace it with soldiers drawn in the main from the Danubian legions which had first supported him. Thereafter replacements for the praetorians were often sought from legionary soldiers in various provinces, though Italians were not excluded. Texts nos. 64 and 65 probably illustrate soldiers who were transferred to the guard by Severus in 193, since Martinus served in XIV Gemina which was the first to support Severus at Carnuntum, and Vibius in X Gemina, which was stationed nearby at Vindobona and soon followed its example.

66 *CIL* 6. 210, inscription, Rome, AD 208

For the welfare of our lords the Emperors, an altar for Hercules the Defender was set up to the spirit of his century in accordance with his vow by Lucius Domitius Valerianus, from Jerusalem, with eighteen years of service, soldier of the tenth praetorian cohort, loyal avenging, in the century of Flavius Caralitanus, selected for the praetorian guard of our Lords from Legion VI Ferrata, Faithful Steadfast, honourably discharged on 7 January, in the consulship of our Lords, Emperor Antoninus Pius Augustus for the third time and Geta, most noble Caesar, for the second time.

This man was transferred into the praetorian guard during Severus' reign, illustrating the practice of recruitment from serving legionaries.

67 *CIL* 3. 2887 = *ILS* 9067, with Breeze 1974, inscription, Corinium, Dalmatia, 2nd C.AD

Aulus Saufeius Emax, son of Publius, of the tribe Camilia, from Ansium (?), soldier of the ninth praetorian cohort, century of Firmius Tertullus, served [_ _ _] years, clerk of a tribune, officer of the watchword, o[rderly], decorated by Emperor [_ _ _] Caesar Augustus, with necklaces [_ _ _

Among the praetorians there was the same range of specialist functions, clerkships, and other posts of limited responsibility as in the legions.

68 *CIL* 6. 2544 = *ILS* 2066, inscription, Rome, 3rd C.AD

(Sculpture of a soldier) To the spirits of the departed, in honour of Pletorius Primus, clerk of the treasury of the fourth praetorian cohort, century of Silvanus, from the province of Lower Pannonia, born at castle Vixillum, who lived thirty-five years, four months, served fifteen years, eight months. Veturia Digna set this up for her estimable husband.

69 *CIL* 9. 5809 = *ILS* 2078, inscription, Recanati, Picenum, 1st (?) C.AD

Gaius Lucilius Vindex, son of Gaius, of the tribe Velina, soldier of the sixth praetorian cohort, lived thirty years, served twelve years as *principalis*, acting as clerk of a tribune, then as orderly (*optio*) in a century, in his will ordered this to be constructed as a mark of esteem and piety and in honour of Gaius Lucilius Secundus, his father, and Lor[enia _ _ _], his mother, and [_ _ _], his grandmother, out of the 2,000 sesterces he bequeathed.

Each praetorian cohort had a small number of cavalry attached to it; these *equites praetoriani* numbered about 900 for the whole guard (Durry 1938: 99–100; Speidel 1965).

70 *CIL* 6. 2440 = *ILS* 2077, inscription, Rome, 2nd C.AD

To the spirits of the departed, in honour of Lucius Naevius Paullinus, son of Lucius, of the tribe Camilia, reservist of the Emperor, (who) served as a cavalryman in the first praetorian cohort, orderly (*optio*) of the cavalry, chief clerk (*cornicularius*) of a tribune, was on active service for sixteen years, was a reservist for three years. Lucius Pessedius Agilis, reservist of the emperor, set this up for his excellent friend.

71 *CIL* 6. 2601 = *ILS* 2055, inscription, near Rome, 3rd C.AD

To the spirits of the departed, in honour of Aurelius Bitus, cavalryman of the sixth praetorian cohort, of Thracian nationality, citizen of Philippopolis, of more or less thirty-five years, who served seventeen years as follows: in Legion I Italica, two years, in the second praetorian cohort as an ordinary soldier, fourteen years; when promoted cavalryman he served for ten months; Valerius Aulusanus, praetorian guardsman, (set this up) to his most worthy and matchless brother.

The *equites singulares Augusti* or mounted imperial bodyguards were established probably by the Flavians with an initial strength of 500, later rising to 1,000, to provide élite cavalry support for the praetorians when they accompanied the emperor on campaign. They were to the praetorian guard what the auxilia were to the legions. The *equites* were recruited from auxiliary cavalry *alae*, with a large proportion of men from Germany, Raetia, Noricum, and Pannonia; they were divided into troops commanded by decurions under the overall charge of a tribune, although the ultimate responsibility rested with the praetorian prefects. The service conditions of the *equites singulares Augusti* were similar to those of the auxilia, but their presence in Rome as an élite unit may have increased the status of the auxiliaries in general (Speidel 1965).

72 *CIL* 6. 715 = *ILS* 2184, inscription, Rome, AD 158

To the unconquered Sun god, in accordance with the vow undertaken, on receiving an honourable discharge from the unit of mounted bodyguards of the Emperor, Publius Aelius Amandus gave this as a gift, in the consulship of Tertullus and Sacerdos.

73 *CIL* 6. 3177 = *ILS* 2196, inscription, Rome, 2nd C.AD

To the spirits of the departed, in honour of Publius Aelius Bassus, armourer, mounted bodyguard of the Emperor, troop of Aelius Crispus, of Bessian nationality, from Claudia Aprum, lived forty-one years, served twenty-one years; Titus Flavius Marcellinus, standard-bearer, heir, and Aurelius Quintus, soldier on double pay, second heir, had this set up to a fellow-townsman and estimable friend.

74 *CIL* 6. 3308 = *ILS* 2210, inscription, Rome, late 2nd/3rd C.AD

To the spirits of the departed, in honour of Ulpius Titus, mounted bodyguard of our Emperor, troop of Emeritus, of Boian nationality, lived thirty-five years, served sixteen years, selected from the first *ala* of Thracians from Upper Pannonia; Ulpius Felicio, his father and heir, and Septimius Provincialis, and Marcellinius Verus, heirs, had this set up to an estimable man, under the charge of Gaius Cestius Severus, veteran of our Emperor. (Figure of a horse.)

We all pray that the earth may be light upon you.

75 *ILS* 2188, inscription, Rome, AD 219

To Hercules Macusanus, for the return of our lord Marcus Aurelius Antoninus Pius Fortunate Augustus, his Antoninian mounted body-guards, Batavian or Thracian citizens selected from the province of Lower Germany, willingly and deservedly fulfilled their vow, on 29 September, in the consulship of our lord Emperor Antoninus Augustus for the second time and Tineius Sacerdos for the second time.

In addition to all the other forces at his disposal in Rome, Augustus instituted a small, special bodyguard of Germans, generally Batavians. It was said that Nero placed special trust in these men precisely because they were outsiders (Tacitus, *Annals* 15. 58). Galba disbanded them (Suet., *Vit. Galb.* 12).

76 Smallwood *GN* 293, inscription, Rome, 1st C.AD

Indus, bodyguard of Nero Claudius Caesar Augustus, in the decuria of Secundus, of Batavian nationality, lived thirty-six years. He lies here. Eumenes, his brother and heir, of the association of Germans, set this up.

77 *CIL* 6. 2896 = *ILS* 2109, inscription, Rome, AD 160

To the spirits of the departed, in honour of Julius Seius Junior, son of Gaius, of the tribe Fabia, from Rome, veteran of the Emperor, served ten years in the eleventh urban cohort, century of Valerius, honourably discharged on 9 January in the consulship of Appius Annius Atilius Bradua and Titus Vibius Varus, lived forty years, twenty days; Julia Palestrice set this up to her estimable husband.

78 *CIL* 6. 217 = *ILS* 2106, inscription, Rome, AD 182

Quintus Tersina Lupus, son of Quintus, of the tribe Scaptia, from Florentia, soldier of the twelfth urban cohort, century of Dexter, ordered in his will that (a statue of) the spirit of the century with a marble base should be set up.

(On the side) Set up on 13 April, in the consulship of Mamertinus and Rufus.

79 *CIL* 9. 1617 = *ILS* 2117, inscription, Beneventum, AD 146

Gaius Luccius Sabinus, son of Gaius, of the tribe Stellatina, town councillor at Beneventum, in his lifetime constructed this for himself and Ofillia Parata, his wife, and Luccius Verecundus, his brother, and his descendants; he served in the first urban cohort at the side of the tribunes, was an attendant (*secutor*), orderly (*optio*) of the hospital, orderly of the prison, aide (*singularis*), clerk (*beneficiarius*) of a tribune, put in charge of the examination of witnesses by Annius Verus prefect of the city, also officer in charge of the watchword, orderly, standard-bearer, clerk of the treasury, orderly in charge of records, senior clerk (*cornicularius*) of a tribune, clerk of Valerius Asiaticus prefect of the city, discharged by Emperor Hadrian Augustus in the consulship of Servianus for the third time and Vibius Varus (AD 134), town councillor, 22 April, in the consulship of Erucius Clarus for the second time. Frontage – twenty feet, twenty feet back (area attached to the tomb).

This career is the most detailed known in any part of the army. Sabinus held six junior posts on the army staff, all three posts in the century, and then four senior staff posts. He may however be unusual in that he served for part of his career in a cohort outside Rome, with fewer soldiers available to perform the necessary duties. The first Flavian urban cohort was reorganized under the Flavians and stationed at Lugdunum. At this time urban cohorts X, XI, XII, and XIV were stationed in Rome, XIII in Carthage.

80 *ILS* 2119, inscription, Lugdunum, late 1st C.AD

Marcus Curvelius Robustus, son of Marcus, of the tribe Aniensis, soldier of the first Flavian urban cohort, century of Herennius, instructed in his will that this should be set up for himself. His heir took charge of its construction.

81 *CIL* 6. 2994 = *ILS* 2172, inscription, Rome

To the spirits of the departed, in honour of Titus Avidius Romanus, soldier of the seventh cohort of *vigiles*, pump-operator, century of Laetorius, Avidia Romana, his mother, to her very dutiful son.

82 *CIL* 11. 1438 = *ILS* 2166, inscription, Pisa, 2nd (?) C.AD

Gaius Virrius Jucundus, standard-bearer (*vexillarius*) of the second cohort of *vigiles*, century of Visertius Latinus, served six years, seven months, nineteen days, during which he was officer in charge of the watchword, orderly (*optio*), standard-bearer, lived twenty-seven years, instructed in his will that an altar with its own base should be constructed; by the decision of Lucilia Lacaena, and Gaius Virrius Jucundus, his son.

2 The officers

CENTURIONS

Centurions were an important part of the command structure of the Roman army and held a more responsible position than that of non-commissioned officers in modern armies. There were 59 centurions in a legion, with six centuries of 80 men in each of the ten cohorts, except the first, which consisted of five centuries of double strength. There were several avenues of promotion to the centurionate: (1) men of equestrian status were sometimes admitted directly from civilian life. Doubtless some sought to escape from troubles at home by enlistment, and the substantial pay rates for centurions might help allay financial anxieties (about 18,000 sesterces in the second century AD, 72,000 for a chief centurion). The fact that equestrians were prepared to enlist demonstrates the status of the centurionate, but also shows that not all centurions were professional, well-trained soldiers. Men of equestrian rank, because of their social standing and superior education could expect rapid promotion; (2) legionaries with long service; serving legionaries will have made up the largest proportion of new centurions in any one year; they were generally men who had held a number of special posts and responsibilities (see pp. 28–32); (3) centurions and decurions of auxiliary units; (4) urban soldiers, especially praetorians, who had completed their term of military service in Rome.

Rules of seniority within the centurionate are obscure, and the reconstruction of elaborate schemes of promotion is not justified on the basis of the evidence of career inscriptions, which cannot tell us why and how a man was promoted. The six centurions in each cohort were *pilus prior, pilus posterior, princeps prior, princeps posterior, hastatus prior, hastatus posterior*, and it is possible that centurions in all cohorts except the first were equal in rank, distinguished only by seniority. Promotion was then to the first cohort, whose five centurions were the most senior and were known as the *primi ordines*; the centurion commanding the first century of this cohort was the chief centurion of the legion (*primus pilus*), with responsibility for the legionary eagle. The *primus pilus* was appointed for one year and usually gained equestrian rank immediately afterwards; then he could advance to the prefecture of the camp (ranking immediately below the senatorial tribune), or a tribunate in the praetorians, urban cohorts, or *vigiles*. After one or more of these posts, the way was now open to the most favoured ex-chief centurions for promotion to procuratorships and equestrian governorships; sometimes a man was first posted back to a legion to hold the chief centurionate for a second time (*primus pilus bis*). See Dobson and Breeze 1969; Dobson 1972; 1974; 1978.

The centurion was responsible for the administration of his century, for the conveyance of orders and the leadership of his men in battle, and for training the troops and maintaining discipline (cf. text no. 17). In mutinies or disturbances it was often centurions who suffered at the hands of a vengeful soldiery (Tacitus, *Annals* 1. 23). Long-serving centurions could be a source of valuable advice for higher officers who were non-specialists and often inexperienced. Sometimes a centurion was temporarily placed in command of a detachment of legionaries or auxiliaries, or given special duties, e.g. the role of messenger to foreign kings or commanders. Since a centurion was likely to be a man of above-average education and general competence, with good promotion prospects and excellent emoluments in the army, he would have little in common with ordinary soldiers. Centurions will probably have formed a tightly-knit group maintaining conservative loyalty to the emperor. It is difficult to say how important a factor this was in times of crisis or civil war. In AD 68–69 centurions often found it safer to fall in with the views of their men (Campbell 1984: 106–9; see also Plate 2).

In the *auxilia*, the *decurio* who commanded a troop (*turma*) of cavalry in an *ala* ranked highest, and it was this officer who was most often promoted to the legionary centurionate; next came the centurions of an infantry cohort, and finally the *decuriones* or centurions of a part-mounted cohort (see Gilliam 1957b).

83 Pliny (1st–2nd C.AD) *Letters*, 6. 25

(Pliny is discussing the mysterious disappearance of a Roman *eques*, Robustus.) Indeed I suspect that something similar has happened to Robustus as once befell my fellow-townsman Metilius Crispus. I had obtained the rank of centurion for him and on his departure had even given him 40,000 sesterces for gear and equipment, but afterwards I did not receive any letters from him or any message about his fate. . .

The emperor was ultimately responsible for approving the appointment of centurions, though it is likely that he intervened personally in a soldier's career only in exceptional circumstances. Powerful patrons like Pliny could approach the emperor directly, or an army commander, to secure his recommendation for a prospective centurion. Vespasian, on finding that a young man of good birth who was unsuited for military service had acquired appointment as a centurion in the army because of his poor financial circumstances, granted him money and an honourable discharge (Frontinus, *Stratagems* 4. 6. 4).

84 Suetonius (1st–2nd C.AD), *On Grammarians*, 24

Marcus Valerius Probus of Berytus, for a long time tried to obtain an appointment as a centurion until he became tired of waiting and devoted his attention to study.

85 *ILS* 2656 = Smallwood *NH* 294, inscription, Rome, 2nd C.AD

To Tiberius Claudius Vitalis, son of Tiberius, of the tribe Galeria, from the rank of Roman *eques* he received the post of centurion in Legion V Macedonica, was advanced from Legion V Macedonica to Legion I Italica, was decorated in the Dacian War with Necklaces, Armbands, Ornaments, and a Rampart Crown, was advanced from Legion I Italica to Legion I Minervia, was again decorated in the Dacian War with Necklaces, Armbands, Ornaments, and a Rampart Crown, was advanced from Legion I Minervia to Legion XX Victrix, was also advanced within the same legion, was again advanced from Legion XX Victrix to Legion IX Hispana, was advanced from Legion IX Hispana to Legion VII Claudia, Loyal and Faithful, was also advanced within the same legion, served in the second cohort as *princeps posterior* for eleven years, lived forty-one years.

Vitalis, after entering the army with equestrian rank, made seven moves in his career, two of them within a legion; he was presumably sent where a need arose and may have taken his century with him in order to reinforce another legion. His advancement on two occasions within a legion may be explained on the hypothesis that he was needed to do a special job in one century for which no other suitably experienced candidate was available (see also texts nos 86–7).

86 *CIL* 8. 217 = *ILS* 2658, inscription, near Cillium, Africa, 3rd C. AD

[_ _ _ Petronius Fortunatus] served for fifty years, four in Legion I Italica as clerk, officer in charge of watchword, orderly (*optio*), standard-bearer; he was promoted to centurion by the vote of the [same] legion, served as centurion of Legion I Italica, centurion of Legion VI F[errata], centurion of Legion I Minervia, centurion of Legion X Gemina, centurion of Legion II A[ugusta], centurion of Legion III Augusta, centurion of Legion III Gallica, centurion of Legion XXX Ulpia, centurion of Legion VI Victrix, centurion of Legion III Cyrenaica, centurion of Legion XV Apollinaris, centurion of Legion II Parthica, centurion of Legion I Adiutrix; in the Parthian expedition he was decorated for bravery with a Wall and Rampart Crown and with Necklaces and Ornaments; he was in his eightieth year at the completion of this monument for himself and for Claudia Marcia Capitolina, his beloved wife, who was in her sixty-fifth year at the time of the completion of this monument, and for his son, Marcus Petronius Fortunatus, who served in the army for six years, centurion of Legion XXII Primigenia, centurion of Legion II Augusta, lived thirty-five years; for their beloved son, Fortunatus and Marcia, his parents, built this as a memorial.

See E. B. Birley 1965. This man's forty-six years of service as a centurion in thirteen legions saw him transferred from Lower Moesia to Syria Palestina (he probably met his wife in Jerusalem), Lower Germany, Upper Pannonia, Britain, Numidia, Syria, Lower Germany, Britain, Arabia, Cappadocia, probably Albanum in Italy, and Upper or Lower Pannonia. These long-distance transfers can hardly be seen as promotions for a soldier who did not reach the *primi ordines*; it seems rather that the government used him as circumstances demanded. There were doubtless many experienced centurions who were not set for higher things and who were proud simply of their status as centurion. For the appointment of a centurion on the vote of the legion, see also *AE* 1976. 540.

87 *CIL* 8. 2877 = *ILS* 2653, inscription, Lambaesis, Africa, 3rd C. AD

(Bust of a man holding a book.) To the spirits of the departed. Titus Flavius Virilis, centurion of Legion II Augusta, centurion of Legion XX Valeria Victrix, centurion of Legion VI Victrix, centurion of Legion XX Valeria Victrix, centurion of Legion III Augusta, centurion of Legion III Parthica Severiana as *hastatus posterior* of the ninth cohort, lived seventy years and served forty-five years. Lollia Bodicca, his wife, and Victor and Victorinus, sons of Flavius, his heirs, had this constructed at a cost of 1,200 sesterces.

Virilis held six posts as centurion, two in one legion at different times; the first four were in Britain, where he presumably met his wife; then he was transferred to Numidia, and finally to Mesopotamia, finishing his career in the junior century of the ninth cohort. This is explicable if it is right that all centurions in cohorts 2–10 had equal rank. He may have served as a legionary before promotion to the centurionate. See also C. Bruun, *Arctos* 1988, 36.

88 *CIL* 8. 2354, inscription, Thamugadi (Timgad), Numidia, 2nd C.AD

Sacred to the Parthian victory of the Emperor, in accordance with the will of Marcus Annius Martialis, son of Marcus, of the tribe Quirina, soldier of Legion III Augusta, soldier on double pay in the *ala* of Pannonians, decurion of the same *ala*, centurion of Legion III Augusta and Legion XXX Ulpia Victrix, honourably discharged by Emperor Trajan Optimus Augustus, Conqueror of the Germans, Conqueror of the Dacians, Conqueror of the Parthians. Protus, Hilarus, Eros, freedmen of Marcus Annius, arranged for the construction of and also dedicated the individual statues (?) from a sum of 8,000 sesterces less the 5 per cent inheritance tax of the Roman people, and themselves added 3,000 sesterces. By decree of the town councillors.

Martialis was promoted to a legionary centurionate from the command of a troop in an auxiliary *ala*.

89 *ILS* 2666, inscription, Tuficum, Umbria, 2nd C.AD

To Sextus Aetrius Ferox, son of Sextus, of the tribe Oufentina, centurion of Legion II Traiana Brave; this man was the first of all those who held the post of chief clerk (*cornicularius*) of the Prefect of the *vigiles* to be appointed centurion in Alexandria, by Emperor Caesar Antoninus Augustus Pius, father of the fatherland, because he conducted himself so diligently in the stages of his military service, by decree of the town councillors and with the agreement of the people, because of his worthiness. This man at the dedication of the statue granted a banquet and 4,000 sesterces to the townsfolk and the local inhabitants of both sexes.

Promotion from the *vigiles* to centurion rank was unusual, and only one other example is known (*CIL* 6. 414b). Another inscription which was perhaps carved on the same stone records the gratitude of the community to Ferox for his help when it was needed, and most recently for helping to persuade Antoninus Pius to permit the community to levy a tax to defray the cost of laying a paved road (*ILS* 2666a – AD 141). Ferox, obviously a man of some wealth, had used his contacts with the emperor to gain a concession for his community.

90 Pflaum, *Carrières* 32 = Smallwood *GN* 283, inscription, Ariminum, AD 66

To Marcus Vettius Valens, son of Marcus, of the Aniensis tribe, soldier of the eighth praetorian cohort, clerk (*beneficiarius*) of the praetorian prefect, decorated in the British war with Necklaces, Armbands, and Ornaments, reservist of the Emperor, decorated with a Gold Crown, centurion of the sixth cohort of *vigiles*, centurion of the Imperial messengers, centurion of the sixteenth urban cohort, centurion of the second praetorian cohort, trainer of the cavalry scouts, chief of the headquarters, [centurion ?] of Legion XIII Gemina from the post of *trecenarius*, [chief centurion] of Legion VI Victrix, decorated for his successful exploits against the Astures with Necklaces, Ornaments, and Armbands, tribune of the fifth cohort of *vigiles*, tribune of the twelfth urban cohort, tribune of the third praetorian cohort, [chief centurion for a second time ?] of Legion XIV Gemina Warlike Victorious, procurator of Emperor Nero Caesar Augustus of the province of Lusitania, patron of the colony, ten scouts (set this up) in his honour, in the consulship of Gaius Luccius Telesinus and Gaius Suetonius Paulinus.

Beginning his military career as an ordinary praetorian guardsman, Valens passed by way of a staff post, imperial reservist, and centurionates in the urban troops, to the post of chief centurion in a legion, after which he acquired equestrian rank, assuming eventually the important procuratorship of Lusitania.

Trecenarius – the meaning is obscure; in the urban troops, perhaps the centurion in command of the *speculatores*, or possibly the title of the most senior centurion.

91 *ILS* 2081 = Smallwood *NH* 300, inscription, Matilica, Umbria, 2nd C.AD

To Gaius Arrius Clemens, son of Gaius, of the tribe Cornelia, soldier of the ninth praetorian cohort, mounted soldier of the same cohort, decorated by Emperor Trajan with Necklaces, Armbands, and Ornaments for service in the Dacian War, aide (*singularis*) of the praetorian prefects, officer in charge of the watchword, orderly (*optio*), clerk in charge of the treasury, chief clerk of a military tribune, reservist of the Emperor, centurion of the first cohort of *vigiles*, centurion of the Imperial messengers (*statores*), centurion of the fourteenth urban cohort, centurion of the seventh praetorian cohort, *trecenarius*, decorated by Emperor Hadrian with an Untipped Spear and Gold Crown, centurion of Legion III Augusta, chief centurion, member of the Board of Two *quinquennalis*, patron of the municipality, curator of the community; the town councillors, the board of six Augustales, and the citizens of the municipality of Matilica (set this up).

This is fairly typical of the more elaborate 2nd century pattern of promotion to the centurionate from the guard: junior staff posts, posts in the century, treasury clerk, senior staff post, reservist, centurionate in Rome.

Quinquennalis was used to describe a municipal magistrate appointed for five years, or as a title bestowed every fifth year on a municipal magistrate charged with conducting the local census.

92 *ILS* 7178, with *AE* 1961. 208, inscription, Oescus (Ghighen), Lower Moesia, 3rd C.AD

To Titus Aurelius Flavinus, son of Titus, of the tribe Papiria, chief centurion and leader of the magistrates of the colony of Oescus, town councillor of the communities of the Tyrani, Dionysiopolitani, Marcianopolitani, Tungri, and the Aquincenses, patron of the guild of engineers, honoured by the divine Great Antoninus Augustus with 50,000 sesterces and 25,000 sesterces and promotion because of his dashing bravery against the enemy forces of the Cenni, and exploits successfully and bravely accomplished. Claudius Nicomedes, town councillor of the community of the Tyrani, (set this up) to his very worthy friend. This site was granted by decree of the town councillors.

This is a good example of the wealth and standing of a chief centurion in his local community and the surrounding area. It is notable how Caracalla intervened personally in his career.

93 *ILS* 2544 = *MW* 393, inscription, Augusta Taurinorum (Turin), 1st C. AD

To Gaius Valerius Clemens, son of Gaius, of the tribe Stellatina, chief centurion, member of the Board of Two *quinquennalis*, priest of the divine Augustus in perpetuity, patron of the colony, the decurions of the *ala* of Gaetulians which he commanded in the Judaean War under the divine Vespasian Augustus, father, (set this up) as a mark of respect. This man, on the occasion of the dedication of statues of him both on horseback and on foot, granted oil to the people of both sexes.

Clemens had probably held this temporary command of an *ala* while he was a centurion.

94 Pflaum, *Carrières* 50 = *MW* 372, inscription, Heliopolis (Baalbek), Syria, late 1st C.AD

To Gaius Velius Rufus, son of Salvius, chief centurion of Legion XII Fulminata, prefect of detachments of nine legions: I Adiutrix, II Adiutrix, II Augusta, VIII Augusta, IX Hispana, XIV Gemina, XX Victrix, XXI Rapax, tribune of the thirteenth urban cohort, commander of the army of Africa and Mauretania sent to crush the peoples which are in Mauretania, decorated by Emperor Vespasian and Emperor Titus in the Judaean War with a Rampart Crown, Necklaces, Ornaments, and Armbands, also decorated with a Wall Crown, two Spears, and two Standards, and in the war involving the Marcomanni, Quadi, and Sarmatians, against whom he took part in an expedition through the kingdom of Decebalus, king of the Dacians, also decorated with a Wall Crown, two Spears, and two Standards, procurator of Emperor Caesar Augustus, Conqueror of the Germans (i.e. Domitian) of the province of Pannonia and Dalmatia, also procurator of the province of Raetia with the right of capital punishment. He was despatched to Parthia and conveyed Epiphanes and Callinicus, sons of king Antiochus, back to Emperor Vespasian along with a considerable body of men who were liable for the payment of tribute. Marcus Alfius Olympiacus, son of Marcus, of the tribe Fabia, eagle-bearer, veteran of Legion XV Apollinaris (set this up).

The mason has made a mistake either by carving VIIII instead of VIII or, if nine is correct, by omitting the name of a legion from the list. It was possibly while he was chief centurion of XII Fulminata that Rufus was sent on a special mission to Parthia to escort into Roman custody the sons of Antiochus of Commagene who had allegedly been intriguing with the Parthians against Rome (Josephus, *Jewish War* 7. 219–43). Thereafter Rufus was given charge of a detachment of legionaries for Domitian's German war in AD 83; as tribune of the urban cohort stationed at Carthage he was chosen to command a force against a revolt in Mauretania, before returning to the Danube to fight in two further campaigns, around AD 86 and 92. His distinguished war record perhaps facilitated his direct advancement to important procuratorships without the tenure of any more tribunates or the post of chief centurion for a second time (Dobson 1978: 216–17).

95 *ILS* 9199 = Pflaum, *Carrières* 36, inscription, Heliopolis (Baalbek), 1st C.AD

To [Lucius] Antonius Naso, son of Marcus, of the tribe Fabia, [centurion] of Legion III Cyrenaica, [centurion] of Legion XIII Gemina, honoured by the emperor in the white drill (?), [prefect ?] of the community of the Colapiani, [chief] centurion of Legion XIII Gemina, tribune of Legion I Italica, [tribune] of the fourth cohort of *vigiles*, tribune of the fifteenth urban cohort, [tribune] of the eleventh urban cohort, tribune of the ninth praetorian cohort, decorated by Emperor Nero with a Rampart Crown, a Gold Crown, two Standards, and two Untipped Spears, [chief centurion for the second time ?] of Legion XIV Gemina, [tribune] of the first praetorian cohort and placed in charge of the veteran soldiers of several armies staying in Rome, procurator of the Emperor in Pontus and Bithynia [_ _ _

See Dobson 1978: 203–4. Antonius Naso is probably the same man who according to Tacitus (*Histories* 1. 20) was dismissed from the praetorians by Galba; he was presumably restored to favour after that emperor's downfall and resumed his military career; he may have won his military decorations during the rebellion of Vindex, or possibly for the suppression of the conspiracy of Piso in 65.

96 *AE* 1978. 286, with Letta 1978: 3–19, inscription, Leccei dei Marsi, 1st C.AD

To Aulus Virgius Marsus, son of Lucius, chief centurion of Legion III Gallica for a second time, camp prefect in Egypt, prefect of engineers, military tribune in the praetorian guard of the divine Augustus and Tiberius Caesar Augustus of the eleventh and fourth praetorian cohorts, member of the Board of Four *quinquennalis* when the office was conferred by the town councillors and people in the Augustan colony in the Troad (Alexandria Troas) and in Marruvium; through his will he granted five silver statues of the Emperors and 10,000 sesterces to the inhabitants of the district of Anninus (in the territory of Marruvium); the inhabitants of Anninus (set this up) in his honour.

This is the earliest clear example of the position of chief centurion twice. The inscription also suggests that the praetorian guard was increased from nine to twelve cohorts in Tiberius' reign, probably soon after AD 23, when, according to Tacitus (*Ann.* 4. 5), there were still only nine.

97 *CIL* 11. 5992 = Smallwood *NH* 297, inscription, Tifernum Mataurense, Umbria, 2nd C.AD

To Lucius Aconius Statura, son of Lucius, of the tribe Clustumina, centurion of Legion XI Claudia Loyal and Faithful, Legion IV Flavia Steadfast, Legion V Macedonica, Legion VII Claudia Loyal and Faithful, decorated by Emperor Trajan Augustus, Conqueror of the Germans, with Necklaces, Armbands, Ornaments, and a Rampart Crown for service in the Dacian War, and decorated by previous emperors with the same awards for service in wars against the Germans and Sarmatians, elevated by the divine Trajan from military service to equestrian rank, priest for a five-year period at Ariminum, *flamen* and priest for a five-year period at Tifernum Mataurense; in accordance with his will, Lucius Aconius Statura, his son, (set this up), at the dedication of which he gave a banquet for the town councillors and people. This site was granted by decree of the town councillors.

A man could be advanced rapidly through imperial patronage. Statura had not reached the *primi ordines*, but his distinguished war record may have been what brought him to Trajan's attention, though we cannot tell if there were other factors involved.

98 Fink, *RMR* 20, papyrus, Egypt, AD 243/4

_ _ _]fidius Victorinus: [enlisted] in the consulship of Praesens and Extricatus (AD 217); promoted decurion from cavalryman of legion II [Traiana Brave] [by _ _ _] most splendid man, who was commander at that time, 3 April, in the consulship of Atticus and Praetextatus (AD 242).

_ _ _]dimus Petosiris: [enlisted] in the consulship of Gratus and Seleucus (AD 221); promoted decurion from the position of soldier receiving pay and a half in the *ala* [_ _ _], [August–October] in the consulship of Atticus and Praetextatus (AD 242), by Basileus, Prefect of Egypt.

Antonius Ammonianus: [enlisted] in the consulship of Maximus and Urbanus (AD 234); promoted decurion from the position of soldier receiving pay and a half in the *ala* [_ _ _] by Basileus, most splendid man, Prefect of Egypt, 24 October in the consulship of Atticus and Praetextatus (AD 242).

Aurelius Hierax: [enlisted _ _ _]; promoted decurion from the position of soldier receiving double pay in the *ala* Gallica Gordiana [by _ _ _ November–December] in the consulship of Atticus and Praetextatus (AD 242).

_ _ _] Origines: [enlisted] in the consulship of the divine Alexander and Dio (AD 229); promoted decurion from cavalryman [_ _ _] [_ _ _] sixth praetorian cohort, [6–12] April, in the consulship of Arrianus and Papus (AD 243).

Third Cohort of Ituraeans

Centurions

Petenefotes Hierax [enlisted] in the consulship of Agricola and Clementinus (230); promoted decurion from [_ _ _] by Januarius, the then Prefect of Egypt, 30 August in the consulship of Agricola and Clementinus (AD 230).

Aurelius Harpocration [enlisted] in the consulship of Agricola and Clementinus (AD 230); promoted centurion from cavalryman [_ _ _] [by _ _ _] prefect of Egypt on the [5–7] of [month, year].

This is a list of centurions and decurions in order of seniority with details of their promotion. The unit mentioned in the first part of the papyrus received at least five new decurions during a year. However this is reasonable if, as seems likely, it was a milliary *ala*, which according to Hyginus (*On the Fortification of Camps* 16) had twenty-four decurions. The battle of Resaina in which Timesitheus, Praetorian Prefect of Gordian III, defeated the Persians and re-established Roman influence in Mesopotamia, took place in AD 243. The promotions recorded in the papyrus may indicate the replacement of losses incurred over the whole campaign, although it is not clear if the text predates the battle itself. For the appointment of auxiliary centurions, see Gilliam 1957b.

PREFECTS AND TRIBUNES

Equestrians commanded auxiliary units and held the tribunates of the urban troops and five of the six tribunates in a legion. By the late first century AD it had been established that these posts were held in a certain order – prefect of a cohort, military tribune (sometimes a milliary unit was commanded by a tribune), prefect of an *ala* – and although *equites* were not obliged to hold all three posts (*tres militiae*), some spent many years in various military assignments. Equestrian military officers might be holding their first post or might be experienced soldiers promoted from the rank of chief centurion (see above, texts nos 90, 94, 95). The promotion of such men not only increased the number of skilled officers but also fostered a degree of social mobility. The prefect of engineers (*praefectus fabrum*) in the late Republic served as a kind of personal adjutant to a military commander, and although the post continued to be held by men of equestrian rank with this function down to the mid-first century AD, it increasingly became a sinecure held by young equestrians, sometimes as a mark of honour. In addition, the patronage of senators or army commanders was often important in securing the advancement of equestrian officers; so the experience and presumed military ability of an applicant will have been only part of the reasons for his appointment. Men who had held one or more of these military posts often went on to occupy a combination of further posts, from financial procuratorships up to the major prefectures, e.g., the corn supply, Egypt, and praetorian guard. At the beginning of the imperial period most equestrian officers were Italians, often from leading municipal families. Gradually this predominance declined as equestrians from the Romanized provinces were advanced (Pflaum, *Carrières*; 1960–1; Saller 1980; 1982; Brunt 1983).

99 Pliny (1st–2nd C.AD), *Letters* 2. 13

Pliny to Priscus. You would willingly seize every opportunity of obliging me, and there is no one to whom I should prefer to be in debt. Therefore for two reasons I decided to approach you rather than anyone else with a request, which I am extremely anxious to obtain. You command a large army and this gives you a plentiful supply of largesse; moreover, the long period of your command has already enabled you to advance your own friends. Please turn your attention to mine – they are not numerous. . .

This is perhaps Javolenus Priscus who was governor of Syria possibly at the end of Domitian's reign. It was in the power of consular governors to appoint some of the officers of the units in their province, though this prerogative was limited by the number of posts available and the need to ensure the emperor's general approval (*Letters*, 4. 4, and texts nos 100, 101, Saller 1982: 105–6, 131–4). Pliny is not always interested in citing the qualities that might recommend his nominee for appointment. Where he does so, his comments are bland and general – friendship with Pliny, good birth, intellect, good conversation, diligence, honesty – implying no special suitability for military command.

100 Pliny, *Letters* 3. 8

Pliny to Suetonius Tranquillus. The manner in which you so discreetly request that I should transfer to your relative Caesennius Silvanus the military tribunate which I obtained for you from the distinguished senator Neratius Marcellus, is in keeping with the respect that you always display towards me. It would have brought me great delight to see you as tribune, but I shall be equally pleased to see some one else in that post through your efforts . . . Your name has not yet been entered in the records, so it is easy for me to substitute Silvanus in your place, and I hope that your kindness is as gratifying to him as mine is to you.

Suetonius, man of letters and biographer of the emperors, had been offered a post in the gift of Neratius Marcellus (consul AD 95), who was governor of Britain by AD 103.

101 Pliny, *Letters* 7. 22

Pliny to Pompeius Falco. You will be less surprised at my rather insistent approach to you to grant a tribunate to a friend of mine, when you discover his identity and character. Since you have given me your word I can now reveal his name and tell you something about him. He is Cornelius Minicianus, whose rank and character together bring prestige to my native district. He is of noble birth and rich, but he loves intellectual pursuits like a man who has to earn his living. Moreover, his honesty as a judge, his courage as an advocate, and his loyalty as a friend are quite outstanding. You will think that you are the person receiving a kindness when you see at first hand that he is the equal of any position or honour that can be conferred upon him. I do not wish to say anything more grandiloquent about a very modest man.

At the time of Pliny's letter, Pompeius Falco was governor of the single-legion province of Judaea, probably about 105–7; he then governed Moesia, around 116–17. An inscription (*ILS* 2722) shows that Minicianus was prefect of the first cohort of the Damascenes in Palestine, presumably the post granted by Falco, and later held a military tribunate in Africa.

102 *ILS* 9007 = *EJ* 224, inscription, Superaequum Paelignorum, 1st C.AD

Quintus Octavius Sagitta, son of Lucius, grandson of Gaius, great-grandson of Lucius, of the tribe Sergia, member of the Board of Two *quinquennalis* on three occasions, prefect of engineers, prefect of cavalry, military tribune by the people's vote, procurator of Caesar Augustus among the Vindelici and Raeti and in the Poenine Valley for four years, and in the province of Spain for ten years, and in Syria for two years.

The post of tribune 'by the people's vote' may be a survival of the tradition that the people should elect a certain number of military tribunes, or was perhaps a largely honorary position.

103 *EJ* 233, inscription, Emona (Ljubljana), Pannonia, 1st C.AD

Titus Junius Montanus, son of Decimus, of the tribe Aniensis, military tribune six times, prefect of cavalry six times, prefect of engineers twice, acting in place of a legate twice.

Montanus probably held each of these posts for a year, although his appointment in place of a senatorial legionary legate will have been a temporary emergency measure.

104 *CIL* 5. 7425 = *ILS* 2720, inscription, Libarna, Liguria, 2nd C. AD

To Quintus Attius Priscus, son of Titus, of the tribe Maecia, aedile, member of the Board of Two *quinquennalis*, priest of Augustus, priest, prefect of engineers, prefect of the first cohort of Spaniards and the first cohort of Montani and the first cohort of Lusitanians, military tribune of Legion I Adiutrix, decorated in the Suebic war by Emperor Nerva Caesar Augustus, Conqueror of the Germans, with a Gold Crown, Untipped Spear, and Standard, prefect of the first Augustan *ala* of Thracians; the people of the town (set this up).

105 *ILS* 9471 = Smallwood *NH* 243, inscription, Alabanda (or Heraclea Salbace ?), Asia, 2nd C.AD

To Lucius (?) Aburnius [_ _ _], prefect of engineers at Rome, military tribune of Legion III Augusta, prefect of the third Augustan part-mounted cohort of Thracians, prefect of the third Syrian part-mounted cohort of Thracians, placed in charge of the first Ulpian cohort of Petraeans, placed in charge of the corn supply on the banks of the Euphrates during the Parthian war, military tribune of Legion VI Ferrata, decorated by the divine Emperor Caesar Nerva Trajan Augustus, Conqueror of the Germans, Conqueror of the Dacians, Conqueror of the Parthians, with a Standard, Untipped Spear, and Gold Rampart Crown, prefect of the first Ulpian *ala* of *singulares*, appointed judicial officer for his native area in respect of the establishment of boundaries, recipient of congratulatory and honorary decrees from many provinces, Lucius Aburnius Torquatus, son of Aburnius Tuscianus, prefect of the second part-mounted Spanish cohort of Roman citizens, military tribune of the third Ulpian cohort of Petraeans, [prefect of the *ala*] of [Roman] c[itizens_ _ _].

106. Pflaum, *Carrières* 121 = Smallwood *NH* 249, inscription, Messana, Sicily, 2nd C.AD

Lucius Baebius Juncinus, son of Lucius, of the tribe Galeria, prefect of engineers, prefect of the fourth cohort of Raetians, military tribune of Legion XXII Deiotariana, prefect of the *ala* of Asturians, prefect of vehicles, judicial official of Egypt.

107 Pflaum, *Carrières* 116 = Smallwood *NH* 246, inscription, Ephesus, Asia, 2nd C.AD

[_ _ _ Aemilius] Juncus, prefect of the first cohort of Pannonians, military tribune of the fifth twin cohort of Roman citizens, military tribune of Legion X Fretensis, prefect of the *ala* of Gallic veterans, decorated by Emperor Trajan in the Parthian war with an Untipped Spear and Rampart Crown, procurator of Cilicia and Cyprus, judicial officer for Egypt at Alexandria, procurator of the province of Asia; the decurions and messengers and cavalrymen who are stationed at Lares Domnici (set this up).

108 Pflaum, *Carrières* 120 = Smallwood *NH* 265, inscription, Camerinum, Umbria, 2nd C.AD

To Marcus Maenius Agrippa Lucius Tusidius Campester, son of Gaius, of the tribe Cornelia, host of the divine Hadrian, father of a senator, prefect of the second Flavian part-mounted cohort of Britons, chosen by the divine Hadrian and sent on the British expedition, military tribune of the first part-mounted cohort of Spaniards, prefect of the first armoured *ala* of Gauls and Pannonians, procurator of the emperor, prefect of the British fleet, procurator of the province of Britain, with the public horse, patron of the municipality; the inhabitants of the Censorglacensis locality, having obtained through the generosity of the best and greatest Emperor Antoninus Augustus Pius, by means of his benevolent intervention, privileges by which their (rights) have been increased and confirmed in perpetuity, (set this up). This site was granted free by decision of the town councillors.

Campester was clearly a man of means, capable of entertaining a Roman emperor in his home, and his personal connection with Hadrian explains why he was singled out by him after only one military post and why he advanced so rapidly to the procuratorship of Britain. Campester's influence with Antoninus Pius also secured benefactions for his native community, and his family's status was enhanced by the fact that his son became a senator.

109 Pflaum, *Carrières* 59 = Smallwood *NH* 268, inscription, Aquileia, AD 105

To Gaius Minicius Italus, son of Gaius, of the tribe Velina, member of the Board of Four for legal jurisdiction, prefect of the fifth part-mounted cohort of Gauls, prefect of the first part-mounted cohort of Breucians, Roman citizens, prefect of the second part-mounted cohort of Varcians, military tribune of Legion VI Victrix, prefect of cavalry of the first *ala* of *singulares*, Roman citizens, decorated by the divine Vespasian with a Gold Crown and Untipped Spear, procurator of the province of the Hellespont, procurator of the province of Asia, which he governed on the orders of the emperor in place of the deceased proconsul, procurator of the provinces of Lugdunensis and Aquitania and also of Lactora, prefect of the corn supply, prefect of Egypt, priest of the divine Claudius, by decree of the town councillors.

On the side of the stone is a longer inscription celebrating the devotion of Minicius Italus to Aquileia, which was probably his home town, and his personal intervention with Trajan on its behalf. After military service in Lower Germany, Italus rose to be procurator of Asia and then acting governor of the province, perhaps after the execution of the proconsul Sextus Vettulenus Civica Cerealis on the orders of Domitian in AD 88; he was in office as prefect of Egypt in AD 103.

SENIOR OFFICERS

Senators held the most important positions in the command of the Roman army. Although only one of the six military tribunes was of senatorial rank, each legion was commanded by a *legatus legionis*, a senator usually of praetorian status. In provinces where only one legion was stationed the commander of the legion was also provincial governor (with the exception of Africa where from the time of Gaius the command of the III Augusta was distinct from the civil administration of the province). Provinces containing several legions and auxiliary units were governed by a senator of consular rank who was supreme commander of all the troops therein. Usually these men had previously held at least one military tribuneship (normally in their early twenties) and legionary legateship (normally in their mid-thirties). Similarly if an army was assembled for a campaign, the senior commanders were senators of consular rank. Only Egypt, and after AD 198 the new province of Mesopotamia, were governed by equestrian prefects, although containing legionary troops.

In their choice of commander emperors were therefore limited by traditional Roman respect for age, experience, and social standing, and the upper class ideal that senators were naturally competent to serve the state in whatever capacity it demanded. There was no military academy in Rome and no systematic preparation of men for military command or for service say, as British or eastern specialists. Senators held a wide variety of posts, including many in civil administration, each one an individuality, and often with periods of inactivity. It is therefore debatable how many senators had significant experience of active service, or indeed how far this was a requirement for advancement. Then, the time spent by senators in command of an army was relatively short, since most held no more than two posts, up to six years in all. However, some senators did acquire long experience of military command, and over a limited period, most notably in the northern wars of Marcus Aurelius, a more concentrated effort was made to assemble and retain men of proven ability in senior commands. Furthermore, an emperor could appoint talented equestrians to senatorial rank and then employ them in posts normally reserved for senators. But emperors were always mindful of their personal security and the need to exercise patronage, and probably preferred non-specialist commanders. In this way no military hierarchy of professional generals could emerge who might plot, or attempt to undermine imperial control of military and foreign policy (for differing views see Birley 1981: 4–35; Campbell 1975; 1984: 325–47; 1987).

Over seventy careers (mainly late 1st–early 3rd century) of consular governors are known in some detail through inscriptions, of which only a small number can be translated here. These generally list posts held in descending order of importance, though the consulship and priesthoods are often placed out of order.

110 *ILS* 1077 = Smallwood *NH* 190, inscription, Rome, 2nd C.AD

To Lucius Aemilius Carus, son of Lucius, of the tribe Camilia, consul, legate of the Emperor with propraetorian power of the province of Cappadocia, legate of the Emperor with propraetorian power and census officer of the province of Lugdunensis, legate of the Emperor with propraetorian power of the province of Arabia, superintendent of the Flaminian way, legate of Legion XXX Ulpia Victorious, praetor, tribune of the plebs, quaestor of the Emperor, military tribune of Legion VIII Augusta, military tribune of Legion IX Hispana, member of the Board of Ten for jurisdiction, member of the Flavian Brotherhood, member of the Board of Fifteen for conducting sacrifices, Gaius Julius Erucianus Crispus, prefect of the first Ulpian *ala* of Dacians, to an excellent friend.

Carus was governor of Arabia (containing one legion) in AD 142/3, and consul in 143 or 144. Although he held two military tribunates (Birley 1981: 10–11), this does not necessarily indicate preparation for a military career; there may have been personal reasons, a wish to serve with a relative, or a temporary shortage of suitable men.

111 *ILS* 1066 = Smallwood *NH* 194, inscription, Minturnae (Minturno), 2nd C.AD

To Lucius Burbuleius Optatus Ligarianus, son of Lucius, of the tribe Quirina, consul, member of the Augustan Brotherhood, legate of Emperor Antoninus Augustus Pius with propraetorian power of the province of Syria, where he died in office, legate of the same Emperor and the divine Hadrian with propraetorian power of the province of Cappadocia, superintendent of the public works and areas, prefect of the public treasury, proconsul of Sicily, *logista* of Syria, Legate of Legion XVI Flavia Steadfast, superintendent of the community of Narbonensis, similarly of Ancona, similarly of Tarracina, superintendent of the Clodian, Cassian, and Ciminian roads, praetor, plebeian aedile, quaestor of Pontus and Bithynia, tribune with the broad stripe of Legion IX Hispana, member of the Board of Three for executions, patron of the colony; Rasinia Pietas, nurse of his daughters, set this up at her own expense. The site was granted by decree of the town councillors.

Ligarianus' career illustrates a combination of military and civil posts, with a preponderance of the latter, culminating in the prestigious province of Syria. He was governor of Cappadocia, 137/8–139/40.

112 Smallwood *NH* 214, with Habicht 1969, inscription, Pergamum, Asia, 2nd C.AD

Gaius Julius Quadratus Bassus, consul (AD 105), priest, appointed army commander in the Dacian War, and companion of Emperor Trajan in the war there, honoured with triumphal ornaments, legate with propraetorian power of the province of Judaea, legate with propraetorian power of Cappadocia-Galatia-Lesser Armenia-Pontus-Paphlagonia-Isau[ria-Phrygi]a, legate with propraetorian power of the province of Syria-Phoenice-Commagene, legate with propraetorian power of the province of [Dacia]; military tribune of Legion XIII (Gemina), member of the Board of Three for bronze, gold, and silver coinage, [quaestor (?) of Cre]te and Cyrene, [curule (?)] aedile, praetor of the Roman people, [legate of] Legion XI Claudia [Loyal and Faithful, and Leg]ion IV Scythica, and Legion [_ _ _], and Legion XII Fulminata, [and Legion] III Gallica, and legion [_ _ _ and leg]ion XIII Gemina and Legion [_ _ _], a man of distinguished birth [whose family] was descended [from kings _ _ _]. Through the agency of the legate [the city of] Seleuceia at Zeugma [set up civic honour for him (?)_ _ _

(On adjacent side of the stone)

This man died while still on active service in Dacia and administering his province, and his body was conveyed back to Asia, borne by soldiers drawn up under the military standard in charge of the chief centurion Quintilius Capito, preceded by a parade in every city and military camp, on the express instructions of the Emperor god Hadrian, and this monument to him was set up out of the emperor's own funds.

Bassus' exceptional career may be tentatively reconstructed: commander of XI Claudia in Upper Germany *c.* AD 99–101 (the other seven legions mentioned probably formed detachments under his command in Dacia and Parthia); commander of a detachment in Dacian war, AD 101–2; governor of Judaea, AD 102/3–5; consul, AD 105; command in second Dacian War, AD 105–6; Cappadocia (including a substantial part of neighbouring territories in a large administrative area), AD 107–10; command in Parthian war, AD 114–15; Syria, AD 115–16/7; Dacia AD 117 (Halfmann, 1979: no. 26).

113 *ILS* 1071 = Smallwood *NH* 234, inscription, Tibur (Tivoli), north-east of Rome, 2nd. C.AD

To Gaius Popilius Carus Pedo, son of Gaius, of the tribe Quirina, consul (AD 147), member of the Board of Seven for organizing banquets, member of the Brotherhood of Hadrian, legate of Emperor Caesar Antoninus Augustus Pius with propraetorian power of Upper Germany and the army encamped in it, superintendent of public works, prefect of the public treasury, superintendent of the old Aurelian road and the new Cornelian road and the Triumphal way, legate of Legion X Fretensis, from which duty he excused himself, praetor, tribune of the plebs, quaestor of the divine Hadrian Augustus, candidate of the emperor in all posts, tribune with a broad purple stripe of Legion III Cyrenaica, granted military decorations by the divine Hadrian for service in the Judaean expedition, member of the Board of Ten for jurisdiction, patron of the municipality, superintendent of exemplary excellence; the senate and people of Tibur (set this up), for a man who deserved very well of the community.

Pedo subsequently became proconsul of Asia. Despite his military distinction in Judaea early in his career, he became governor of Germany (c. 151) with little experience; seemingly through the goodwill of Hadrian he acquired the standing of a legionary legate without holding the post.

114 *AE* 1956. 124 = Pflaum, *Carrières* 181 bis, inscription, Diana Veteranorum (Zana), Numidia, 2nd C.AD

To Marcus Valerius Maximianus, son of Marcus Valerius Maximianus who was local censor and priest, priest of the colony of Poetovio, with the public horse, prefect of the first cohort of Thracians, tribune of the first cohort of Hamians, Roman citizens, placed in charge of the coastline of the peoples of Pontus Polemonianus, decorated in the Parthian war, chosen by Emperor Marcus Antoninus Augustus and sent on active service in the German expedition with the task of bringing food by boat down the river Danube to supply the armies in both provinces of Pannonia, placed in charge of the detachments of the praetorian fleets of Misenum and also of Ravenna and also of the British fleet, and also of the African and Moorish cavalry chosen for scouting duties in Pannonia, prefect of the first *ala* of Aravacans, while on active service in Germany praised in public by emperor Antoninus Augustus because he had killed with his own hand Valao, chief of the Naristi, and was granted his horse, decorations, and weapons; in the same *ala* he achieved the honour of his fourth military post, prefect of the *ala* of lance-bearers, decorated in the war against the Germans and Sarmatians, placed in charge with the honour of centenarian rank of the cavalry of the peoples of the Marcomanni, Naristi, and Quadi journeying to punish the insurrection in the east (i.e. the revolt of Avidius Cassius, AD 175), with an increased salary appointed to the procuratorship of Lower Moesia and at the same time placed in charge of detachments and sent by the Emperor to drive out a band of Brisean brigands on the borders of Macedonia and Thrace, procurator of Upper Moesia, procurator of the province of Dacia Porolissensis, chosen by our most revered emperors for admission to the senatorial order among men of praetorian rank, and soon after legate of Legion I Adiutrix, also legate of Legion II Adiutrix, placed in charge of the detachments in winter quarters at Laugaricio, also legate of Legion V Macedonica, also legate of Legion I Italica, also legate of Legion XIII Gemina, also legate of the Emperor with propraetorian power of [Legion III Augusta], decorated by the most noble Emperor Marcus Aurelius Commodus Augustus on the second German expedition; the most distinguished council of the people of Diana Veteranorum (set this up) with the money contributed.

Maximianus, from a wealthy family of Poetovio in Pannonia, had performed valiant service as an equestrian officer and had attracted imperial attention and support, indicated by his promotion to senatorial rank at praetorian level and his immediate advancement to a series of legionary commands. We know from another inscription that he later became consul (c. AD 186). Serious trouble had begun on the Danube in AD 168, and in AD 170/171 Greece and the approaches to Italy were invaded by tribes including the Marcomanni and Quadi. Marcus Aurelius was prepared to promote men of military ability from outside the senatorial order in the interests of the state, and Maximianus initially performed a crucial role by ensuring supplies to the armies in Pannonia; cf. text no. 115.

115 *ILS* 1107 = Pflaum, *Carrières* 188, inscription, Rome, 2nd C. AD

To Marcus Macrinius Avitus Catonius Vindex, son of Marcus, of the tribe Claudia, consul (c. AD 173), augur of the Roman people, legate of the Emperor with propraetorian power of the province of Lower

Moesia, legate of the Emperor with propraetorian power of the province of Upper Moesia, superintendent of the community of Ariminum, procurator of the province of Dacia Malvensis, prefect of the *ala* of lance-bearers, prefect of the third *ala* of Thracians, military tribune of Legion VI Victrix, prefect of the sixth cohort of Gauls, decorated by Emperor Marcus Aurelius Antoninus Augustus in the German war with two Untipped Spears, two Standards, and a Mural and Rampart Crown; Junia Flaccinilla to her beloved husband and Macrinia Rufina to her devoted father (set this up); he lived 42 years, five months.

116 Dio (2nd–3rd C.AD), 68. 32

Later, however, when the Dacian war had begun and Trajan needed the help of the Moors, he (Lusius Quietus) came to him on his own initiative and performed exceptional exploits. After being honoured for this he achieved even more numerous and more distinguished deeds in the second war, and in the end he advanced to such a pitch of courage and good luck in this war that he was enrolled among men of praetorian rank, became consul, and then governor of Palestine (Judaea). It was because of this especially that he was envied and despised and met his downfall.

Since the holding of important office was generally believed to be the prerogative of men of high rank, the promotion of men of talent from outside the traditional governing class often fostered resentment. The consulship of Helvius Pertinax, who was to become emperor in AD 193, caused disquiet in some quarters because of his low birth, despite his military success (Dio, 71. 22). Dio (78. 13) vehemently criticized Macrinus, who became emperor in 217 from the position of praetorian prefect, for appointing men of dubious antecedents, for example, Marcius Agrippa who had been a slave and lady's hairdresser and who was sent to govern Dacia.

117 Tacitus (1st–2nd C.AD), *Annals* 1. 80

It was also Tiberius' practice to prolong tenure of posts and to keep some men in the same army commands or governorships up to the day of their death. Various reasons for this have been recorded; some think that he found new responsibilities tedious and preferred to let one decision stand indefinitely, others think that he was jealous that too many people might enjoy the fruits of office; others believe that precisely because he had a cunning mind he found it difficult to make a decision; for he did not seek out the exceptionally talented, but he also hated the corrupt, since he feared that the meritorious would be a threat to him and that the bad would bring about public disgrace.

Here Tacitus characteristically summarizes the dilemma faced by all emperors in trusting and controlling talented men who might be ambitious and use their army command to raise revolt (cf. Dio, 52. 8). Moreover, the expectations of the upper classes also had to be satisfied, as Tacitus (*Annals* 4. 6) illustrates in his comments on Tiberius' appointments in the early part of his reign – 'birth, military excellence, distinction in civilian pursuits, everyone agreed that he chose the best people'. See also chapter 7.

3 The Emperor as commander-in-chief

When Octavian adopted the designation *imperator* as part of his name, probably in 38 BC, he was making a claim to be the outstanding military leader in Rome. In his campaign against Sextus Pompey he needed the aura of authority and the prestige associated with victory which it imparted (Syme 1958). Once established in power, Augustus tied the army closely to his person, and it was his legacy that all emperors bore the attributes of a Roman general (by the 70s *imperator* was the usual designation of emperors). Since all campaigns were conducted under their auspices, the glory belonged to them, and acclamations as general were added to their titles, while other names and epithets expressed the humiliation of Rome's enemies (e.g. *Parthicus* – 'Conqueror of the Parthians'), and aggressive military prowess (e.g. 'extender of the empire'). In public images imperial military responsibilities played a significant role and the emperor was depicted wearing military dress on statues, reliefs, triumphal arches, and coins, often as a conquering hero or a dignified but firm military leader, most strikingly illustrated by the statue of Augustus from Prima Porta (see Zanker 1988: 190–1). Moreover, every emperor was personally associated with his troops – as paymaster, comrade, benefactor – and sought to demonstrate that he was a worthy and courageous fellow-soldier, deserving of their complete loyalty. Not surprisingly therefore emperors increasingly assimilated to their role as military leaders and by the end of the first century AD were taking personal command of all major campaigns. They could, therefore, spend more time with their troops, but this made the conduct of administration more difficult since the whole apparatus of government had to follow them. In one sense the imperial role as commander-in-chief was in keeping with Roman ideology, which held military prowess in high esteem and associated military command with the leading men in the state; but emperors also saw their successful command of the army and their popularity with the soldiers as protection against revolt (Campbell 1984: 17–156; chapter 7 this volume; significance of the emperor's public image – Zanker 1988).

THE EMPEROR WITH HIS TROOPS

118 Epictetus (1st–2nd C.AD), *Discourses*, 1. 14. 15

For they (the soldiers), on entering military service, swear an oath to value the safety of the emperor above everything . . .

119 Suetonius (1st–2nd C.AD), *Augustus* 25. 1

After the civil wars he (Augustus) did not address any of the soldiers as 'comrades' in either speeches or edicts, but always 'soldiers', and indeed did not permit any other form of address to be used even by his sons or stepsons who held military commands. For he thought that the former term was too flattering for the demands of military discipline, the peaceful nature of the times, and his own majesty and that of his house.

It is not clear when the term 'comrades' was first employed after this in public documents or speeches, but it was in common use during the civil wars of AD 68/69, and thereafter was the normal mode of address. In instructions issued to provincial governors about the wills of soldiers, Trajan speaks of the justness of his feelings for his 'excellent and outstandingly loyal fellow-soldiers' (text no. 263).

120 Dio (2nd–3rd C.AD), 56. 42

The senate and the equestrian order, their wives, the praetorians, and virtually all the others who were present in the city at that time, attended and participated in the funeral ceremony (of Augustus). When the body had been placed on the pyre in the Campus Martius, first all the priests walked round it, then the equestrians, both those belonging to the order and the others, and then the praetorian guardsmen ran round it and threw onto it all the military decorations which any of them had ever received from him for bravery. Then, as the senate had decreed, the centurions lifted their torches and set fire to the pyre from underneath.

121 Velleius Paterculus (1st C.BC–1st C.AD), 2. 104

At the sight of him (Tiberius) there were tears of joy from the soldiers as they ran up to him and welcomed him with tremendous and unprecedented enthusiasm, eagerly taking him by the hand and unable to restrain themselves from blurting out: 'Is it really you that we see, general? Have we got you back safely?' 'I served with you in Armenia, general'.'And I was in Raetia'. 'I received military decorations from you in Vindelicia'. 'And I in Pannonia'. 'And I in Germany'. It is difficult to express this adequately in words and indeed it may seem incredible.

Velleius was a friend of the imperial family and his successful equestrian career culminated in the acquisition of senatorial rank and eventual election to a praetorship. His description here of the return of Tiberius to take command of the German legions in AD 4 is doubtless exaggerated, but nevertheless Tiberius had a reputation for looking after his men well and for sharing the rigours of military life, and the enthusiasm of the troops was probably genuine. Later, Tiberius tried to exploit his comradeship with the army by reminding the mutinous Pannonian legions that 'he himself had an outstanding concern for the courageous legions in whose company he had endured numerous campaigns' (Tacitus, *Ann.* 1. 25).

122 Dio, 69. 9

So that the soldiers should be inspired by watching him (Hadrian) everywhere, he adhered to a rigorous lifestyle, walked or rode on every occasion, and never during this period mounted a chariot or a four-wheeled cart. He did not cover his head in hot or cold weather, but went about bare-headed in the snows of Germany and in the heat of Egypt.

For Hadrian's personal conduct when visiting the army see also *Historia Augusta, Life of Hadrian*, 10. 2. Vespasian (Tacitus, *Hist.* 2. 5), Trajan (Dio, 68. 8; no. 131), and the Severans (texts nos 123–4) had a similar reputation. By the second century an emperor on campaign was expected to behave as a 'fellow-soldier'.

123 Herodian (2nd–3rd C.AD), 2. 11

He (Septimius Severus) shared the hardships of the soldiers, using a cheap tent and taking the same food and drink as he knew was available to everyone. He never exhibited any trappings of imperial luxury. Therefore he won even greater approval from his fellow-soldiers. They respected the fact that he not only joined personally in all their toils but also was the first to start any job, and therefore carried out all their duties enthusiastically.

Cf. Herodian 3. 6; Dio, 74. 15.

124 Dio, 77. 13

In essential and urgent campaigns, however, he (Caracalla) was temperate and unaffected, and performed menial tasks enthusiastically on equal terms with the rest. So, he marched on foot with the soldiers and ran with them, did not wash, or change his clothes, joined in every task with them, and chose exactly the same kind of rations as they had.

Cf. Herodian, 4. 7 – Caracalla used wooden utensils, baked his own bread, avoided extravagance, marched on foot with his men, sharing their labours and sometimes carrying a legionary standard. He seems to have gone further than other emperors in his efforts to identify himself personally with the troops, since he not only called the troops 'comrades', but wanted them to address him in this way instead of 'emperor'.

125 *BMC* 1, p. 151, no. 33, = Smallwood *GN* 276, sestertius, AD 37–8

Obverse. Head of Gaius, laureate.

GAIUS CAESAR AUGUSTUS GERMANICUS, CHIEF PRIEST, TRIBUNICIAN POWER.

Reverse. Gaius standing on a platform, speaking to five soldiers, four of whom carry standards.

SPEECH TO THE COHORTS (of the praetorian guard).

Dio, 59. 2 describes how in AD 37 Caligula drilled the praetorians before the senate and paid Tiberius' bequest, doubling it in his own name. It is possible that the coin type illustrated above was originally minted specifically to celebrate the formal *adlocutio*, though it continued until AD 40/41.

126 *BMC* 1, p. 218, no. 122 = Smallwood *GN* 292, sestertius, AD 64–6

Obverse. Head of Nero, laureate.

NERO CLAUDIUS CAESAR AUGUSTUS GERMANICUS, CHIEF PRIEST, TRIBUNICIAN POWER, *IMPERATOR*, FATHER OF THE FATHERLAND.

Reverse. Nero standing on a platform accompanied by the praetorian prefect, addressing three soldiers, two of whom hold standards.

SPEECH TO THE COHORTS (of the praetorian guard). BY DECREE OF THE SENATE.

127 Josephus (1st C.AD), *Jewish War* 6. 33

Titus, thinking that the enthusiasm of soldiers involved in warfare is best stimulated by a confident speech of encouragement, and that inspiring words and promises often persuade them to forget danger and sometimes even to despise death, assembled his toughest companions and tested the spirits of his men. 'Fellow-soldiers', he began . . .

Josephus places this speech during the siege of Jerusalem. The belief that a commander should encourage his troops in routine tasks (see text no. 17) and particularly on the eve of battle, was part of Roman tradition. Such speeches could convey information about the nature of the enemy and the commander's intentions, and in this way often had political overtones (see pp. 184–5; 187).

THE EMPEROR AS GENERAL

128 Augustus, *Res Gestae* 4. 2

The senate decreed on fifty-five occasions that thanksgivings should be offered to the immortal gods for successful operations conducted on land and sea by me or by my officers acting under my auspices. The days on which thanksgivings were offered in accordance with senatorial decrees amounted to eight hundred and ninety.

129 *IRT* 301, inscription, Africa, 1st C.AD

Sacred to Mars Augustus. Under the auspices of Emperor Caesar Augustus, chief priest, father of the fatherland, under the command of Cossus Lentulus, consul (1 BC), member of the Board of Fifteen for conducting sacrifices, proconsul, the province of Africa was liberated from the Gaetulian war. The city of Lepcis (made this).

The provinces for which Augustus was directly responsible, and to which he was legally empowered to appoint governors and commanders, contained most of the army. Therefore he was effectively commander-in-chief and military operations were conducted under his auspices (in the Republic the commander had the right to take the *auspicia*), even though others directed individual campaigns. By the end of his reign Africa remained as the only province containing legionary troops governed by a proconsul chosen by lot by the senate. But Lentulus (proconsul AD 5–6) distinguishes between his leadership and the overall authority of Augustus; possibly the emperor's *maius imperium* granted in 23 BC implied his control of the auspices even in the case of senatorial proconsuls; or Lentulus may have been directly appointed by Augustus as a special commander (see Campbell 1984: 350–1).

When an emperor went on campaign he was in personal charge of every aspect of military life, though of course depending on his experience he would take advice from his commanders. It is hard to believe that during his short visit to Britain Claudius made much difference to the plans worked out by Aulus Plautius (cf. Dio, 60. 21; Suetonius, *Claudius* 17). We may contrast the more direct leadership of Domitian, Trajan, Marcus Aurelius, or Septimius Severus (Dio, 75. 11–12 – siege of Hatra).

130 Frontinus (1st–2nd C.AD), *Stratagems* 1. 3. 10

When the Germans in their usual way kept emerging from woodland and concealed hiding-places to attack our soldiers while keeping a safe escape route through the recesses of the forest, Emperor Caesar Domitian Augustus by extending the frontier along a length of 120 miles, not only altered the character of the war, but subjected the enemy to his control because he had uncovered their hiding-places.

See also text no. 158.

131 Dio, 68. 23

He (Trajan) always marched on foot with the body of the army, looked after the dispositions of the troops during the entire campaign, drawing them up first in one formation, then another, and forded on foot all the rivers that they did. Sometimes he even circulated false reports through the scouts so that the soldiers might simultaneously practise their manoeuvres and be fearlessly ready to face any eventuality.

Dio is referring to the Parthian war. The ideal of Trajan's personal leadership in the Dacian wars is graphically expressed in the sculptures on his commemorative column, where the emperor is to the forefront of many scenes (see Plates 3 and 4).

132 Fronto (2nd C.AD), *Ad Verum Imp.* 2. 3 (Loeb, vol. II, pp. 194–6), AD 166

(Lucius Verus to Fronto). . . I am ready to agree to any suggestions as long as my achievements are highlighted by you. Naturally you will not omit my speeches to the senate and addresses to the army. I shall also send you the text of my negotiations with the enemy. They will be a great help to you . . . You should spend a lot of time on the causes and early stages of the war, and particularly on the poor progress in my absence. You should come slowly to my role. Moreover, I think that it is essential to make clear how much the Parthians had the upper hand before my arrival, so that the extent of my achievements may be highlighted.

Cornelius Fronto was intending to write a history about the campaign led by the emperor Lucius Verus against the Parthians (AD 163–6). This letter illustrates the importance in imperial life of personal involvement in all aspects of military command and personal responsibility for victory.

133 *BMC* 3, pp. 497–504 = Smallwood *NH* 337, *sestertii, c.*
AD 134–8

Obverse. Bust of Hadrian, laureate or bare-headed.

HADRIAN AUGUSTUS, CONSUL FOR THE THIRD TIME, FATHER OF THE FATHERLAND.

Reverse. Hadrian, in military dress, sometimes accompanied by an officer, addressing soldiers from a platform in some versions, in others, from horseback.

THE ARMY OF BRITAIN. BY DECREE OF THE SENATE.

These coins are part of a series issued by Hadrian celebrating the army stationed in the provinces. Similar examples are known for the armies of Cappadocia, Dacia, Dalmatia, Germany, Spain, Africa, Moesia, Noricum, Raetia, Syria, and Thrace; there is also a type which shows Hadrian addressing the praetorians. They serve to emphasize his concern for the troops and leadership of the army, qualities also demonstrated in his personal visits to army camps; for his speech in Africa, see text no. 17.

134 *ILS* 419, inscription, Moguntiacum (Mainz), Upper Germany, AD 197

In honour of Lucius Septimius Severus Pius Pertinax Augustus, unconquered Emperor, and Marcus Aurelius Antoninus Caesar, for Legion XXII Primigenia, Loyal and Faithful, in recognition of its distinction and courage, the community of the Treveri (Trier) after being defended by it during a siege (set this up).

It is significant that the Treveri make their dedication in the first place in the name of the emperors, who are seen as the directing force behind the army's success (for emperors as commanders, see Campbell 1984: 59–69; 1987: 28–9).

IMPERIAL MILITARY HONOURS

135 Augustus, *Res Gestae* 4. 1; 3

I celebrated two ovations and three curule triumphs (29 BC) and was acclaimed *imperator* on twenty-one occasions. The senate voted more triumphs to me, all of which I declined. I deposited the laurel leaves which decorated my *fasces* in the Capitol, after fulfilling the vows which I had undertaken in each war . . . (Section 3) In my triumphs nine kings or children of kings were led in front of my chariot.

Cf. text no. 128. Laurel leaves symbolized the crown of the *triumphator.* After 19 BC senators were not permitted to hold a triumph, which was confined to members of the imperial family.

136 *BMC* 1, p. 168, no. 29 = Smallwood *GN* 43 (a), *aureus*, AD 46–7 (see Plate 5)

Obverse. Head of Claudius, laureate.

TIBERIUS CLAUDIUS CAESAR AUGUSTUS, CHIEF PRIEST, IN THE SIXTH YEAR OF HIS TRIBUNICIAN POWER, *IMPERATOR* FOR THE TENTH TIME.

Reverse. Triumphal arch surmounted by an equestrian statue between two trophies; on the architrave of the arch.

(VICTORY) OVER THE BRITISH.

137 *ILS* 213 = Smallwood *GN* 44, inscription, Rome, AD 49

Tiberius Claudius Caesar Augustus Germanicus, son of Drusus, chief priest, in the ninth year of his tribunician power, *imperator* for the sixteenth time, consul for the fourth time, censor, father of the fatherland, having increased the territory of the Roman people, extended and demarcated the boundary of the pomerium.
(On the top) Pomerium
(On the side) 8.

Cf. Dio, 60. 22–23; Suetonius, *Claudius* 17; 21. The pomerium was the formal boundary of Rome. Claudius, weak and unpopular, aimed to enhance his prestige by a display of military prowess.

138 *ILS* 264 = *MW* 53, inscription, Rome, arch in the Circus Maximus, AD 80

The senate and people of Rome to Emperor Titus Caesar Vespasianus Augustus, son of the divine Vespasian, chief priest, in the tenth year of his tribunician power, *imperator* for the seventeenth time, consul for the eighth time, father of the fatherland, their own leader (*princeps*), because under the direction, advice, and auspices of his father, he subdued the Jewish race and destroyed the city of Jerusalem, which had been either besieged fruitlessly or left completely untouched by all the commanders, kings, and peoples before him.

139 Josephus, *Jewish War* 7. 132–57 (extracts)

It is impossible to describe properly the huge number of wonderful sights and their magnificence in every conceivable way, either as works of art or in variety of wealth or as rarities of nature. (Section 133) Virtually all the things which men of exceptional good fortune have acquired individually, the marvellous and priceless achievements of other peoples, these were assembled on that day and demonstrated the magnitude of the Roman empire . . . (A description of the riches in the procession). (Section 136) Moreover, the images of their (Roman) gods of astonishing size and brilliantly worked craftsmanship were carried in the procession, and there was nothing which was not made from an expensive material. Many types of animals were also led past, all decorated with the proper trappings. (Section 137) The men who had charge of each group of these animals were adorned with clothing of purple and gold, while those chosen to participate in the procession itself had on their persons the most remarkable and astonishingly rich adornment. (Section 138) Furthermore, even the mob of captives did not lack ornaments, and the elaborate and beautiful nature of their garments hid from view any unsightly mutilation of their bodies . . . (Description of various tableaux depicting the course of the campaign.) (Section 148) The spoils were carried piled up in heaps, but those taken from the temple in Jerusalem were more conspicuous than all the rest . . . (Description of the spoils including the seven-branched-candelabrum.) (Section 150) A copy of the Jewish Law was carried after this, as last of all the spoils. (Section 151) Next came many people carrying statues of Victory, all made from ivory and gold. (Section 152) Behind them first drove Vespasian with Titus following, while Domitian rode beside them magnificently dressed, and his horse too was a wonderful sight.

(Section 153) The triumphal procession reached its conclusion at the temple of Jupiter Capitolinus where they came to a halt. It was an ancient custom to wait there until the death of the general of the enemy should be announced. (Section 154) This man was Simon, son of Gioras, who had just taken part in the procession with the prisoners; then a noose was placed round his neck and he was whipped by his escort as he was dragged to the place near the forum where Roman law demands that those condemned to death for villainy should be executed. (Section 155) When it was announced that Simon was dead there was a roar of approval and they began the sacrifices, which were conducted in due form with the customary prayers, before the imperial family withdrew to the palace. Some people were entertained to dinner by the imperial family, while for all the others arrangements had been made for handsome banquets in their own homes. All that day the city of Rome celebrated the victory of the campaign against its enemies, the end of civil war, and the beginning of hopes for a happy future.

See in general Versnel 1970; Künzl 1988.

140 *BMC* 3, p. 221, no. 1035 = Smallwood *NH* 50, *sestertius*, AD 116–17 (See Plate 6)

Obverse. Bust of Trajan, laureate.

TO EMPEROR CAESAR NERVA TRAJAN BEST AUGUSTUS, CONQUEROR OF THE GERMANS, CONQUEROR OF THE DACIANS, CONQUEROR OF THE PARTHIANS, CHIEF PRIEST, TRIBUNICIAN POWER, CONSUL FOR THE SIXTH TIME, FATHER OF THE FATHERLAND.

Reverse. Trajan in military dress, standing with the seated figure of Armenia at his feet between two reclining river gods.

ARMENIA AND MESOPOTAMIA BROUGHT INTO THE POWER OF THE ROMAN PEOPLE. BY DECREE OF THE SENATE.

This grandiloquent celebration of Trajan's Parthian campaign proved premature since all conquered lands were soon evacuated.

141 *ILS* 425, inscription, Rome, arch in the forum, AD 203

To Emperor Caesar Lucius Septimius Severus Pius Pertinax Augustus, son of Marcus, father of the fatherland, Conqueror of the Parthians and the Arabians and Conqueror of the Parthians and the Adiabenici, chief priest, in the eleventh year of his tribunician power, *imperator* for the eleventh time, consul for the third time, proconsul, and Emperor Caesar Marcus Aurelius Antoninus Augustus Pius Fortunate, son of Lucius, in the sixth year of his tribunician power, consul, proconsul, [father of the fatherland, excellent and most courageous emperors], because of the restoration of the state and the extension of the power of the Roman people through their outstanding qualities at home and abroad, the senate and people of Rome (set this up).

Plates

1 Ti. Claudius Maximus

Source: Kavalla Museum

2 Centurion monument from Colchester, Colchester Museum

3 Trajan as commander-in-chief
Source: Lepper and Frere 1988, by courtesy of Mr F Lepper

4 Trajan addresses the army; receives an embassy
Source: Lepper and Frere 1988, by courtesy of Mr F Lepper

5 Aureus, AD 46–7: Claudius' triumph over the British
Source: *BMC* I, p. 168, no. 29

6 Sestertius, AD 116–17: conquest of Armenia and Mesopotamia
Source: *BMC* III, p. 221, no. 1035

7 Model of a Roman camp, The Grosvenor Museum, Chester

8 The Roman siege ramp at Masada
Photograph: Richard Stoneman

9 Reconstruction of a Roman catapult from Masada, made for a film version of the siege of Masada
Photograph: Richard Stoneman

10 Roman ceremonial helmet, AD 3–4. Rijksmuseum van Oudeiden, Leiden

11 The Mithraeum at Carrawburgh on Hadrian's Wall. The stone
is pierced to allow a light placed behind it to create a halo for the god
Photograph: Richard Stoneman

12 Aureus, AD 41–2: Claudius and the praetorians
Source: *BMC* I, p. 165, no. 5

13 Bronze diploma – interior faces
Source: Roxan 1985: 79

14 Bronze diploma – exterior faces showing holes for binding wire
Source: Roxan 1985: 79

15 Bronze diploma – interior face
Source: Roxan 1985: 102

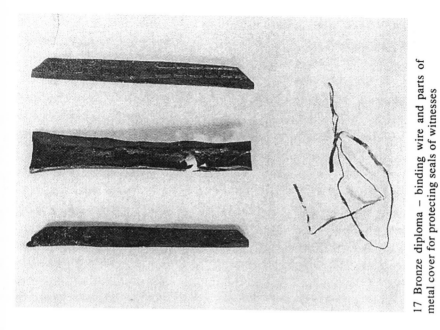

17 Bronze diploma – binding wire and parts of metal cover for protecting seals of witnesses

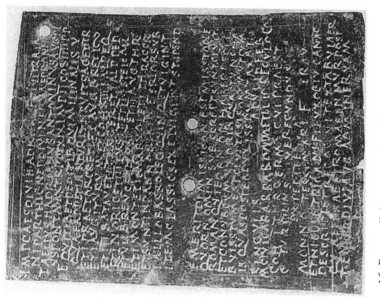

16 Bronze diploma – exterior face
Source: Roxan 1985: 102

18 Bronze diploma – exterior face with metal cover in position
Source: Roxan 1985: 102

4 The army in the field

THE DISPOSITION OF THE ARMY

There were twenty-five legions in service in AD 14, around 140,000 men, with probably an equal number of auxiliaries. Augustus apportioned legions and other units to individual provinces where he perceived a need, either because of inadequate pacification, or because he intended a province to be a platform for aggrandizement. Indeed Augustus greatly extended Roman territory in directions that suited him, enhancing his own reputation, acquiring revenue, and bringing prestige to the Roman state. In winter, the troops were scattered and stationed in winter quarters, before being assembled in camps for summer campaigns. These camps and winter quarters were not permanent, though they might have stone-built accommodation, especially in the cold northern provinces; in Syria the troops could be billeted in towns. The Romans did not recognize any formal barriers or limits to their power, and friendly kingdoms on the periphery of Roman territory provided troops and an easy route to further expansion when required. Britain was annexed in AD 43 and other peripheral areas like Thrace were absorbed. Gradually, permanent bases emerged, often accommodating two legions and a number of auxiliary units; but during the first century AD these bases became smaller, containing only one legion (see Figure 1; cf. also Plate 7), and consequently more dispersed, while some auxilia units were stationed in separate forts; the earliest auxiliary fort which is known in detail is Valkenburg in southern Holland, built c. AD 40 (see Figure 2).

By the late first and early second centuries AD, it is legitimate to speak of frontier zones, and in some areas in the second century a line was clearly demarcated by the building of artificial barriers, as in Upper Germany, Britain, Raetia, and Numidia. However, important areas, like Dacia, lacked them. Furthermore, artificial barriers did not necessarily have a common purpose, and while doubtless intended to contain any

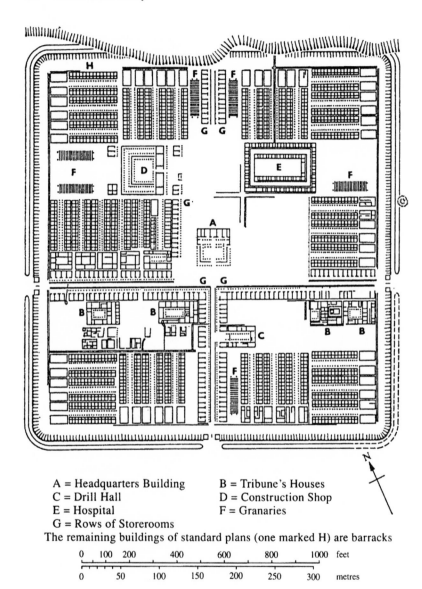

A = Headquarters Building   B = Tribune's Houses
C = Drill Hall   D = Construction Shop
E = Hospital   F = Granaries
G = Rows of Storerooms
The remaining buildings of standard plans (one marked H) are barracks

Figure 1 Legionary fortress at Inchtuthil, Scotland, *c.* AD 86 (20 hectares)

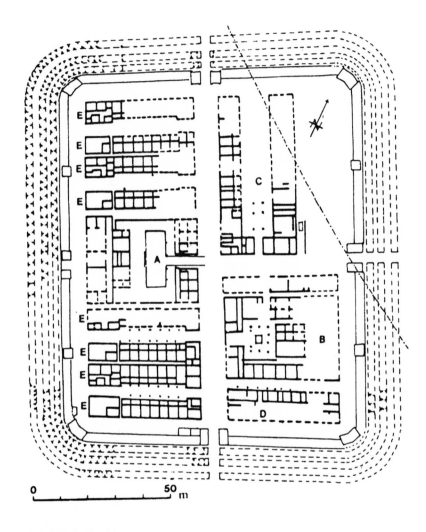

A = Headquarters   B = Prefect's House
C = Long Barracks   D = Hospital
E = Barracks

Figure 2 Auxiliary fort at Valkenburg, Holland, *c.* AD 40 (1.5 hectares)

fighting at the current limits of Rome's direct control, may also have served to improve communications and to direct and control traffic; the gates in Hadrian's Wall allowed Roman roads to run northwards and there were camps beyond the wall. It is also possible that a barrier subsequently used for defensive purposes was originally contructed for quite different reasons. Indeed the eventual frontiers of the empire may have been simply where Roman advance had temporarily faltered for a variety of reasons, with no overall plan. So, it is unsafe to argue that a strategy of 'defence in depth' had emerged by the early third century, or that Rome had given up ideas of further conquests; the annexation of Mesopotamia by Septimius Severus shows that imperial military ambitions still flourished.

At all times of course Roman troops wherever they were stationed acted as an army of occupation, keeping order among subject peoples. But it must be emphasized that part of their role was to defend Roman sovereignty against outside threat, and that this was probably of greater significance by the end of the second century. Frontier zones or lines do indicate that the areas directly controlled by Rome were now more precisely demarcated. Significantly, by the early third century the main concentration of troops was on the Rhine and Danube, rather than in the east, the last area to see expansion. It was politically important for emperors to maintain the territorial integrity of the empire, and they should be credited with a wish to protect the peace and prosperity of their peoples, many of whom now served in the army, while the provincial upper classes increasingly contributed senators. Plautius Silvanus celebrated his military achievements in Moesia not merely as victorious conquest but as consolidation of the peace of his province (*ILS* 986). For discussion, see Mann (1974, 1979); Luttwak (1976); Isaac (1992).

142 Tacitus (1st–2nd C.AD), *Annals* 4. 5

Italy was protected by two fleets, one on each of the seas on either side, at Misenum and Ravenna; the adjacent coast line of Gaul was protected by the warships which Augustus had captured in his victory at Actium and stationed at Forum Julii with a strong complement of rowers. Our principal force, however, was close to the river Rhine, where eight legions were stationed as a defence against the Germans or the Gauls. The Spanish provinces, recently subdued, were in the charge of three legions. King Juba had received the people of Mauretania as a gift of the Roman people. The rest of Africa was guarded by two legions, and Egypt by an equal number. Then all the great sweep of territory from the borders of Syria to the river Euphrates was kept under control by four legions; bordering on this are the Iberians and Albanians and other kings who were protected against external regimes by the greatness of our power. Rhoemetalces and the sons of Cotys ruled Thrace, while the bank of the river Danube was guarded by two legions in Pannonia and two in Moesia. A further two legions were stationed in Dalmatia, geographically behind the other four, and could be summoned from close by if Italy needed rapid help. Rome however had its own garrison in the form of three urban and nine praetorian cohorts, recruited mainly from Etruria and Umbria or the old territory of the Latins, and the ancient Roman colonies. In suitable locations in the provinces were stationed allied ships, auxiliary cavalry *alae* and infantry cohorts, virtually equivalent in strength to the legions. But it is difficult to trace them all since they were moved to different locations as circumstances demanded, and their numbers increased or decreased from time to time.

Tacitus is referring to AD 23, when the Pannonian Legion IX Hispana had been transferred to Africa to help put down the rebellion of Tacfarinas.

143 Dio (2nd–3rd C.AD), 55. 23

Twenty-three, or as some argue, twenty-five legions were being maintained at this time (after AD 9). At the present moment only nineteen of them still exist: the second, Augusta, with its winter quarters in Upper Britain; the three third legions – the Gallica in Syria Phoenice, the Cyrenaica in Arabia, the Augusta in Numidia; the fourth, Scythica, in Syria; the fifth, Macedonica, in Dacia; two sixth legions, of which one, Victrix, is in Lower Britain, and one, Ferrata, in Judaea; the seventh, generally called Claudia, in Upper Moesia; the eighth, Augusta, in Upper Germany; the two tenth legions, one, Gemina, in Upper Pannonia and one (Fretensis) in Judaea; the eleventh, Claudia, in Lower Moesia; for two legions were named after Claudius in this way because they had not fought against him in the revolt of Camillus; the twelfth, Fulminata, in Cappadocia; the thirteenth, Gemina, in Dacia; the fourteenth, Gemina, in Upper Pannonia; the fifteenth, Apollinaris, in Cappadocia; the Twentieth, named Valeria Victrix, in Upper Britain. These then in my view were the troops Augustus took over and kept, along with those of the legion called the twenty-second and stationed in Upper Germany, even if this legion was certainly not called Valeria by everyone and does not employ this name now. These are the legions that are still in existence out of those of Augustus. As regards the remainder, some were completely disbanded, others were joined with other legions by Augustus himself and by other emperors, as a result of which they have the name Gemina.

Since I have once been led into discussing the legions, I shall describe the other legions existing at the present day and the occasions of their enlistment by emperors after Augustus, so that anyone who wishes to find out about them can easily discover all the material assembled in one place. Nero recruited the first legion, called Italica, which has winter quarters in Lower Moesia; Galba the first, Adiutrix, which is stationed in Lower Pannonia, and the seventh, Gemina, in Spain; Vespasian the second, Adiutrix, in Lower Pannonia, the fourth, Flavia, in Upper Moesia, the sixteenth, Flavia, in Syria; Domitian the first, Minervia, in Lower Germany; Trajan the second, Aegyptia, and the thirtieth, Germanica, both of which he also named after himself (Traiana and Ulpia respectively); Marcus Antoninus the second, in Noricum, and the third, in Raetia, both of which were named Italica; Severus the Parthicae, the first and third of which are in Mesopotamia, the second in Italy.

Dio is mistaken in calling the twenty-second legion Valeria. Augustus' twenty-second legion was called Deiotariana, and the XXII Primigenia was probably recruited by Caligula. For the origins and naming of legions, see Mann 1983; Keppie 1984a: 205–15.

144 *CIL* 6. 3492 = *ILS* 2288, inscription, Rome, 2nd C.AD

Names of the legions

Second, Augusta (Britain)	Second, Adiutrix (Lower Pannonia)	Fourth, Scythica (Syria)
Sixth, Victrix (Britain)	Fourth, Flavia (Upper Moesia)	Sixteenth, Flavia (Syria)
Twentieth, Victrix (Britain)	Seventh, Claudia (Upper Moesia)	Sixth, Ferrata (Judaea)
Eighth, Augusta (Upper Germany)	First, Italica (Lower Moesia)	Tenth, Fretensis (Judaea)
Twenty-second, Primigenia (Upper Germany)	Fifth, Macedonica (Lower Moesia)	Third, Cyrenaica (Arabia)
First, Minervia (Lower Germany)	Eleventh, Claudia (Lower Moesia)	Second, Traiana (Egypt)
Thirtieth, Ulpia (Lower Germany)	Thirteenth, Gemina (Dacia)	Third, Augusta (Numidia)
First, Adiutrix (Upper Pannonia)	Twelfth, Fulminata (Cappadocia)	Seventh, Gemina (Spain)
Tenth, Gemina (Upper Pannonia)	Fifteenth, Apollinaris (Cappadocia)	Second, Italica (Noricum)
Fourteenth, Gemina (Upper Pannonia)	Third, Gallica (Syria)	Third, Italica (Raetia)
First, Parthica (Mesopotamia)	Second, Parthica (Italy)	Third, Parthica (Mesopotamia).

This inscription appeared on two columns, only one of which now survives, and listed the legions in geographical order from west to east, starting with Britain; legions in an upper province are mentioned before those in a lower. However the second and third Italica legions, recruited by Marcus Aurelius, and the three Parthicae legions recruited by Septimius Severus, are not in order and have been added at the end. This indicates that the list was inscribed, or at least compiled, early in Marcus' reign. The purpose of the inscription is obscure; perhaps it was intended to celebrate Roman military prowess, or it may have served as an official record of army units.

The army list gives a good picture of Roman priorities in the disposition of the legions; there were sixteen legions in the northern areas of the empire, including eleven along the Danube, whereas the eastern frontier areas had eleven (two of these being in Judaea with the primary function of controlling the Jews, and two in the new province of Mesopotamia). Britain, with three legions and a large force of auxiliaries, was always considered to need a large garrison. See Figures 3 and 4.

145 Arrian (2nd C.AD), *Periplous* 6. 1–2

Before midday we journeyed more than sixty miles to Apsarus, where five cohorts are stationed. (Section 2) I gave the soldiers their pay and inspected the weapons, and the fortifications, and the ditch, and the sick, and the existing supply of food. The opinion I formed on these matters I have written down in my Latin report.

Apsarus lay in the south-east corner of the Black Sea, which was within the responsibility of Arrian as governor of Cappadocia (c. AD 135). He toured small military establishments of auxiliary soldiers in the area and wrote reports for Hadrian. The *Periplous* is an account in Greek of his experiences including points of topographical and antiquarian interest.

146 Arrian, *Periplous* 9. 3–5

As regards the fort (near the river Phasis), where four hundred picked soldiers are stationed, in my opinion it is very strong because of the nature of the terrain, and very suitably placed for the protection of those sailing in the area. The wall is encircled by two ditches, each one of which is wide. (Section 4) Formerly the wall was made of earth and the towers were of wood. But now the wall is constructed from baked bricks, and the towers as well. The wall has strong foundations and war machines have been positioned upon it, and in a word, everything is fitted out so as to prevent any of the barbarians from approaching it and to ensure that those manning the fort incur no risk of a siege. (Section 5) Since the harbour needed to be secure for ships, and also the territory

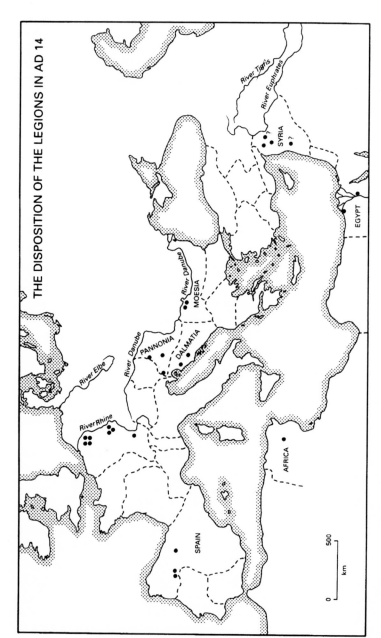

Figure 3 The disposition of the legions in AD 14

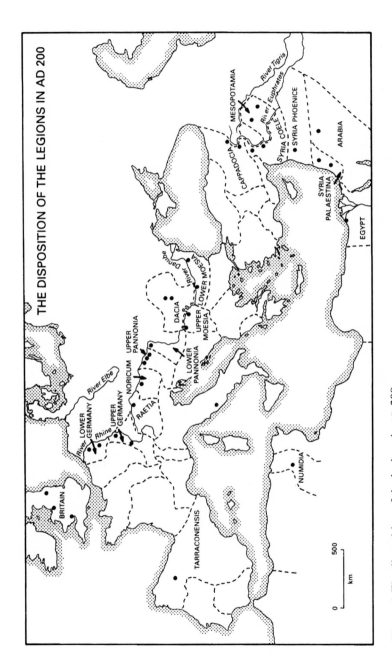

Figure 4 The disposition of the legions in AD 200

outside the fort where it was occupied by veteran soldiers and some other people engaged in trade, I decided to build, starting from the double ditch which encircles the wall, another ditch down to the river; this will enclose the harbour and the homes outside the wall.

Arrian refers to other outposts on the Black sea: 3 (at the river Hyssus); 10. 3 (Sebastopolis); 17. 2 (Dioscurias), which he says marked the limit of Roman power in this area. Although the major concentrations of troops were generally in the less civilized parts of the empire, forts and outposts manned by auxiliary soldiers, guarding roads, communications, coastal trading stations, and tax-collecting offices, were common in many areas; the army was not always concentrated in large camps. The fort at the mouth of the river Phasis contained 400 men and must have been a sizable structure, in a region clearly on the periphery of direct Roman control; here at least is a specific example of the conversion of a temporary structure into a permanent fort. For veterans, see chapter 8.

147 *ILS* 950 = *EJ* 214, inscription, Tibur (Tivoli), north-east of Rome, 1st C.AD

In memory of Torquatus Novellius Atticus, son of Publius, member of the Board of Ten for judging lawsuits, military tribune of the first legion, tribune of detachments of four legions, I, V, XX, XXI, quaestor, aedile, praetor of the centumviral court, supervisor of public areas, officer in charge of conducting the census and levy and proconsul of the province of Narbonensis; at the end of his term in this office he died at Forum Julii in his forty-fourth year.

When legions and auxiliary units were situated in permanent bases, the movement of large bodies of troops round the empire to deal with an immediate crisis became more difficult, since it would leave some areas with an inadequate garrison. Furthermore, the troops might be reluctant to leave an area where they had their roots and perhaps their families. Therefore, especially from the late first century onwards, it became common practice to transfer temporarily detachments (*vexillationes*) from a legion or several legions or auxiliary units (Saxer 1967).

148 *CIL* 3. 1980 = *ILS* 2287, inscription, Salonae (Solin), Dalmatia, AD 170

To Emperor Caesar Marcus Aurelius Antoninus Augustus, chief priest, in the twenty-fourth year of his tribunician power, consul for the third time, the detachments of Legion II Pius and III Concord, two hundred feet (of wall), under the direction of Publius Aelius Amyntianus, centurion *frumentarius* of Legion II Traiana.

The two legions are II and III Italicae, recruited by Marcus, and the detachments were sent to fortify Salonae.

149 *BGU* 2492, with Rea 1977, papyrus, Egypt, 2nd C.AD

I therefore ask you, mother, that you write to me about yourself. What did you do in Memphis? Do not fail. You should know that Gemellus has joined the fleet; he said to me: 'Your mother is going to court with your father in Memphis, before the chief justice'. Please, mother, as soon as you receive this letter send Germanus to me, because the word is that our cohort is leaving for Mauretania. Up to the moment, the *ala* of Moors and the cohort [_ _ _] of Africans have left. That cohort is being brought up to full strength by men from our cohort; men from three years of enrolment (?) are leaving . . .

This letter from a soldier in Egypt shows that despite local recruitment and permanent camps, it was always possible for a soldier to be posted permanently or temporarily to another province. Speidel (1981a) points out that '*ala* of Moors' is soldiers' usage for the first Mauretanian *ala* of Thracians.

FIGHTING

As far as we can tell, the Romans had an organized but uncomplicated approach to military tactics, in which the main principles were: the use of cavalry for flank attacks and encirclement, the placing of a force in reserve, the deployment of a combat line that could maintain contact, readiness to counterattack, flexibility in the face of unexpected enemy manoeuvres. Generals tended to look back to stratagems and tactics successfully employed by previous commanders; this was possible in an age of slow technological progress. However, the Romans were capable of adapting tactics in an original way to suit immediate requirements, e.g., in dealing with Parthian cavalry and archers. Unfortunately Roman writers rarely discussed the technical organization of the army or its battle preparations and tactics. The history of the Roman army at war amounts to a series of vignettes relating to different ages and circumstances. So, we know how the Romans won or lost certain battles, but not who decided tactics or what factors influenced this, or if there was an archive of official military battle plans, or if the tactics described were typical, or how much notice contemporaries took of new tactics. Army tactics and individual battles are discussed in Connolly 1981; Keppie 1984a; Webster 1985; tactics and military text books in Campbell 1987.

Furthermore, our sources and probably also emperors and their advisers, will have found it very difficult to get information about potential enemies of Rome. Some reports may have come from traders, Roman citizens on business, friendly kings, or Roman officers in the course of their duties (Arrian as governor of Cappadocia travelled extensively by ship round the Black Sea and reported to Hadrian on matters relating particularly to the Cimmerian Bosporus where king Cotys had just died – *Periplous*, 17–25). Normally there was little chance of an accurate assessment of other peoples, on which could be based discussion of appropriate tactics (Millar 1982: 15–20). Indeed we hear little of what the Romans thought of the military capacities of hostile nations, except in general terms about the Germans and the Parthians. This need not of course be merely the result of lack of evidence; it may be that the Romans had little interest in these matters, believing their own propaganda that their imperial power was invincible.

150 Tacitus (1st–2nd C.AD), *On Germany* 37

From this year (113 BC) if we reckon up to the second consulship of the emperor Trajan (AD 98), there is a total of about two hundred and ten years. This is the time we are taking to conquer Germany. In the space of this long period we have inflicted and incurred many losses. Not the Samnites, not the Carthaginians, not the Spanish and the Gauls, not even the Parthians have chastised us more often. Indeed German liberty is a tougher opponent than the empire of the Arsacids (Parthia). For what else can the east cast up to us except the death of Crassus, while it lost its own Pacorus and was subjected to Ventidius? But the Germans routed or captured Carbo, Cassius, Aurelius Scaurus, Servilius Caepio and Mallius Maximus, and all together deprived the Roman people of five consular armies, and stole Varus and his three legions even from Augustus.

It suits Tacitus' theme here to emphasize the strength of the Germans; elsewhere the Parthians are treated as the major opponents of Rome. It is interesting that the relative threat of peoples outside the empire is calculated partly by counting up the number of defeats they have inflicted on Roman armies. Aurelius Scaurus is wrongly included instead of Junius Silanus as an army commander.

151 Dio (2nd–3rd C.AD), 40. 14

(An account of the Parthian empire at the invasion of Crassus in 53 BC) . . . They (the Parthians) finally rose to such a pitch of distinction and power that they actually made war on the Romans at that time, and from then onwards down to the present day were considered comparable to them. They are indeed formidable in warfare, yet their reputation is greater than their achievements, since, although they have never taken anything from the Romans and have moreover surrendered certain parts of their own territory, they have never been completely conquered, but even now are a match for us in their wars against us when they become involved in them . . . (There follows a description of the Parthian army and the climatic conditions). For this reason they do not campaign anywhere during this season (winter, when the damp weather affected their bowstrings). For the rest of the year, however, they are very difficult to fight against in their own land and in any area that resembles it. For they can endure the blazing heat of the sun because of their long experience of it, and they have found many remedies for the shortage of water and the difficulty of finding it, with the result that they can easily drive away anyone who invades their land. Outside this land, beyond the Euphrates, they have now and again won some success in battles and sudden raids, but they cannot wage a continuous, long-term war with any people, both because they face completely different conditions of climate and terrain, and because they do not prepare a supply of provisions or money.

This is about the only detailed, rational analysis we have of a power on the periphery of the Roman empire that might be perceived as a threat. Dio is probably expressing a late-second century view based on the accumulated wisdom of Roman experiences in the east. Note also his comments (80. 3) on the rise of the Persians, who around AD 224 replaced the Parthians as the dominant force east of the Euphrates.

152 Josephus (1st C.AD), *Jewish War* 3. 115–26

But Vespasian, eager to invade Galilee himself, marched out from Ptolemais after drawing up his army in the usual Roman marching order. (Section 116) He ordered the auxiliary lightly-armed troops and the archers to go on ahead to cut off any sudden attacks by the enemy and to investigate woodland which was suspicious because of its suitability for ambushes. Next followed a detachment of heavily-armed Roman soldiers, both infantry and cavalry. (Section 117) After them marched ten men from each century carrying their own equipment and the implements for measuring out the camp. (Section 118) Next came the engineers whose task was to straighten bends in the road, level rough areas, and cut down woodland which was blocking the way, so that the army should not be exhausted by a difficult march. (Section 119) Behind these men Vespasian placed his personal equipment and that of his subordinate commanders and a strong cavalry guard to protect it. (Section 120) He himself rode behind these with infantry guards and mounted guards and his personal bodyguards. Next followed the legionary cavalry, for one hundred and twenty cavalry are attached to each legion. (Section 121) After these came the mules carrying the siege towers and the remaining siege engines. (Section 122) After them came the legionary commanders, the commanders of cohorts, and the military tribunes, surrounded by guards. (Section 123) Next came the standards surrounding the eagle, which goes at the head of every Roman legion, since it is the king and most courageous of all birds; it is thought by the Romans to be a symbol of empire and a portent of victory no matter who their opponents may be. (Section 124) The trumpeters followed these holy objects, and behind them the packed marching column, six abreast. According to the usual procedure a centurion accompanied them to supervise the marching ranks. (Section 125) Behind the infantry the servants attached to each legion followed in a group, bringing the soldiers' equipment on mules and other beasts. (Section 126) Behind all the legionaries came a mixed group of auxiliaries, and finally for security a rearguard consisting of light and heavy infantry and a large force of cavalry.

153 Arrian (2nd C.AD), *Ectaxis contra Alanos* 1–11

At the head of the entire army are to be stationed the mounted scouts divided into two sections with their own commander. After these should come the Petraean mounted archers also divided into two sections, and under the command of their decurions. After these should be stationed the men drawn from the *ala* of the Aurianians. Drawn up with them should be the men of the fourth cohort of Raetians under the command of Daphne the Corinthian. Next to them should come the men from the *ala* of Colonists. Drawn up with them should be the Ituraeans and Cyrenaicans and then men from the first cohort of Raetians. Demetrius should be commander of all these men. (Section 2) After these should come the German cavalry, also divided into two sections, under the command of the centurion in charge of the camp.

(Section 3) After these the infantry should be drawn up, holding their standards in front of them, the Italians, and the Cyrenaicans who are present. Pulcher, who commands the Italians, should be in command of them all. After these should come the Bosporan infantry under their commander Lamprocles, and after these the Numidians under their commander Verus. (Section 4) They should be drawn up with four infantrymen abreast. The attached archers should be at the head of this group. Their own cavalry should protect both flanks of the marching column. After these should come the mounted guards (of the legionary legate) and after these the legionary cavalry, and then the catapults. (Section 5) Next should come the standard of the fifteenth legion (Apollinaris) with Valens the commander of the legion, the second in command, the military tribunes who have been assigned to the expedition, and centurions of the first cohort (of the legion). In front of the standard of the infantrymen should be drawn up the spearmen; the infantrymen should march drawn up four abreast. (Section 6) After the fifteenth legion the standard of the twelfth legion (Fulminata) should be positioned, with the military tribunes and centurions around it; this phalanx (the legion) should also march drawn up four abreast.

(Section 7) After the heavy infantry the allied force should be drawn up, heavy infantry from Lesser Armenia and Trapezus, and spearmen from Colchis and Rhizion. After them should be drawn up the infantry of the [Apulians]. Secundinus, commander of the [Apulians] should be commander of the allied force. (Section 8) After this should come the baggage train. The *ala* of the Dacians and its prefect should form the rearguard. (Section 9) Centurions who have been appointed for this purpose should keep the flanks of the infantry in order; to provide protection the *ala* of Gauls should ride along both flanks in a single column, and also the Italian cavalry. Their commander should patrol along the flanks. (10) The commander of the entire force, Xenophon (i.e. Arrian), should generally take up position in advance of the infantry standards, but should also make the rounds of the whole army; he should ensure that they march according to their formation, bring to order those who have got into disorder, and praise those who are in proper formation. (11) This should be the marching formation.

Arrian's *Ectaxis* is an account of the military dispositions and tactical preparations he made for repelling the invasion of the Alani, a nomadic people living north of the Caucasus, while he was governor of Cappadocia *c.* AD 135. It is interesting that he refers to himself as Xenophon, the famous Greek commander of the fourth century BC. All the military units mentioned have been identified in Cappadocia except the 'Aplanoi', which is probably a manuscript mistake; the cohort of 'Apulians' (known from another source) has been substituted in the translation. As a description of battle plans the *Ectaxis* is a unique document (also text no. 159); see Bosworth 1977; Campbell 1987.

154 Onasander (1st C.AD), prologue 4–7

Finally I may say confidently that my work will be a training school for good generals and will give pleasure to past commanders in this period of imperial peace. Even if I achieve nothing else, I shall make clear why some generals have blundered and suffered mishap, while others have been successful and become glorious . . . (Section 7) Therefore I think that I must say in advance that the examples of military technique collected in this book are all based on experience of real exploits, and indeed exploits of the kind of men to whom Rome owes her inherited superiority in race and courage right down to the present.

Onasander was a Greek who addressed his military handbook to Quintus Veranius, consul in AD 49 and governor of Britain *c*. AD 58. He is typical of writers on the art of generalship in that he claims that his work is relevant to contemporary military life (cf. Frontinus, *Strategemata* 1, *prooem*. – 'Therefore commanders will be equipped with examples of good planning and foresight, which will foster their own ability to devise and execute similar operations'). Collections of stratagems and textbooks on generalship were perhaps of value in an age of non-specialist and often inexperienced commanders (Campbell 1987).

155 Josephus, *Jewish War* 2. 578–80

(Josephus, placed in charge of Galilee by the Jewish leaders during the revolt from Rome in AD 66, describes how he trained his army in Roman methods). He (Josephus) introduced various distinguishing ranks for the soldiers and made them subordinate to decurions and centurions, who in turn were subordinate to tribunes, and above these were commanders who were in charge of larger bodies of soldiers. (Section 579) He taught them the transmission of signals, trumpet calls for advance and retreat, attack using the wings and encircling manoeuvres, the necessity of bringing assistance from the victorious part of the army to those troops in trouble, and of helping any part which is hard pressed . . . (Section 580) In particular he trained them for war by explaining on every occasion the discipline of the Romans, telling them that they would be fighting against men who through fortitude of body and courageous spirit ruled over virtually the entire world.

156 Tacitus, *Annals* 3. 74

Since his army was no match in fighting strength but much superior in making raids, he (Tacfarinas) attacked using many small groups of soldiers, avoided direct contact, and set up ambuscades. Therefore the Romans divided their attacking force into three independent formations. One of these, under the command of the legate Cornelius Scipio, occupied the route which Tacfarinas had used to attack the town of Lepcis, using the Garamantes as a secure base. On the other flank the son of Blaesus commanded a detachment with the task of ensuring that the communities around Cirta should not be attacked with impunity. Blaesus himself, the commander-in-chief, with picked troops took up position in the centre; he established forts and armed outposts in strategic locations, penned the enemy in and harassed them on all fronts, because whatever way they turned there was part of the Roman army in front of them, on the flanks, and often in the rear. In this way many were killed or captured. Then Blaesus split up his three formations into smaller detachments under the command of centurions of proven courage. When the summer was over he did not withdraw his forces or establish them in winter quarters within the province of Africa itself, as was the usual practice; instead he built a series of forts, as if he were beginning the campaigning season, and then by employing lightly-armed columns with desert experience, he continually forced Tacfarinas to keep on the move. . .

In AD 17 Tacfarinas, who had been a Roman auxiliary, led a rebellion of nomad peoples living on the fringe of the province of Africa. The war dragged on partly because of the incompetence of some of the senatorial proconsuls and because the Roman army found it difficult to deal with Tacfarinas' clever tactics. Despite the success of Blaesus, the war was not concluded until AD 24.

157 Josephus, *Jewish War* 2. 542–55 (extracts)

(Cestius Gallus, governor of Syria, had in AD 66 marched against the Jewish rebels in Jerusalem, taking the Legion XII Fulminata with detachments from the other three legions in Syria, six auxiliary infantry cohorts and four *alae*, and troops supplied by friendly kings. He subsequently decided to withdraw from the city) . . . On the following day by continuing with his retreat, Cestius encouraged the enemy to further opposition, and pressing closely round the rearguard they killed many men; they also advanced along both sides of the road and pelted the flanks with spears. (Section 543) The rearguard did not dare to turn to face the men who were wounding them from behind, since they thought that an immense throng was on their heels, and they did not try to repel those who were attacking them in the flanks since they themselves were heavily armed and were afraid to break up their ranks since they saw that the Jews were lightly equipped and ready for sudden incursions. Consequently the Romans suffered a lot of damage without being able to strike back against their enemies. (Section 544) For the entire journey men were being hit, or dislodged from the ranks, and falling to the ground. After many had been killed, including Priscus, commander of the sixth legion, Longinus, a tribune, and a prefect of an *ala* called Aemilius Jucundus, with great difficulty the army reached Gabao, the site of their earlier camp, after abandoning much of their baggage . . . (Cestius decides to continue the retreat). (Section 546) To speed up the retreat, he ordered the disposal of everything that hampered the army. They therefore killed the mules and asses and all the draught animals except for those which carried missiles and artillery pieces, which they kept because they needed them and also because they were afraid that the Jews might capture them and use them against themselves. Cestius then led the army on towards Beth-horon. (Section 547) The Jews made fewer attacks on the open ground, but when the Romans were packed together in the narrow defile of the descending roadway, some of the Jews got in front and prevented them from emerging, while others drove the rearguard down into the ravine, and the main body positioned above the narrowest part of the road pelted the column with missiles. (Section 548) In this position, even the infantry had great difficulty in defending themselves, and the cavalry's situation was even more dangerous and precarious, since under the bombardment of missiles they could not advance in order down the road, and it was impossible for horses to charge the enemy up the steep slope. (Section 549) On both sides there were cliffs and ravines down which they fell to their death. Since no one could discover a means of escape or of self-defence, they were reduced in their helplessness to lamentation and groans of despair, to which the Jews responded with war-cries and yells of intermingled delight and rage. (Section 550) Indeed Cestius and his entire army would almost certainly have been overwhelmed if night had not fallen, during which the Romans were able to escape to Beth-horon, while the Jews encircled them and watched for them to come out.

(Section 551) Cestius now gave up hope of continuing the march openly and planned to run away. Having selected about four hundred of his most courageous soldiers, he stationed them on the roofs of houses with orders to shout out the watchwords of the camp sentries so that the Jews would think that the entire army was still there. He himself with the rest of the army advanced silently for three and a half miles. (Section 552) At dawn when the Jews saw that the Romans' quarters were deserted, they charged the four hundred men who had deceived them, quickly killed them with their javelins, and then went after Cestius. (Section 553) He had got a considerable start on them during the night and after daybreak quickened the pace of his retreat with the result that the soldiers in a terrified panic abandoned their artillery and catapults and most of the other war engines, which the Jews then captured and subsequently used against the men who had left them behind ... (Section 555) They (the Jews) had suffered only a few casualties, while the Romans and their allies had lost 5,300 infantry, and four hundred and eighty cavalry.

158 Frontinus (1st–2nd C.AD), *Stratagems* 2. 3. 23

The Emperor Caesar Augustus Germanicus (Domitian), when the Chatti by retreating into woodland repeatedly interrupted a cavalry battle, ordered his cavalrymen, as soon as they reached impassable ground, to jump from their horses and fight on foot; by this ploy he ensured that his victory should not be denied by difficulties of terrain.

159 Arrian, *Ectaxis contra Alanos* 11–31

When the army has arrived at the appointed place, all the cavalry by wheeling in a circular movement is to adopt a square formation; scouts should be sent to high ground to watch for the enemy. Next, at a signal the men will prepare their arms in silence and when this has been done take their place in formation. (Section 12) Battle formation should be as follows. Each wing of the infantry (auxiliary) should hold the high ground, since that will be its formation in terrain like this. The Armenians under the command of Vasakes and Arbelos should be drawn up on the right wing, holding the highest point on that wing, because they are all archers. (Section 13) The men of the Italian cohort should be drawn up in front of them, and they will all be under the command of Pulcher who commands the Italian cohort. And Vasakes and Arbelos and their cavalry and infantry should be positioned in support of him.

(Section 14) The allied force from Lesser Armenia, the light-armed troops from Trapezus, and the Rhizionian spearmen should be drawn up on the left wing and hold the highest ground on this wing. The two hundred [Apulians] should be drawn up in front of them and one hundred of the Cyrenaicans so that their heavily-armed men can be a protection for the spearmen, who can shoot over their heads from the high ground. (Section 15) The heavy infantry of the fifteenth legion should occupy all the central area on the right, beyond the mid-point of the entire area, because these troops are by far the most numerous. The infantry of the twelfth legion should occupy the remaining area on the left side, right up to the outer limit of the left wing. The infantry should be drawn up eight ranks deep, in a closely packed formation. (Section 16) The first four ranks shall consist of pike-bearers, whose pikes will end in long, slender iron points. The men in the first rank should hold their pikes at the ready, so that if the enemy comes near, they can thrust the iron tip of their pike especially at the breasts of the horses. (Section 17) The men of the second (?), third, and fourth ranks should hold their pikes forward to jab and wound the horses where they can, and kill the riders. When the pike has been lodged in the heavy body armour, because of the softness of the metal it will bend and make the horseman ineffective. (Section 18) The remaining ranks behind them should be of spearmen. Behind them should be a ninth rank of infantry archers from the Numidians, Cyrenaicans, Bosporans, and Ituraeans. (Section 19) The artillery should be positioned on each wing so that it can fire its missiles at the advancing enemy from the longest possible range, and behind the whole infantry formation.

(Section 20) All the cavalry drawn up in *alae* and squadrons, which will be eight in number, should be positioned beside the infantry on both wings, with the infantry and archers in front of them as a defensive screen, two companies of them, while in the middle of the infantry formation, six companies [_ _ _] (Section 21) The mounted archers among these troops should be stationed close to the infantry formation, in order to shoot over it. Spearmen, pikemen, knifemen, and battleaxe-men should keep watch over both flanks and wait for the signal. (Section 22) The mounted bodyguards should be stationed around Xenophon himself (i.e. Arrian), and also up to two hundred bodyguards from the infantry phalanx, and the centurions assigned to the mounted guards, and the commanders of the bodyguards, and the decurions of the mounted guards. (Section 23) They should take up position round him [_ _ _] one hundred light-armed spearmen, so that as he tours the entire formation, where he sees anything lacking, he should take note of it and correct it. (Section 24) Valens, commander of the fifteenth legion, should take command of the entire right wing along with the cavalry. The tribunes of the twelfth legion should take command of the left wing.

(Section 25) When the troops have been drawn up like this there should be silence until the enemy come within weapon range. When they have come within range, everyone should utter a huge and ferocious warcry; missiles and stones should be discharged from catapults, arrows from bows, and the spearmen should throw their spears, both the light-armed troops and those carrying shields. Stones should be thrown at the enemy by the allied forces on the high ground; there should be a general bombardment from all sides, so concentrated as to throw the horses into confusion and bring destruction to the enemy cavalry. (Section 26) Because of the incredible weight of missiles we may hope that the advancing Scythians (i.e. Alani) will not get very close to our infantry formation. But if they do get close, then the first three ranks should lock their shields together, and, standing shoulder to shoulder, withstand the charge with all possible strength in the most concentrated formation, joined together in the strongest possible way. The fourth rank [shall hold up their pikes, so that they can kill any enemy horsemen, but not hold them straight up, so that the spearmen overshoot with their spears], while the first rank should wound and stab the horses and their riders ceaselessly with their pikes. (Section 27) When the enemy has been repulsed, if there is an obvious rout, the infantry formation should open up and the cavalry should advance, though not all the squadrons, only half of them. The vanguard of this formation should consist of those who are first to advance. (Section 28) The other half should follow those who have advanced first, but in good order and not in full-blooded pursuit, so that if the rout becomes complete, the first pursuit can be sustained by fresh horses, and if there is a sudden enemy counter-attack, they can be attacked as they turn. (Section 29) Simultaneously the Armenian archers should advance and shoot, to prevent the retreating forces from turning, and the light-armed spearmen should attack at the run. The infantry formation should not remain in the same spot but should advance more quickly than a walking pace, so that if any stronger resistance is encountered from the enemy it can again provide a protective screen in front of the cavalry.

(Section 30) This is what should happen if the enemy are routed at the first attack. But if they wheel about and aim at an encirclement of our wings, the wings of our light-armed archers should extend their position onto the higher ground. I do not think that the enemy, noting that our wings were weaker as a result of this extension, would thrust their way through them and break up the infantry. (Section 31) But if the enemy should overcome one wing or both of them, it is absolutely inevitable that their cavalry will expose their flank to us and their pikes will be at right angles to us. Then our cavalry should attack them not with a bombardment of missiles, but with swords and battleaxes. The Scythians (Alani) being unprotected and with their horses unprotected (the text breaks off here).

Cf. text no. 153. The text is damaged at Section 26; the restoration of Bosworth 1977: 240 has been translated. Arrian's tactics give the major role to the infantry, not the cavalry, and it seems that he adapted his defensive formation from the model of the Greek phalanx in order to deal with a massed cavalry attack from the Alani; Roman commanders had tried various ways of protecting the legions against archers, and attacks by massed and sometimes armoured cavalry, especially in the context of warfare in Parthia (Campbell 1987: 24–7).

160 Dio, 49. 30

The nature and construction of the 'tortoise' (*testudo*) are as follows. The baggage animals, lightly-armed troops, and cavalry are positioned in the centre of the army. The infantry who use the oblong, curved, and cylindrical shields, are drawn up on the outside, forming a rectangular shape; facing outwards, and holding their weapons in front of them, they enclose the other troops. The rest who have flat shields are packed together in the centre and raise their shields over their heads and over the heads of all the others, so that nothing except shields can be seen throughout the entire formation, and all the men are protected from missiles by the close-packed arrangement . . . They use it in two ways. Either, they advance to make an assault on a fort, and often enable some men to climb the very walls, or, when surrounded by archers they all kneel down together, and even the horses are trained to kneel or lie down, and therefore give the enemy the impression that they are beaten; then as the enemy approach they suddenly spring up and throw them into confusion.

161 Josephus, *Jewish War* 3. 166–8

Vespasian now positioned his artillery pieces, of which in total there were one hundred and sixty, in a circle round the place and gave orders to shoot at the defenders on the wall. (Section 167) In one great barrage the catapults fired bolts, the stone-throwers hurled stones weighing nearly a hundredweight, there were fire-brands and showers of arrows, making it impossible for the Jews to man the ramparts or the interior area which was within range of the missiles. (Section 168) For a throng of Arab archers and all the javelin men and slingers joined in the bombardment with the artillery.

Josephus is here describing the siege of Jotapata during the Jewish revolt.

162 Josephus, *Jewish War* 7. 304–20 (extracts)

When the Roman general had built a wall all round the exterior of the place, as I described above, and exercised the strictest vigilance to make sure that no one escaped, he turned his attention to the siege. He discovered that there was only one location capable of sustaining earthworks. (Section 305) For behind the tower which controlled the road from the west to the palace and the ridge, there was a very broad outcrop of rock which jutted out to a significant degree, though still being about 450 feet (300 cubits) below the level of Masada. It was called White (cliff). (Section 306) After he had climbed up and occupied this high point, Silva ordered the soldiers to build up a siege mound. Because of the enthusiasm of their work and the number of people helping, a solid mound was built to a height of about 300 feet (200 cubits). (Section 307) However they thought that it was not stable or wide enough as a base for the siege engines, and on top of it they built a platform of great stones fitted closely together, seventy-five feet (50 cubits) broad and seventy-five feet (50 cubits) high . . . (Section 309) Moreover, a tower ninety feet (60 cubits) high was built entirely enclosed by iron, from which the Romans, using catapults and stone-throwers, speedily drove the defenders from the walls and prevented them from appearing. (Section 310) At the same time Silva having got ready a mighty battering ram, ordered it to be directed in a series of repeated attacks against the wall, which was breached with difficulty and then destroyed. . . (The defenders built up a second wall of wooden beams and earth which was not so vulnerable to the battering ram.) (Section 315) Noting this, Silva decided that it would be more effective to use fire against this wall, and ordered the troops to bombard it with a volley of flaming torches. (Section 316) Since it was largely constructed of wood, it rapidly caught fire and because of its hollow interior this spread right through and blazed up in a mighty conflagration. (Section 317) When the fire first started, the Romans were alarmed by a north wind, which, diverting the fire from above, blew it against them, and they were virtually in despair in case all the siege engines were burned. (Section 318) Then the wind suddenly changed, as if by divine prescience, and blowing fiercely in the opposite direction, spread the flames over the wall, which was totally engulfed from top to bottom. (Section 319) The Romans, therefore, assisted by divine intervention, returned delightedly to their camp with the intention of attacking their enemy next day, and throughout the night kept a particularly careful watch in case any of them should escape in secret. (The defenders of Masada committed suicide before the final Roman assault.)

In the field the Roman army was supported by well-organized artillery. Vegetius tells us that a large, rock-throwing engine was attached to each legionary cohort; smaller engines, which fired iron bolts and were mounted on carts pulled by oxen, were attached to each century. Roman technological achievement in siege warfare probably did not surpass that of the Hellenistic Greek kings, but Roman commanders were adept in deploying all their resources of artillery and skills of siege and circumvallation, even in very unhelpful terrain such as Masada (see

Plate 8), to eliminate all places of refuge for an enemy, whom the legions could always defeat in open battle. For artillery, siege engines (see Plate 9), weaponry, and armour (see Plate 10), which are outside the scope of evidence that can be presented in this book, see Marsden 1969; 1971; Connolly 1981: 281–303; Webster 1985; Bishop and Coulston 1993.

163 Dio, 71. 3

Rivers are very easily bridged by the Romans since the soldiers are always practising it like any other military exercise, on the Danube, Rhine, and Euphrates. The procedure, which is probably not familiar to everyone, is as follows. The ships used for bridging a river are flat-bottomed and are anchored some distance upstream from the intended place for the bridge. When the signal is given, they first let one ship drift down with the current close to the bank that they occupy, and when it is opposite the place where the bridge is to be made, they throw into the water a basket full of stones fastened by a cable, which acts as an anchor. Since it is secured by this, the ship remains anchored close to the bank, and by means of planks and fastenings which the ship carries in large amounts, they immediately lay out a floor up to the landing spot. They then launch another ship downstream adjacent to the first, and another one adjacent to that, until the bridge has been extended to the opposite bank. The ship closest to the hostile bank has on board towers and a gate and archers and catapults.

164 *On the Fortifications of a Camp* (2nd C.AD), 57

Particular attention should be paid to the road which borders the sides of a camp. Furthermore, whatever the strategic position of a camp, it should have a river or a source of water on one side or the other. Unfavourable terrain, called 'a stepmother' by previous writers, should be avoided at all costs; so, the camp should not be overlooked by a mountain, which the enemy could use to attack from above or from which they could spy on activities in the camp; there should be no forest in the vicinity which might offer concealment to the enemy, and no ditch or valleys which might allow a surprise attack on the camp; and care must be taken that the camp is not inundated and destroyed by a sudden overflowing of the waters of a neighbouring river.

'Step-mother' was presumably soldiers' talk using the pejorative sense of the word common in Roman literature. This treatise, wrongly ascribed to Hyginus, the writer on surveying, dates from the second century (possibly Trajan's reign), and is an account of the construction of a camp for a hypothetical army, and the measurement of the internal areas; see M. Lenoir, 1979; camp construction – Webster 1985: 167–220; in Britain – Frere and St. Joseph 1983; Maxwell and Wilson, 1987.

MEDICAL SERVICE

Medical staff were attached to the legions, urban troops, and auxilia, and the most important of these were skilled doctors (*medici*), often of Greek origin, perhaps on a short commission and having the status and pay of an equestrian officer before their return to civilian life. While in the army they enjoyed exemption from civic duties and may have taken their seniority from the type of unit in which they served. Some military doctors were called *medici ordinarii*, and although the meaning of this term is disputed, it is possible that they had a long-term commission with a rank equivalent to that of a centurion, though not a tactical command. There were other junior medical attendants and orderlies, some of whom were also designated *medici*, and who ranked as *immunes* (text no. 35). However the numbers, organization, and status of medical staff remain obscure since most of the evidence comes from inscriptions, which offer only a brief notation of posts held with no further explanation.

Considerate commanders were noted for their care for sick soldiers – (Germanicus and Agrippina – Tac., *Ann.* 1. 69; 71; Trajan – Dio, 68. 8), and the sick and wounded were treated in well-designed and carefully built hospitals which provided insulation, quietness, and reduced likelihood of infection (Davies 1969b; 1970; 1971; 1972; Webster 1985; Fink *RMR* 74 p. 278, n.3 (= text no. 11, above; see also texts nos 145, 239).

165 *CIL* 11. 3007 = *ILS* 2542, inscription, Viterbo, 2nd C.AD

To the spirits of the departed, in honour of Marcus Ulpius Telesporus (?), son of Claudius, doctor of the *ala* Indiana and the third *ala* of Ast[u]rians, and salaried doctor of the most distinguished community of Ferentium, Ulpius Protogenes, freedman, erected this to his estimable patron.

It seems that this military doctor returned to a medical post in civilian life.

166 *CIL* 13. 6621 = *ILS* 2602, inscription, Obernburg, Upper Germany

Sacred to Apollo and Aesculapius, Welfare, Fortune, for the welfare of Lucius Petronius Florentinus, prefect of the fourth part-mounted cohort of Aquitanians, Roman citizens, Marcus Rubrius Zosimus, doctor of the cohort mentioned above, from Ostia on the Tiber, willingly, happily, and deservedly paid his vow.

Zosimus has a Greek name and was presumably posted to the cohort of Aquitanians from civilian life in Ostia.

167 *CIL* 6. 20 = *ILS* 2092, inscription, Rome, AD 82

In honour of Asclepius and the good health of his fellow soldiers, Sextus Titius Alexander, doctor of the fifth cohort of praetorians, made this offering in the consulship of [Domitian] Augustus for the eighth time and Titus Flavius Sabinus.

168 *CIL* 7.690 = *RIB* 1618, inscription, Vercovicium (Housesteads), Britain

To the spirits of the departed, in honour of Anicius Ingenuus, doctor *ordinarius* of the first cohort of Tungrians, lived twenty-five years.

169 *CJ* 10. 53(52). 1, 3rd C.AD

The Emperor Antoninus to Numisius. Since you say that you are doctor of Legion II Adiutrix, you will not be forced to undertake civic duties during the time when you are absent on state business. But when you have ceased to be absent (on state business), after the termination of your exemption on that basis, if you belong to that group to whom are applicable the privileges granted to doctors, you will benefit from that exemption.

INCENTIVES AND PUNISHMENTS

Soldiers could be rewarded after a successful campaign with a distribution of booty, extra rations, or promotion. Military decorations were more a symbolic recognition of an individual soldier's courage, and in the Republic were bestowed unsystematically in a way that emphasized the nature of the action rather than the status of the recipient. In the imperial period donatives replaced booty as a reward for the troops. Moreover, by the end of the first century AD the award of military decorations had been reorganized in a much more hierarchical structure in which there were a limited number of decorations whose design was largely based on items of captured enemy equipment or Roman weaponry or celebrated acts of valour, like storming a town or fort. According to his rank and status, a man received a combination of the various types of decoration and a certain number of each type, with the most important being reserved for senators of consular standing, although the *corona civica* could be won by any soldier (text no. 170). Awards of military decorations were normally made to Roman citizens, but a few examples show that non-citizen auxiliaries could be decorated, though this may have been restricted to junior officers. In the second century entire auxiliary units were sometimes granted a title derived from a decoration (e.g. *torquata*).

It was the emperor's responsibility on the recommendation of his officers to decide on military decorations, which he could award personally if present on campaign. Otherwise the duty fell to the recipient's immediate commander. Soldiers proudly record their military decorations on memorial inscriptions and significantly represent them as a personal grant from the emperor (Maxfield 1981).

In Roman tradition, fortitude and disciplined readiness for battle were at the root of their conquest of Italy and the Mediterranean, and '*Romana disciplina*' distinguished them from their rivals. Military law was strict particularly in respect of cowardice and desertion. But the enforcement of discipline was uneven since it was the responsibility of individual commanders, and not all emperors were politically secure enough to give a strong lead (Campbell 1984: 190–8; 300–11).

170 *ILS* 2637 = *EJ* 248, inscription, near Tibur (Tivoli), north-east of Rome, early 1st C.AD

Marcus Helvius Rufus Civica, son of Marcus, of the tribe Camilia, chief centurion, bestowed a bath building on the townsmen and residents.

Helvius Rufus, as a legionary soldier, had been decorated in AD 20 by L. Apronius, proconsul of Africa, with necklaces and spear, and by Tiberius himself with the civic crown for bravery in action and for saving the life of a fellow-soldier (Tacitus, *Annals* 3. 21; Aulus Gellius, *Attic Nights* 5. 6. 14). Rufus in order to commemorate his distinction had apparently adopted the nickname 'Civica'. Although the civic crown could be won by all soldiers, this is the last known example of the award of a spear to anyone of lower rank than a senior centurion.

171 *CIL* 12. 2230 = *ILS* 2313, inscription, Cularo (Grenoble), Narbonensis, 2nd C.AD

To the spirits of the departed, in honour of Titus Camulius Lavenus (?), son of Lucius, veteran of the Legion III Gallica, granted an honourable discharge by Emperor Antoninus Augustus Pius, and on the wishes of

Emperor Hadrian Augustus decorated with golden Necklaces and Armbands, according to the vote of the legion, Camulia Soror (?) and Partegoria [_ _ _] because of his worthiness, in honour of an excellent and devoted patron.

This is the only known example of the award of decorations by an emperor in response to the wishes of the recipient's colleagues. The standard award for ordinary soldiers consisted of necklaces, armbands, ornaments.

172 *CIL* 2. 4461 = *ILS* 2661, inscription, Aeso (Avella), Spain, 2nd C.AD

To Lucius Aemilius Paternus, son of Lucius, of the tribe Galeria, chief centurion, prefect of engineers, centurion of Legion VII Gemina, centurion of Legion I Minervia, centurion of Legion VII Claudia, [Loyal and Faithful], centurion of Legion XIII Gemina, centurion of the tenth [urban] cohort, centurion of the fourth praetorian cohort, *trecenarius* of Legion II Augusta, and chief centurion, decorated on three occasions by Emperor Trajan with Necklaces, Armbands, Discs, and a Rampart Crown, twice in Dacia and once in Parthia, Atilia Vera, daughter of Lucius, to her (father) who deserved well of her.

Paternus was a praetorian centurion when last decorated. Centurions received necklaces, armbands, necklaces and one crown, while senior centurions could additionally receive a spear.

173 *CIL* 3. 1193 = *ILS* 2746, inscription, Apulum (Alba Iulia), Dacia, 2nd C.AD

In honour of Gaius Julius Corinthianus, son of Gaius, from Thevestis, prefect of the seventh cohort of Gauls, tribune of the first cohort of Britons, also of the detachment of Dacians in Parthia, on whom because of his bravery the most revered emperors conferred a Wall Crown, an Untipped Spear, and a silver Standard, prefect of the *ala* of Campagonians, also prefect of a milliary *ala*, lived 39 years, Marcius Arrianus and Julius Clinias and Pisonianus, his heirs, had this erected.

Cf. Maxfield 1981: 178. Equestrian officers normally received one or two crowns and spears, and a standard (cf. nos 114–15), while senators received decorations according to their seniority; a consular could normally expect four crowns and either three or four spears and standards, for example, Quintus Glitius Atilius Agricola – 'decorated with military decorations by the same emperor (Trajan) in the Dacian war, a Wall Crown, Rampart Crown, Naval Crown, gold Crown, four Untipped Spears, four Standards' (*ILS* 1021–1021a).

174 Suetonius (1st–2nd C.AD), *Augustus* **25. 3**

As military decorations he rather more readily bestowed ornaments and necklaces, which were valuable for the gold and silver they contained, than rampart and wall crowns, which conferred high distinction; these he granted as sparingly as possible, and impartially, and often even to ordinary soldiers.

Augustus apparently attempted to preserve the tradition of awarding military decorations by merit alone.

175 Josephus (1st C.AD), *Jewish War* **7. 13–15**

Therefore he (Titus) immediately ordered the men appointed for this purpose to read out the names of soldiers who had performed a distinguished exploit during the war. (Section 14) Summoning each man by name, he applauded them as they came forward, being just as delighted as if it had been his own achievement, granted them gold crowns, gold necklaces, small gold spears and standards made from silver, (Section 15) and promoted each man to a higher rank; moreover, out of the spoils he generously distributed to them silver and gold and clothing and other booty. When they had all been honoured as he judged each one deserved, he offered prayers for the entire army, then descended amid tremendous acclamations and went on to offer sacrifice for his victory (at Jerusalem).

176 Suetonius, *Augustus* **24. 2**

(Augustus exercised discipline extremely severely) He dismissed the entire tenth legion in disgrace for insubordination, and he also dis-banded, without the benefits associated with completion of service, other units which were improperly clamouring for discharge. If any units abandoned their position in battle, he decimated them and fed the remainder on barley. If any centurions abandoned their position, he executed them, just as he did ordinary soldiers; for other kinds of offences he imposed various humiliating penalties; for example he would order men to stand all day in front of the general's headquarters sometimes clad only in their tunics and without sword-belts, or sometimes holding a ten-foot pole or even a piece of earth.

After the disorder of the civil wars when discipline was frequently subverted and soldiers were encouraged to desert their commanders, Augustus attempted to re-establish traditional military practices and the authority of the *imperator*. He needed to show that he was not at the mercy of his troops.

177 *D* 49. 16. 3. 10; 15–16; 6. 3–6; 7

*(*Modestinus (3rd C.AD) **Book IV On Punishments)**

The soldier who flees to the enemy and then comes back, shall be tortured and then condemmed to the wild beasts or the gallows, although soldiers are not normally liable to either of these punishments . . . (Sections 15–16) The soldier who in time of war does anything forbidden by the commander or who does not carry out his orders, is executed even if his action was successful. The man who leaves the ranks will, according to the circumstances, be beaten with rods or demoted to another branch of the service . . .

*(*Section 6. 3–6) (Menander (2nd C.AD) **Book III On Military Matters)**

The soldier who was the first to take flight in battle must be be executed in full view of the soldiers as an example. Scouts, who have passed on secret information to the enemy are traitors and are executed. Moreover, a rank and file soldier who pretends to be ill through fear of the enemy, is in the same situation . . . (Section 7) (Taruttienus Paternus (2nd C.AD) Book II On Military Matters) Traitors and deserters are generally tortured and executed after having been discharged. For they are considered to be enemies not soldiers.

178 Tacitus, *Annals* 13. 35

But Corbulo had more trouble with the inefficiency of his soldiers than with the duplicity of the enemy. His legions had been transferred from Syria where they had grown lazy because of the long peace and could scarcely cope with routine camp duties. It is reliably stated that there were long-serving soldiers in that army who had never kept guard or served as look-out, who found ramparts and ditches a novel and unusual experience, who had no helmets or armour, who were sleek business men spending their military service in towns . . . The entire army was kept under canvas although the winter was so severe that the frozen ground had to be dug up before tents could be pitched. Many soldiers lost limbs through frostbite and others froze to death during guard duty. One soldier was seen carrying a bundle of firewood with hands frozen so stiff that they fell off his arms still fastened to their load. Corbulo himself, in light clothing and bare-headed, appeared personally with the troops as they marched and toiled, praising the enthusiastic, encouraging the sick, and providing an example for everyone. But the severity of the climate and service conditions caused many to refuse their duties or desert. Corbulo sought the answer in toughness. For he did not, like other commanders, extend a pardon to first and second offenders, but immediately executed anyone who deserted the standards. Experience showed that this was beneficial and more effective than leniency, since Corbulo had fewer deserters from his army than those commanders who were indulgent.

Cf. Fronto *Principia Historiae* 12 = Loeb, vol. 2, p. 208. The legions stationed in the east seem to have had a particularly bad reputation for ill-discipline. That is perhaps because in Syria the soldiers were quartered in towns, not camps, and were consequently more difficult to control. But it may simply be that we have more evidence for Syria than for other provinces because of the eastern campaigns of Corbulo and Lucius Verus, reported by Tacitus and Fronto, who may indeed have exaggerated the extent of earlier indiscipline in the Syrian army.

5 The army in peacetime

MILITARY LIFE IN AND AROUND THE CAMPS

Many documents illustrate the routine duties of Roman soldiers in time of peace, on guard duty, patrols, foraging expeditions, as messengers and guards of the provincial governor. Soldiers could be detached from their unit for long periods to serve in a neighbouring outpost, and the better educated were often seconded for secretarial work either in their base or at headquarters (for the daily life of soldiers, see Davies 1974).

Detailed records were needed to list the whereabouts and activities of every soldier in a unit, and keep a running check on the total strength available. Three types of report have been identified: a morning report including orders of the day, the number of junior officers and men, their duties; a monthly inventory of personnel; a *pridianum* – a yearly record of a unit on 31 December, stating accessions, losses, and those absent on duty (Fink *RMR* 64 is the only certain example; it uses the word *pridianum* – the only technical name for any of these reports to be mentioned in papyri). However, it is doubtful if so precise a distinction is possible, or if a *pridianum* was required yearly, or if these types of record were used uniformly everywhere. The strength report discovered in 1988 at Vindolanda (text no. 182) may be an interim summary, from several of which a *pridianum* could have been compiled later (Fink *RMR* pp. 179–82; Bowman and Thomas 1991).

Foremost among the army's duties was the maintenance of order in the provinces. Since there was no regular police force, much responsibility lay with the governing élite of the local cities who had only limited resources and who might in turn require the support of Roman troops not only against brigands, but against internal dissension. In certain respects the Roman army was like an army of occupation, most notably in Judaea where religious and nationalist feelings against Roman rule were strong. Government operations like the corn supply, or tax collecting, or the maintenance of routes for communication and trade, could require a more or less permanent military presence. From this kind of activity the army's role could be extended to more routine guard or police duties in the community. For the incidence of urban unrest and brigandage in the imperial period, see MacMullen 1966: 163–241; 255–68; availability of weapons in local communities – Brunt 1975; the army as an internal security force in the east – Isaac 1992: 101–60.

179 Vegetius (4th C.AD), 2. 19

Seeing that there are several posts in the legions which require soldiers of some education, the men in charge of scrutinizing recruits, although it is right for them to examine the size, strength, and mental attitude of every recruit, should also select some men on the basis of their skill in writing and their ability in calculating and working out accounts. For the record of the entire legion in relation to services, military duties, and pay, is written out every day in the registers with virtually more care than details of supply and civil matters are recorded in the public account books. Soldiers chosen in turn from all the centuries and tents even in time of peace perform daily guard duties, and also man outposts or keep watch; the names therefore of those who have done their turn of duty are entered in the records so that no one is overworked contrary to what is just or escapes with doing nothing.

180 *P. Dura* 82 = Fink, *RMR* 47, papyrus, Dura Europus, AD 223–5 (extracts)

col. i
27 March: net total of rank and file soldiers, 923, among these nine centurions, eight men on double pay, one on pay and a half; camel riders, 34, among these one man on pay and a half; cavalry, 223, among these five decurions, seven men on double pay, four on pay and a half of the twentieth cohort of Palmyreni, Severiana Alexandriana. Julius Rufianus, tribune, sent the password (chosen) from the seven planets, "Holy(?) Mercury".
Sent [_ _ _] five soldiers, among these [_ _ _] camel riders, one cavalryman: century of Marianus, Aurelius Licinnius; century of Pudens, Aurelius Demetrius; century of Nigrinus, Aurelius Romanus and Aurelius Rufus; troop of Antoninus, Iarhaboles, son of Odeatus.
Returned, formerly detailed with [_ _ _] Appadana (?) [_ _ _] troop of Tiberinus [_ _ _]
Timinius Paulinus, decurion, announced the orders of the day. We shall

do whatever may be ordered; we shall be ready for every command. Those standing guard at the standards of our lord Alexander Augustus: decurion, Timinius Paulinus; shrine-keeper, Aurelius Silvanus; [_ _ _], son of Vabalathus; supervisor, Aurelius Rubathus; inspector of sentries, Iarhaeus, son of Malchus; second supervisor, Claudius Agrippa; cavalryman. . .

col. ii

29 March: net total of rank and file soldiers 9[14] of the twentieth cohort of Palmyreni, Severiana Alexandriana [_ _ _]

Julius Rufianus tribune [_ _ _]

sent to obtain barley [_ _ _] soldiers, among these [_ _ _] cavalrymen [_ _ _]

sent as escorts for the barley collectors, [_ _ _] soldiers; century of Marianus [_ _ _]

Returned: those formerly detailed to Adatha, two soldiers: century of Nigrinus, Julius Zabdibolus [_ _ _]

Returned: those formerly detailed to the headquarters of the governor with letters [_ _ _]

Check! Returned: from those formerly detailed with the men present at the headquarters of the governor from the second part-mounted cohort [_ _ _]

Sent: to collect wood for the bath, one soldier, of the century of Nigrinus, Zebidas, son of Barneus [_ _ _] . . .

This is perhaps a morning report of cohort XX Palmyreni.

181 *AE* 1979. 643, with Marichal 1979, ostracon from Bu-Njem, Tripolitania, 3rd C.AD

December 24, number (of soldiers)	57
among these:	
clerk	1
orderly	1
scout – (erased)	(1)
cavalry	8
on exercises (?)	22
on watchtower	1
at the gate	1
at commanding officer's	1
doing building work (?)	1
sick:	3
Sulpicius Donatus	

Titus Buzuris
Aurelius Rufus
at flogging   1
the rest, noted (?):   17
at the bakehouse (?)   15
at the bath   2

At Bu-Njem were discovered 146 Latin ostraca of which 117 contained records of a military unit which was stationed here in the early-mid third century – a detachment of the III Augusta, at least up to AD 238 when the legion was disbanded. The ostracon translated forms part of a daily report presumably sent to the commanding officer, and from which information could be extracted for a more detailed report.

182 Bowman and Thomas 1991, tablet, Vindolanda, Britain, *c.* AD 90

18 May, net total of the first cohort of Tungrians which is commanded by Julius Verecundus, prefect, 752, including six centurions.
From these there are absent:

Guards of the governor	46
in the office of Ferox	
in Coria (Corbridge)	337
	including two (?) centurions
in London	(?) a centurion
[_ _ _]	6
	including one centurion
[_ _ _]	9
	including one centurion
[_ _ _]	11
In [_ _ _]	(?) 1
	45
Total absent	456
	including five centurions
Remainder, present	296
	including one centurion
From these:	
Sick	15
Wounded	6
Suffering from inflammation of the eyes	10
Total of these	31
Remainder, fit and well	[265]
	including one centurion

This is probably an interim strength report, and is the only extant example of a report for a milliary infantry cohort; the first cohort of Tungrians must have been one of the earliest of such units to be constituted. At Vindolanda it was apparently divided into two, with the larger detachment forming an element of the garrison at Corbridge away from the main base. There is evidence for an increasing sejunction of units at least on the British frontier at this time. A milliary infantry cohort is usually thought to have had ten centuries, but this document shows only six centurions; the editors suggest that this may have been a temporary arrangement during reorganization of the cohort (see also p. 34).

183 Fink, *RMR* 63, papyrus, Egypt, AD 105 or 106

col. i . . .

16 September

[According to ?] the *pridianum* of the first cohort of Spaniards Veterana, at Stobi
[_ _ _] Arruntianus, prefect
[Total of soldiers], 31 December   546
including 6 centurions, 4 decurions, cavalry   119,
including [_ _ _] men on double pay, 3 men on pay and a half; one
infantry man on double pay, and [_ _ _] men on pay and a half

ADDITIONS AFTER 1 JANUARY

(Fragmentary)
[Total]   596
col. ii including 6 centurions, 4 decurions; cavalry [_ _ _] including 2 men on double pay, 3 on pay and a half, [_ _ _] infantrymen on pay and a half.

FROM THESE THERE HAVE BEEN LOST:

given to the Fleet Flavia Moesica [_ _ _] on the orders of Faustinus the legate
[_ _ _] on the orders of Justus the legate, including one cavalryman
[_ _ _]
sent back to Herennius Saturninus
transferred to the army of Pannonia
died by drowning
killed by bandits, one cavalryman
killed in battle (?)

Total lost including [_ _ _]
restored from the stragglers
the remainder, net total [_ _ _]
including 6 centurions, 4 decurions; cavalry 110 (or more) including 2 men on double pay and 3 on pay and a half;
infantrymen on double pay [_ _ _], 6 men on pay and a half.

FROM THESE ABSENT:

in Gaul to obtain clothing
similarly to obtain [grain (?)]
across the river (?) Erar (?) to obtain horses, including [_ _ _] cavalrymen
at Castra in the garrison, including 2 cavalrymen
in Dardania at the mines
total absent outside the province including [_ _ _] cavalrymen

INSIDE THE PROVINCE

guards of Fabius Justus the legate, including Carus, decurion [_ _ _]
in the office of Latinianus, procurator of the Emperor
at Piroboridava in the garrison
at Buridava in the detachment
across the Danube on an expedition, including [_ _ _] men on pay and a half
23 cavalrymen, 2 infantrymen on pay and a half
similarly across (the river) to protect the corn supply
similarly on a scouting mission with the centurion A[_ _ _]vinus [_ _ _] cavalrymen
in (?) at the grain ships, including one (?) decurion
at headquarters with the clerks
to the Haemus (mountains) to bring in cattle
to guard beasts of burden, including [_ _ _] men on pay and a half
similarly on guard duty [_ _ _]
Total absent of both types
including one centurion, 3 decurions; cavalry including [_ _ _] 2 infantrymen on pay and a half.
The remainder present
including 5 centurions, one decurion; cavalry including [_ _ _] men on double pay, one infantryman on double pay, [_ _ _] men on pay and a half
from these sick, among them [_ _ _]

For the date and historical context, see Lepper and Frere 1988: 244–59. The unit mentioned was the part-mounted *cohors I Veterana Hispanorum equitata*, known from a diploma to have been in Lower Moesia in AD 99 and in Dacia in 129 and 140; during the period described in the papyrus, it was based at Stobi in Macedonia though many of its soldiers were on detachment in Moesia and elsewhere. Marichal has argued that this document is not itself a *pridianum* but an extraordinary strength report during the Dacian wars which made use of a *pridianum* (Bruckner and Marichal 1963). It may have been subsequently brought to Egypt by the official who received it.

184 Daris, *Documenti* 10 (3) = Fink, *RMR* 10, papyrus, Egypt, AD 80–87

Marcus Papirius Rufus C[_ _ _]
departed (from camp) to the granary at Neapolis (in Alexandria) in accordance with the letter of Titus Suedius Clemens, prefect of the camp, in the third year of Emperor [Titus _ _ _]. He returned on 21 January of the same year. He departed to the granary in the Mercurium in the first year of Emperor Domitian [_ _ _]. He returned in the same year on 13 July. He departed on guard duty (?) [_ _ _] in the fourth year of Domitian on 21 April. He returned in the same year [_ _ _]. He departed to the granary in the Mercurium, year [_ _ _]. He returned in the same year on 7 July.

　　Titus Flavius Satur[ninus _ _ _]
departed for the purpose of dredging harbours, [year _ _ _] 14 January. He returned in the same (?) year [_ _ _]. He departed with Timinius, centurion [_ _ _]. He returned in the same year on 28 November. He departed with Maximus the freedman [_ _ _].

　　Titus Flavius Vale[_ _ _]
departed for the purpose of making papyrus, year [_ _ _] on 15 January. He returned in [_ _ _]. He departed for the mint, in the first year of Emperor Domitian [_ _ _]. He returned in the same year on 17 January. [_ _ _] He departed to the granary in the Mercurium [_ _ _]. He returned in the same year on 14 July. [He departed _ _ _] from the countryside in the seventh year of Domitian on 19 September.

　　Titus Flavius Celer
departed to the granary in Neapolis, year [_ _ _] on 11 February. He returned in the same year [_ _ _]. He departed with the river patrol [_ _ _]. He returned in the same year on 24 May. He departed [_ _ _] on 3 October in the first year of Emperor Domitian. He returned [in the same year] on 20 February. He departed with the grain convoy, year [_ _ _], on 19 June. He returned in the third year of Domitian [_ _ _

This record (perhaps derived from a morning report) of detached service for individual soldiers may refer to Legion III Cyrenaica. The soldiers are absent for a minimum of about four months and a maximum of ten and a half months.

185 Daris, *Documenti* 66, terracotta jar, Oxyrhynchus, Egypt, 2 BC

From the Ox(yrhynchite) nome.

Ammonios, son of Ammonios, helmsman of the public boat whose emblem is [_ _ _] through the agency of Lucius Oclatius, soldier on marine escort duty, of the twenty-second legion, second cohort, century of Maximus Stoltius, and Hermias, son of Petalos, helmsman of another boat whose emblem is Egypt, through the agency of Lucius Castricius, soldier on marine escort duty, of the twenty-second legion, fourth cohort, century of Titus Pompeius. This is a specimen of what we placed on board out of the produce of the twenty-eighth (year) of Caesar; Ammonios (filled) up to the bulwarks with $433^{1/4}$ *artabae* (about 22,529 litres) of wheat, and similarly Hermias with $433^{1/4}$ *artabae* of wheat; all these were placed on board by Leonidas and Apollonios, corn collectors of the eastern section of the lower toparchy, $866^{1/2}$ *artabae* (about 45,058 litres) of wheat, and we made a further measurement of a half *artabe* (about 26 litres) of wheat for every hundred *artabae* (5,200 litres). (This is for the purpose of tax.) We carried out the loading from the 2nd of Hathyr to the 4th of the same month, and we have sealed it (the jar) with both our seals, that of Ammonios whose figure is Ammon, and that of Hermias whose figure is Harpocrates. Year twenty-nine of Caesar, 4th Hathyr. (Added in different hand) We, Hermias and Ammonios have placed our seals on the specimens. Year twenty-nine of Caesar, 19th Hathyr.

This writing is on a terracotta jar containing the specimen of wheat from the Oxyrhynchus nome which would be opened in Alexandria to test its purity. The twenty-second legion is the Deiotariana, stationed at Alexandria.

186 Guéraud 1942, nos 1 and 13, ostraca, Egypt

No. 1

Rustius Barbarus to his brother Pompeius, greetings. Why is it that you have not written back to me if you received the loaves of bread? I sent you fifteen loaves with Popilius and Dutuporis, then fifteen more and a vase (?) with the carter Draco; you have used up four *matia* (one third of an *artabe*) of wheat. I sent you six loaves with the cavalryman

Thiadices, who said he could take them. I request, brother, that you have some scales (?) made for my personal use, as beautiful as possible, and write to me so that in payment for them I can make you bread or send you money, whichever you wish. Now, I want you to know that I am going to get married. As soon as I have married, I shall write to you at once to come. Farewell. Regards to [_ _ _].

No. 13

[_ _ _] to Terentius and [_ _ _] and Atticus [_ _ _], fondest greetings. First of all I pray that you are in [good health]; my dearest wish [_ _ _] is for you and the children to remain in good health. I received from Ca[_ _ _] the bunch of radishes (?) that you sent. You are going to get gourds and citrus fruit (from me); divide them with your brothers as you yourselves wish. Regards to your comrades in the army. Isidorus sends you his best wishes. I pray that you are well.

These are examples of Latin and Greek ostraca, dating from late first-mid second century AD, found near a quarry and gold mine on the road from Coptos in Egypt to the Red Sea. A small detachment of soldiers was stationed here perhaps to guard the mine and the trade route.

187 *ILS* 9073, inscription, Rusicade (Skikda), Numidia, AD 268–70

In honour of Jupiter Best and Greatest, I have fulfilled my vow to the *Genius* of Emperor Caesar Marcus Aurelius Claudius Unconquered Pius Fortunate Augustus, Aelius Dubitatus, soldier of the ninth praetorian cohort, century of Etrius; for nine years I have looked after the staging post at Veneria Rusicade, and my fellow-soldiers have been safe and fortunate [_ _ _

Rusicade was a colony which, along with Cirta, Milev, and Chullu, formed a loose confederation; it was an important port and the terminus for the road from Cirta which Hadrian had rebuilt, and along which grain was transported for export from Numidia. In the third century there was apparently a detachment from the ninth praetorian cohort based here.

188 Frend 1956: 46, inscription, Sulmenli (Eulandra ?), Asia, AD 213

[In the consulships of Emperor Antoninus for the third time and Caelius B]albinus, 11 October, at Prymnessus, the procurator Philocurius: '[_ _ _] they are showing dissension in respect of matters that have been decided; those who are showing dissension [shall be punished in accordance with] the decisions'. Valens: 'The Anosseni request that they should be granted a soldier on police duty'. [Philocurius the procurator: 'To guarantee (?)] the decisions I shall provide a soldier'.

This is an extract from a document dealing with a dispute (continuing until AD 237) between two villages in Asia, Anossa and Antimacheia, over contributions in animals, fodder, and carts, that they were obliged to make for people on official business using the local roads. They belonged to an imperial estate and so were under the jurisdiction of a procurator. The initial hearing with the people of Anossa as the plaintiffs took place about AD 200 before the procurator, who ordered an *optio* to carry out his decision. At a further hearing in AD 213 the people of Anossa seem to be complaining that the earlier decision was not being properly implemented; it is interesting that they ask for a soldier to be sent to them – it was not always the case that local communities wished to avoid contact with the military (below, pp. 170–80).

189 Pliny (1st–2nd C.AD), *Letters* 10. 19–20

Pliny to Emperor Trajan. I request, sir, that you guide me with your advice since I am uncertain whether I ought to employ public slaves of the local communities on prison guard duty, as has been the practice up to now, or use soldiers. For I am apprehensive that public slaves are not sufficiently reliable guards and on the other hand that a not inconsiderable number of soldiers would be detained on this duty. For the moment I have added a few soldiers to serve as guards with the public slaves. I see that there is a danger, however, that this very action will cause carelessness on both sides since they will be confident that each can direct the blame on to the other for any mistake for which they were both responsible.

Trajan to Pliny. My dear Pliny, there is no need to transfer more fellow-soldiers to prison guard duty. We should adhere to the custom which pertains in that province, namely that prisons are guarded by public slaves. For it is your responsibility through your discipline and watchfulness to ensure that they carry out this duty reliably. The most important point is, as you say in your letter, the fear that if soldiers are mixed in with public slaves, both sides may become more neglectful of their duty by relying on each other. Moreover, we should adhere to the general rule that as few soldiers as possible should be diverted from military duties.

As governor of Bithynia-Pontus, Pliny had some auxiliary troops under his command.

190 *P. Dura* 60B, with Chaumont 1987, papyrus, Dura-Europus, Syria, early 3rd C.AD

Marius Maximus to tribunes, and prefects, and commanders of units, greetings. I have enclosed what I have written to Minicius Martialis, procurator of our Emperors, so that you may take note of this. I hope that you are well.

Copy

You should take care that the treasuries of the units through which Goces is passing, envoy of the Parthians to our lords the most steadfast Emperors, offer him hospitality according to the customary procedure. And write to inform me of whatever you spend in each unit.

   Gazica
   Appadana
   Du[r]a
   Ed[da]na
   Bi[blada]

Lucius Marius Maximus Perpetuus Aurelianus governed Syria Cole, where he is attested in post by AD 207. The five place names indicate the route that Goces was to take where Roman camps or outposts had been established. For the use of soldiers as messengers and escorts in eastern diplomacy, see Campbell 1993.

191 *D* 1. 18. 13

(Ulpian (3rd C.AD), **Book VII On the Duties of a Proconsul**)

It is right for a competent and conscientious governor to see to it that the province of which he has charge is peaceful and quiet. He will achieve this without difficulty if he carefully ensures that evil men are expelled, and hunts them out. He should hunt out sacrilegious persons, brigands, kidnappers, and thieves, and punish each one according to his crime, and he should also bring force against those who harbour them, since a criminal cannot escape detection for long without their help.

SOLDIERS AS BUILDERS AND ENGINEERS

Many soldiers had experience of building and labouring in the normal course of military life, while others acquired special technical skills, since the army tried to be as self-sufficient as possible, by making the items it needed and by building and maintaining forts, accommodation, bathing facilities, and aqueducts. The army also had to build roads and bridges, and these activities often benefited the local community in the vicinity of military establishments, since roads and bridges once built or repaired would be used in the main by civilians. Products of military workshops could also be sold outside the camp. There is much evidence for smithies (*fabricae*) in army camps; the workshop at Corbridge, established probably in the late second century, had about 560 square metres of floorspace and accommodation for 100/150 men who worked in the factory producing weapons and iron tools well beyond the requirements of the troops in the camp. Such operations, however, will have taken business away from local smiths. Bricks and tiles were made in large quantities in legionary camps, and the use of bricks stamped with a legion's number in private housing may suggest that bricks constituted a kind of commerce, in that they could be exchanged for local produce or services. In all these cases the army's role was closely connected with its military responsibilities. But soldiers were also used to assist local communities in the construction of public buildings that have no ostensible military purpose, although the exact circumstances in which this occurred are obscure. Military engineers and surveyors were often sent to assist local communities (see MacMullen 1959; 1967: 23–48).

192 *D* 49. 16. 12. 1

(Macer (3rd C.AD), **Book I On Military Affairs**)

Paternus has also written that the man who is attentive to the responsibilities of the command of an army should grant leave very sparingly, not permit a horse which belongs to the military to be taken outside the province, and not send soldiers to carry out any private job, or to fish or hunt. In the rules of discipline established by Augustus it is laid down as follows: 'Although I know that it is not inappropriate for soldiers to be occupied in building work, I am nevertheless afraid that if I grant permission for anything to be done which might be in my interest or yours, it would not be done in a fashion which would be acceptable to me'.

193 *D* 1. 16. 7. 1

(Ulpian (3rd C.AD), **Book II On the Duties of a Proconsul**)

He should visit temples and public buildings in order to inspect them and find out if they are properly maintained and in good condition, or if they require any repairs. Moreover, he should ensure that building projects which have been begun are completed in so far as the resources of that community permit, he should formally appoint conscientious inspectors of public works, and he should arrange for groups of soldiers to assist the inspectors if necessary.

194 Tacitus (1st–2nd C.AD), *Annals* 11. 20

Soon afterwards the same honour (an honorary triumph) was acquired by Curtius Rufus, who had sunk a mine in the territory of the Mattiaci in a search for silver. The output from this mine was small and did not last for long. But the legionaries endured much costly toil as they dug channels and laboured underground in a way which would have been onerous even if they had been in the open. Exhausted by this, and because troops in several provinces were undergoing similar toils, the soldiers wrote secretly in the name of all the armies to beg the emperor that when he was about to appoint a commander, he should grant him an honorary triumph before he took up his command.

195 *CIL* 10. 3479 = *ILS* 2857, inscription, Naples

To the spirits of the departed. Gaius Terentius Longinus, orderly (*optio*) in charge of the squad of builders, lived thirty years, served eleven years, Tullius Titianus, tribune of the praetorian fleet at Misenum, his heir, erected this for an estimable man.

196 *CIL* 6. 8991 = *ILS* 7741, inscription, Rome, 2nd C.AD

I, Lucius Marius Vitalis, son of Lucius, lived seventeen years, fifty-five days; accomplished in learning, I persuaded my parents that I should learn a craft; I left the city in the praetorian guard of Hadrian Augustus Caesar and while I was studying there the fates envied me, and snatching me away from my craft, deposited me in this place.

Maria Malchis his heart-broken mother, to her most worthy son.

197 *CIL* 5. 8003 = Smallwood *GN* 328, milestone near Meran, AD 46

Tiberius Claudius Caesar Augustus Germanicus, chief priest, in the sixth year of his tribunician power, designated consul for the fourth time, *imperator* for the eleventh time, father of the fatherland, built the road Claudia Augusta which his father Drusus had laid out after he had opened up the Alps by war, from the river Po to the river Danube, over a distance of 350 miles.

This illustrates the military aspect of Roman road building. Drusus' victory over the Raeti in 15 BC had led to the creation of the province of Raetia. This part of the road ran in a north-westerly direction, passing through Tridentum (Trent), Pons Drusi (Bolzano), and the Resia pass, providing access to the upper Danube. *ILS* 208 (= *EJ* 363a), found near Feltria, shows that the road began at Altinum near the mouth of the Po. For the construction of roads, see Chevallier 1989.

198 *ILS* 5834 = Smallwood *NH* 420, milestone near Thoana, Arabia, AD 110–111

Emperor Caesar Nerva Trajan Augustus, Conqueror of the Germans, Conqueror of the Dacians, son of the divine Nerva, chief priest, in the fifteenth year of his tribunician power, *imperator* for the sixth time, consul for the fifth time, father of the fatherland, when Arabia had been reduced to the position of a province, opened up a new road from the borders of Syria right up to the Red Sea, and paved it, through the work of Gaius Claudius Severus, legate of the emperor with propraetorian power. Fifty-four miles.

Thoana lies about 54 miles north of Petra. The construction of this road, which ran from Bostra to the Red Sea, presumably began immediately after the annexation of Arabia in AD 106 and was intended to link southern Syria with the Arabian peninsula. It followed the course of an old caravan route previously used by the Nabataeans. It can be inferred from text no. 36 dated to March 107, that the soldiers cutting stones near Petra were possibly engaged in this road construction.

199 *ILS* 5863 = Smallwood *NH* 413, cliff face inscription on the south bank of the Danube, above Orshova, Upper Moesia, AD 100

Emperor Caesar Nerva Trajan Augustus, Conqueror of the Germans, son of the divine Nerva, chief priest, in the fourth year of his tribunician power, father of the fatherland, consul for the third time, cut back the mountains, constructed the projecting arms (*ancones*) underneath, and built the road.

200 *AE* 1973. 473, inscription about 100 metres upstream from the inscription in text no. 199

Sacred to Hercules, the stonemasons, who were engaged in making the projecting arms (*ancones*), of Legion III[I Flavia] and Legion VII C[laudia, Loyal and Faithful], paid their vow.

The reference to stonemasons here shows that the *ancones* mentioned in texts nos 199 and 200 must be built structures and not merely 'corners'. They can be identified as brackets underneath the roadway to support a wooden super-structure which gave the cliff road additional width. Another possibility is that Trajan was remaking the road and removing the existing stone brackets because he decided to have the rock face of the cliff itself cut back to provide more width. The road may have been intended primarily as a tow path for the movement of supply ships upstream (see Lepper and Frere 1988: 287–9).

201 Van Berchem 1983, inscription, left bank of river Orontes, AD 75

Emperor Vespasian Caesar Augustus, chief priest, in the sixth year of his tribunician power, *imperator* for the twelfth time, father of the fatherland, consul for the sixth time, designated for a seventh, censor, Emperor Titus Caesar, son of Augustus, chief priest (*sic*), in the fourth year of his tribunician power, [consul] for the fourth time, designated for a fifth, censor, [Domitian] Caesar, son of Augustus, consul for the third time, when Marcus Ulpius Trajan was legate of the emperor with propraetorian power, arranged for the [construction] of a channel 3 miles long for the river Dipotamia, with bridges, by the soldiers of four legions – [III Gal]lica, IV Scythica, VI Ferrata, XVI Flavia – [and also] (by the soldiers) of twenty auxiliary cohorts [and also (?)] (by the militiamen ?) of Antioch. Mile 1.

This refers to the construction of a canal north of Antioch probably at the confluence of the Orontes and the Karasou. The inscription also shows that XVI Flavia was in Syria at this time, not in Cappadocia as previously supposed, and that Syria had a garrison of four legions; it is possible, however, that the channel was built by detachments from the four legions and that XVI Flavia was not permanently based in Syria (Keppie 1986: 421).

202 *EJ* 268, inscription, valley of river Strymon, Macedonia, early 1st C.AD

Under Emperor Caesar Augustus, son of a god, Legion X Fretensis under Lucius Tarius Rufus, legate with propraetorian power, built the bridge.

203 *ILS* 510, inscription, Romula, Dacia, AD 248

Emperor Caesar Marcus Julius Philip Pius Fortunate Unconquered Augustus, in the fifth year of his tribunician power, consul for the third time, father of the fatherland, and Marcus Julius Philip the Younger, *imperator*, consul, proconsul, leader of the youth, son of Philip Augustus, and Marcia Otacilia Severa our most blessed Augusta, restorers of the whole world, in order to protect the community of their own colony of

Romula, built the circuit of the walls from the base up by means of a body of soldiers.

204 *CIL* 8. 2728 = *ILS* 5795, inscription, Lambaesis, Africa, AD 152 (extracts)

Endurance   Courage   Hope

[To Marcus Valerius] Etruscus (legate of III Augusta): The most illustrious community of Saldae and I, along with the citizens of Saldae, ask you, sir, that you ask Nonius Datus, veteran of the legion III Augusta, surveyor, to come to Saldae to complete what remains of his work.

I (Nonius Datus) set out and on the way encountered bandits; stripped and wounded I got away with my companions and came to Saldae. I met the procurator, Clemens. He took me to the mountain, where they were lamenting the tunnel as a doubtful piece of work which they thought would have to be abandoned . . .

(There follows a description of how the tunnelling procedure had gone wrong). When I was allocating the work so that they should know who was responsible for each section of the tunnelling, I arranged for there to be rivalry in the work between men from the fleet and the auxiliary troops, and on this basis they worked together in tunnelling through the mountain. Therefore I, who had originally conducted the survey and marked out the course, decided that it should be done in accordance with the plan which I had given to the procurator Petronius Celer (procurator of Mauretania Caesariensis in AD 137). When the work was completed and the water was sent through the channel, Varius Clemens the procurator (AD 152) dedicated it. Five *modii* (quantity of water flowing in the channel at one moment ?).

I have appended some letters so that my work on this tunnel at Saldae may emerge more clearly.

Letter of Porcius Vetustinus (procurator of Mauretania, AD 150) to Crispinus (legate of III Augusta, AD 147–50): You acted very kindly, sir, and in keeping with your consideration and goodwill on other occasions, in sending me Nonius Datus, reservist, so that I could discuss with him the work which he undertook to look after. So, although I was pressed for time and was hurrying to Caesarea, nevertheless I made the journey to Saldae and inspected the water channel which had started well, although it was a large undertaking and could not be completed without the attention of Nonius Datus, who dealt with the matter carefully and conscientiously. I was therefore going to ask that we be permitted to detain him for several months to take charge of the work, if he had not been taken ill as a result of [_ _ _

The town of Saldae (Bejaia or Bougie) in Mauretania Caesariensis required assistance with its building project from the III Augusta at Lambaesis in the neighbouring province of Africa. Datus' involvement apparently dated from the procuratorship of C. Petronius Celer in AD 137 when a plan was drawn up and the tunnel for the water channel begun. After the work had run into some problems, Vetustinus, procurator in AD 150, persuaded Crispinus, legate of the III Augusta (AD 147–50), to send Datus to supervise, in the hope that he could stay for some months. After a further approach to the new legate, Valerius Etruscus (AD 151–2), presumably from the procurator Varius Clemens (AD 152), Datus had to return to see the work through, and the water channel was duly dedicated in AD 152. In the later stages of this project, between AD 147 and 152, Datus was seemingly the only person in both provinces who was competent to give advice, and his commanding officer could spare him only for short periods. The tunnel (428 metres long) was part of the Toudja aqueduct, bringing water to the town over a distance of 21 kilometres.

205 *ILS* 9375 = *EJ* 264, boundary stone, Africa, AD 29–30

Legion III Augusta established boundaries in the third year of the proconsulate of Gaius Vibius Marsus; seventieth (*centuria*) to the right of the *decumanus*, and two hundred and eightieth beyond the *kardo*.

In land division the surveyor established two basic lines – the *decumanus maximus*, generally running from east to west, and the *kardo maximus*, generally running from north to south; these lines (*limites*) had a certain defined width and served partly as access roads. The intersection of the two *limites* was the central point of the survey and the addition of further parallel *decumani* and *kardines* at regular intervals produced a series of squares or rectangles (*centuriae*), which usually contained 200 *iugera*. The *centuriae* were subdivided as required. One specific stone in each *centuria* was carved with the co-ordinates, that is, to the right or left of the *decumanus maximus*, or on the far side or the near side of the *kardo maximus*, depending on the original orientation, and the *centuriae* were numbered accordingly (Dilke 1971).

In AD 24 the proconsul Cornelius Dolabella had put an end to the long war against Tacfarinas, the territory of whose supporters was perhaps being divided by the III Augusta in preparation for distribution to veteran soldiers or other settlers.

206 Blume *et al.* (1848, 1852): I. p. 251, inscription, 2nd C.AD.

On the authority of Emperor Titus Aelius Hadrian Antoninus Augustus Pius, father of the fatherland, a decision was delivered by Tuscenius Felix, chief centurion for the second time, after Blesius Taurinus, soldier of the sixth praetorian cohort, land surveyor, had fixed the boundaries of the territory of the people of Ardea.

This is apparently a transcription of the wording on a boundary stone from Ardea in Latium. For the activities of another military land surveyor, in Pannonia, see text no. 355.

RELIGION

In the Republic official religious observances associated with the army served the state's need to establish divine goodwill and ensure military success – the observation of omens and signs before campaigns and battles, the ritual purification of arms after the campaigning season, the worship of divinities important in Roman life, especially Jupiter, Juno, Minerva, and Mars. Augustus, who sought to place his personal rule inside a framework of traditional practice, was probably responsible for the organization of the military calendar, a late version of which has been found at Dura-Europus, with its emphasis on traditional religious festivals and veneration of the imperial family. In the camps the emperor was presented to his troops as a divinely inspired and invincible commander-in-chief, a worthy object of their loyalty; that was confirmed by imposing titulature, imperial statues in military dress in the camp shrine, and imperial portraits on military standards, which were also located in the shrine and received religious observances.

The Romans were non-sectarian, and although the calendar excluded non-Roman divinities, neither individuals nor groups of soldiers were prevented from worshipping other gods privately as long as this was not deemed detrimental to good discipline. Nevertheless, it was doubtless important to preserve the framework of Roman state worship in the army, since by the second century AD most soldiers were Romanized provincials, while the auxilia were in the main non-citizens. The identification with the emperor and the traditions of the Roman state, and the focus of official loyalty thereby established, will in the long term have helped to enhance the Roman character of the army whatever the private religious beliefs of some soldiers (von Domaszewski 1895; Birley 1978; Helgeland 1978; Le Bohec 1989b: 548–72).

207 Fink *et al*. 1940, with Fink, *RMR* 117, papyrus, Dura-Europus, *c*. AD 223–227

Col. i

[1 January _ _ _]
[3 January. Because] vows [are fulfilled and undertaken] both for the welfare of our lord Marcus Aurelius Severus Alexander Augustus and

for the eternity of the empire of the Roman people, [to Jupiter Best and Greatest an ox, to Queen Juno a cow, to Minerva a cow], [to Jupiter Victor] an ox, [to Juno Sospes (?) a cow _ _ _, to Father Mars a bull, to Mars the Victor] a bull, to Victoria a cow.

7 January. [Because honourable discharge with entitlement to] privileges [is granted to soldiers who have served their time], or because [pay] is distributed [to the soldiers, to Jupiter Best and Greatest an ox, to Juno a cow], [to Minerva] a cow, to Welfare a cow, to Father Mars a bull [_ _ _].

8 January. For the birthday of the deified [empress _ _ _], supplication to [_ _ _].

[9–23] January. For the birthday of [Lucius Seius (?)] Caesar, [_ _ _] of Lucius [_ _ _] Caesar.

24 January. For the birthday [of the divine Hadrian, to the divine Hadrian an ox].

28 January. For the victories [_ _ _] and the greatest Parthian victory of the divine Severus, and for [the imperial power of the divine Trajan], to the Parthian [Victory] a cow, to the divine Trajan [an ox].

4 February. For [the imperial power of the divine Antoninus the Great], a supplication; to the divine Antoninus the Great an ox.

1 March. For the celebrations [of the birthday of Father Mars the Victor], to Father Mars the Victor a bull.

6 March. For the imperial power of [the divine Marcus Antoninus and the divine Lucius Verus], to the divine Marcus an ox, [to the divine Lucius] an ox.

13 March. Because Emperor [Caesar Marcus Aurelius Severus Alexander] was acclaimed Emperor, to Jupiter an ox, [to Juno a cow, to Minerva a cow], to Mars an ox; and because Alexander our Augustus was [first] acclaimed Imperator by the soldiers [of Emperor Augustus Marcus Aurelius Severus Alexander, a supplication _ _ _].

14 March. Because Alexander our [Augustus] was named [Augustus and father of the fatherland and] chief priest, a supplication; [to the *Genius* of our lord] Alexander [Augustus a bull _ _ _].

Col. ii

19 March. For the festival of the Quinquatria (in honour of Minerva), a supplication; similar supplications until 23 March.

4 April. For the birthday of the divine Antoninus the Great, to the divine Antoninus an ox.

9 April. For the imperial power of the divine Pius Severus, to the divine Pius Severus an ox.

11 April. For the birthday of the divine Pius Severus, to the divine Pius Severus an ox.

21 April. For the birthday of the Eternal City of Rome, [to the Eternal City of Rome a cow].

26 April. For the birthday of the divine Marcus Antoninus, [to the divine Marcus] Antoninus [an ox].

7 May. For the birthday of the divine Julia Maesa, to the divine Maesa [a supplication].

10 May. For the Rose Festival of the standards, a supplication.

12 May. For the circus races in honour of Mars, to Father Mars the Avenger a bull.

21 May. Because the divine Severus was acclaimed Imperator [_ _ _] to the divine Pius Severus.

24 May. For the birthday of Germanicus Caesar, a supplication to the memory of Germanicus Caesar.

31 May. For the Rose Festival of the standards, a supplication.

[9] June. For the Festival of Vesta, to Mother Vesta, a supplication.

[26] June. Because our lord Marcus Aurelius Severus Alexander was acclaimed Caesar and was clothed in the toga of manhood, to the *Genius* of Alexander Augustus a bull.

[1] July. Because Alexander our Augustus was designated consul for the first time, a supplication.

[4] July. For the birthday of the divine Matidia, to the divine Matidia a supplication.

[10] July. For the imperial power of the divine Antoninus Pius, to the divine Antoninus an ox.

[12] July. For the birthday of the divine Julius, to the divine Julius an ox.

[23] July. For the day of the Festival of Neptune, a supplication and sacrifice.

[1 August]. For the birthday of the divine Claudius and the divine Pertinax, to the divine Claudius an ox, [to the divine Pertinax] an ox.

[5 August]. For the circus races in honour of Welfare, to Welfare a cow].

[14–29] August. For the birthday of Mamaea [Augusta], mother of our Augustus, to the Juno of Mamaea Augusta [a cow].

[_ _ _

[15–30] August. For the birthday of the divine Marciana, [to the divine] Marciana [a supplication].

Col. iii

31 [August]. For the birthday of [the divine Commodus, to the divine] Commodus [an ox].

[7] September [_ _ _

[18] September. For [the birthday of the divine Trajan and the imperial power of the divine Nerva; to the divine Trajan an ox, to the divine Nerva an ox].

[19] September. For [the birthday of the divine] Antoninus [Pius, to the divine Antoninus an ox].

[20–22] September. For the birthday of the divine Faustina, to the divine Faustina a supplication.

[23] September. For the birthday of the divine [Augustus], to the divine Augustus [an ox].

(October 16-November 12 – about nine entries).

Col. iv

[17] December [_ _ _] birthday (?) [_ _ _] supplication, continued until 23 December [_ _ _].

This calendar was discovered in the temple of Artemis Azzanathkona which served as the archive office of the twentieth cohort of Palmyrenes stationed at Dura-Europus. That it was a military calendar is confirmed by the festivals for discharge and pay. Julius Caesar, Augustus, Germanicus, and Trajan may also have had a special significance for soldiers. The exclusion of cults of local gods and the traditional nature of the calendar, which was written in Latin, suggest that it was designed for use by military garrisons all over the empire. Augustus himself had probably been responsible for the original conception.

The family of Severus Alexander, including his mother Julia Mamaea and grandmother Julia Maesa, feature prominently; since the Severi claimed descent from Trajan, Hadrian, and the Antonines, the entries for these emperors and female members of their family are also relevant in that they demonstrated the legitimacy of Alexander's rule. The overall effect of the calendar will have been to bring to the soldiers' attention the emperor and his family, his achievements, his military prowess, and the benefits he bestowed on them. Moreover, many festivals were accompanied by a sacrifice, a bull for the living emperor, an ox for gods and deified emperors, a cow for goddesses and empresses; so, the soldiers could enjoy feasting and a break from military duties. These observances were not merely routine. Many soldiers probably did believe that divine goodwill would assist their military career; and successful campaigns meant fewer casualties and more donatives.

208 *ILS* 2182, inscription, Rome, AD 139

To Jupiter Best and Greatest and the *Genius* of Titus Aelius Hadrian Antoninus Augustus Pius, father of the fatherland, the citizens from Thrace honourably discharged on the appropriate day from the force of cavalry bodyguards of the emperor, whose names have been carved on the sides, happily and willingly set up this marble statue with its own base, in the consulship of Emperor Antoninus Augustus for the second time and Bruttius Praesens for the second time, on 1 March, under Petronius Mamertinus and Gavius Maximus, praetorian prefects, and (V)alerius (?) Maximus, tribune, and the centurions and trainers Flavius Ingenuus, Julius Certus, Ulpius Agrippa, Valerius Bassus; these soldiers began their military service in the consulship of Vopiscus and Hasta (AD 114).

The names of thirty-nine soldiers are carved on the sides of the base. The *genius* was the male spirit or inherent power of an individual which ensured the continuity and development of the family as represented by the paterfamilias. Reverence was paid to the *genius* of the emperor as the great protector who sustained the whole Roman state. This worship could be combined with the *genius* of various parts of the army, and the proliferation of worship of the *genii* of associations of junior officers and military institutions suggests that it was spontaneous and not organized from the top (Speidel 1978a).

209 *CIL* 7. 1030 = *RIB* 1262, inscription, Bremenium (High Rochester), Britain, 3rd C.AD

To the *Genius* of our lord and of the standards of the first cohort of Vardulli and the Gordian unit of scouts from Bremenium, Egnatius Lucilianus, legate of the emperor, (set this up), under the charge of Cassius Sabinianus, tribune.

Lucilianus was governor of Lower Britain *c.* AD 238/41.

210 *CIL* 3. 6577 = *ILS* 2290, inscription, Egypt

To the holy *Genius* of the legion and of my splendid fellow-soldiers, Quintus Caecilius Kalendinus, orderly (*optio*), set this up.

211 *ILS* 4920 = *RIB* 152, inscription, Aquae Sulis (Bath), Britain, 2nd (?) C.AD

This holy place which had been destroyed by arrogant action, Gaius Severius Emeritus, centurion of the region, cleaned up and restored to the Virtue and Spirit (*Numen*) of the Emperor.

212 Tertullian (2nd–3rd C.AD), *Apologeticus* 16. 8

Among the Romans, the entire basis of the religious life of soldiers is to worship the military standards, swear by the standards, and place the standards ahead of all other gods.

Although Tertullian may be exaggerating, he is right to emphasize the emotional symbolism of military standards. Probably from the time of Marius, the eagle represented the continuity and identity of individual legions, and to lose it in battle was considered a great disgrace. It was made of gold or silver-gilt and resided in a small chapel in the legionary camp, with the other military standards (perhaps one for each cohort), and the portraits of the emperor. The standards were objects of almost religious veneration, and in this shrine men could indeed seek sanctuary; here too the camp bank was located under the care of the standard-bearers (Vegetius, 2. 20). The principal festival in honour of the eagle was the *natalis aquilae* which celebrated the day on which the legion had been established. The Feriale Duranum (see text no. 207) mentions the *Rosaliae signorum*, which may however be an adaptation of a civil festival to suit a martial environment.

It is significant that statues and portraits of the imperial family, which were a prominent feature of camp life, were closely associated with the eagles and standards. The statue represented the emperor himself, the embodiment of the loyalty and devotion of the army, and to tear down his portrait was tantamount to rebellion (see Campbell 1984: 96–9).

213 Dio (2nd–3rd C.AD), 40. 18

The so-called eagle refers in fact to a small shrine and in it is placed a golden eagle. This is established in all the regular legions and is never moved from winter quarters unless the whole army marches out. One man carries it on a long pole which tapers to a sharp spike so that it can be fixed in the ground.

214 Tacitus (1st–2nd C.AD), *Annals* 2. 17

(Germanicus leads the Roman attack on the Cherusci.) Then a splendid portent attracted the commander's attention as eight eagles were observed to make for the woods and enter them; he shouted that the army should advance and follow the birds of Rome, the legions' very own spirits.

215 Tacitus, *Annals* 1. 39

(The mutinous German legions attempt to murder the senator, Munatius Plancus.) In his moment of danger the only place of refuge was the camp of the first legion. There he grasped the standards and the eagle and sought safety in the protection of the gods. But if the eagle-bearer Calpurnius had not defended him from murderous attack, an envoy of the Roman people, in a Roman military camp, would have stained the altars of the gods with his blood, an unheard of occurrence even among enemies.

216 *CIL* 2. 6183 = *ILS* 2293, inscription, Emporiae (Ampurias), Spain

In honour of Jupiter Best and Greatest, the detachment of Legion VII Gemina Fortunate, under the direction of Junius Victor, centurion of the same legion, for the birthday of the eagle (set this up).

217 *CIL* 3. 6224 = *ILS* 2295, inscription, Moesia, AD 224

In honour of the military deities, *Genius*, Courage, the holy Eagle, and the standards of Legion I Italica Severiana, Marcus Aurelius Justus from the community of Horreum Margi in Upper Moesia, chief centurion from the position of *trecenarius*, granted this gift. (On the side) Dedicated on 20 September in the consulship of Julianus for the second time and Crispinus, through Annius Italicus, legate of the Emperor with propraetorian power.

218 *CIL* 3. 3526 = *ILS* 2355, inscription, Aquincum (Budapest), Lower Pannonia, AD 216

Publius Turranius Firminus, veteran, after being a horn-player of Legion II Adiutrix Antoniniana, at his own expense entirely restored the sentry-box for the safeguarding of the standards and sacred statues, in the consulship of Sabinus for the second time and Anullinus.

For imperial statues, see also texts nos 232–3.

219 *CIL* 8. 2634 = *ILS* 2296, inscription, Lambaesis, Africa, AD 253

To the God Mars, powerful in military life, this statue in honour of Legion III Augusta Valeriana Galliena Valeriana was provided in fulfilment of his vow by Sattonius Jucundus, chief centurion, who, when the legion was reconstituted, was the first to place his centurion's stick beside the eagle; it was dedicated by Veturius Veturianus, most distinguished man, legate of the three Emperors with propraetorian power.

This legion, named after Valerian and Gallienus and the latter's son, had been disbanded by Gordian III, and was reconstituted by Valerian in 253.

220 *CIL* 3. 11082, inscription, Arrabona (Györ), Upper Pannonia, AD 207

To the Victory of our Emperors and of Legion I Adiutrix Loyal and Faithful Antoniniana, Publius Marcius Sextianus, son of Publius, from Ephesus, (set this up) at public expense through the decree of the town council, dedicated by Egnatius Victor, legate of the Emperors with propraetorian power, and Claudius Piso, legate of the fifth legion, on 13 June, in the consulship of Aper and Maximus.

Victory was one of the most important of the deified abstractions worshipped by the Romans; associated with the name of an emperor or legion, it signified their role in a particular military victory, while *Victoria Augusta* symbolized the perennial military success of emperors.

221 Dio, 65. 14

(Flavian forces at the battle of Cremona, AD 69.) As the sun was rising the soldiers of the third legion, called the Gallic, which had its base in Syria and was, as it happened, at that time on the side of Vespasian, suddenly greeted it as they usually did. . .

Cf. Tacitus, *Histories* 3. 24. The third Gallic legion had been serving in Syria since the battle of Philippi and had participated in Antony's campaign against the Parthians. Over this period the legion had acquired a tradition of worship of an oriental solar deity.

222 *CIL* 7. 506 = *RIB* 1330, inscription, Condercum (Benwell), Britain, 2nd C.AD

To Jupiter Best and Greatest, of Doliche, and the spirits of the Emperors, for the welfare of Emperor Caesar Titus Aelius Hadrian Antoninus Augustus Pius, father of the fatherland, and of Legion II Augusta, Marcus Liburnius Fronto, centurion of the same legion, willingly and deservedly fulfilled his vow.

Cf. text no. 41. Doliche was a hill in Commagene (Tell Dülük) with a long tradition of worship. The priests of the cult associated it with various other deities, and its popularity within the army may be connected with the role of iron in the lore surrounding *Dolichenus*.

223 *CIL* 6. 30947 = *ILS* 4302, inscription, Rome

In honour of Jupiter Best and Greatest, of Doliche, where iron is born, Gaius Sempronius Rectus, centurion of the *frumentarii*, gave this gift.

224 *RIB* 1546, inscription, Brocolitia (Carrawburgh), Britain, 3rd. C.AD

To the invincible god Mithras, Marcus Simplicius Simplex, prefect, willingly and deservedly fulfilled his vow.

This is one of the three altars found in the Mithraeum close to the fort (see Plate 11). There is a recess at the back to carry a lamp; on the front is a relief of Mithras, carrying a whip, representing the sun, with which he was sometimes identified. His crown is constructed with pierced openings through which the rays of the lamp could shine. The Mithraeum at Carrawburgh was an underground cavern, originally built in the early third century though modified later; it will have held between ten and twelve people (Richmond and Gillam 1951).

Mithras was an ancient Iranian spirit of light which seems first to have come to the attention of the Romans early in the first century BC. Among the attributes of Mithras were those of a victorious warrior, which may have recommended him to soldiers, among whom his worship became increasingly popular in the later second century AD; moreover the initiation tests and close-knit structure of Mithraism may have appealed to the self-contained world of army life, and perhaps especially to the officer class; the three altars at Carrawburgh were dedicated by prefects of the first cohort of Batavians.

225 *CIL* 7. 646 = *RIB* 1600, inscription, Vercovicium (Housesteads), Britain, AD 252

To the invincible Sun-god Mithras, Everlasting Lord, Publicius Proculinus, centurion, on behalf of himself and his son Proculus, willingly and deservedly fulfilled his vow, in the consulship of our lords Gallus and Volusianus.

226 *ILS* 4721 = *RIB* 989, inscription, Bewcastle, Britain, 3rd (?) C.AD

To the holy god Cocidius, Quintus Peltrasius Maximus, tribune, promoted from the rank of chief clerk of the praetorian prefects, most eminent men, willingly and deservedly fulfilled his vow.

227 *RIB* 1583, inscription, Vercovicium

To Jupiter Best and Greatest and the god Cocidius and the *Genius* of this place, the soldiers of Legion II Augusta on garrison duty, willingly and deservedly fulfilled their vow.

Cocidius was a Celtic god of war apparently sometimes linked with Mars, and common in the vicinity of Hadrian's Wall.

MILITARY *COLLEGIA*

Collegia (associations of people involved in the same occupation, or for a particular purpose) were common in the Roman world. The government, fearing threats to public order, required all to have a licence, but in practice permitted many burial societies or religious associations, which fulfilled the needs of ordinary people, to exist unlicensed. Rank and file soldiers were forbidden to associate in *collegia*, presumably because the presence of private clubs inside the normal structure of a military unit was held to be prejudicial to discipline, and possibly divisive. *Principales*, however, and other soldiers performing specialist tasks were permitted to associate; they already belonged to a restricted group, and emperors, who were prepared to allow association if some benefit could be expected, doubtless hoped that *collegia* which they sanctioned, by identifying with the imperial family and honouring imperial achievements, would set an example to other soldiers.

Military *collegia* are found in all parts of the empire by the time of Hadrian, but evidence that there was a substantial increase in their numbers in the reign of Septimius Severus may be misleading, since it is based entirely on inscriptions, largely from the camp of the III Augusta at Lambaesis in Africa. Perhaps, because of the pay rise that Severus granted to the army, more *collegia* than before chose to set up honorary inscriptions; and the situation in Africa need not have been typical of other military camps.

Army *collegia* often fulfilled a religious purpose; the *schola* or meeting hall of the *collegium* was used as a sanctuary for military divinities and statues of the imperial family and the emperor, who acted as a protecting spirit of the *collegium*. The *collegia* at Lambaesis charged a joining fee (*scamnarium*) from which they provided mutual assistance for their members who were discharged, or left the *collegium* because of a transfer or promotion to another unit, and on behalf of soldiers who had died; certain essential military expenses could also be met from the common fund. So, military *collegia* shared the functions of the *collegia tenuiorum* which the government tolerated among civilians. Veteran soldiers often organized themselves in the same way (*collegia* – Meiggs 1973: 311–36; military *collegia* – De Ruggiero, *Diz. epig.*, s.v. *collegia*, pp. 367–9).

228 Digest 47. 22. 1

(Marcianus (3rd C.AD), Book III The Institutes)

In their instructions emperors have ordered provincial governors not to permit the existence of corporate clubs, and not to permit soldiers to form clubs in the camps.

Although Marcianus wrote in the reign of Caracalla, the wording shows that this ban on *collegia* in the military camps was a rule of long standing confirmed by successive emperors. We may attribute it to Augustus, who acted toughly against *collegia* in general.

229 ILS 2353, inscription, Brigetio (Szöny), part of the province of Lower Pannonia after AD 214, AD 229

Sacred to Minerva Augusta, the association of trumpet players in fulfilment of their vow set this up in the consulship of our lord Emperor Alexander for the third time, and Dio.

The trumpet players will have belonged to the first Adiutrix legion stationed at Brigetio. The epithet attached to Minerva is in honour of Alexander's mother, Julia Mamaea.

230 CIL 3. 3524 = ILS 2375, inscription, Aquincum (Budapest), Lower Pannonia, AD 228

The meeting hall of the scouts of Legions I and II Adiutrix, Loyal and Faithful, Severianae, was restored by the men whose names are written below, and dedicated by Flavius Aelianus, legate of the Emperor with propraetorian power, on 1 October in the consulship of Modestus and Probus (20 names follow), under the supervision of Aurelius Pertinax, *frumentarius*.

This *collegium* included the scouts from two legions, since I Adiutrix also served in Lower Pannonia after the reorganization of the provincial boundaries in AD 214. There were ten scouts attached to each legion.

231 CIL 8. 2557 = ILS 2354, inscription, Lambaesis, Numidia, AD 203

For the good fortune and security of the era of our lords the Emperors, Lucius Septimius Severus Pius Pertinax Augustus and Marcus Aurelius Antoninus Augustus, [Conqueror of the Parthians, Conqueror of the British, Greatest Conqueror of the Germans] (added later in place of the names of Geta and Plautilla), and Julia Augusta, mother of our Emperor and of the Camps [and of the senate, and of the fatherland] (added later) of our Antoninus Augustus the Invincible, the horn players of Legion III Augusta, Loyal and Avenging: Lucius Clodius Secundus orderly (*optio*), Gaius Julius Felix (34 more names). As an entrance fee, those who have been made members of the association will pay 750 *denarii*. If anyone from the association sets out on a journey overseas when he has been promoted, he will receive travel expenses (?), a soldier 200 *denarii*, a cavalryman, however, 500 *denarii*; similarly, as a payment to veterans on discharge – 500 *denarii*. Similarly, if anyone leaves the association as a result of promotion, he will receive 500 *denarii*. Similarly, if someone passes away, his heir or his representative will receive 500 *denarii*. Similarly, if anyone is demoted, an occurrence which we deplore, he will receive 250 *denarii*. Similarly (?), those who have discharged their responsibility to the common fund, and any recruit who from this day has made the proper payment to the fund, will receive whatever he is owed. These rules were established on 22 August in the consulship of [_ _ _] (Plautianus' name has been erased) for the second time and Geta for the second time. Ceninis, Antoninus, Filinus, Marcus (the significance of these names is obscure).

232 *ILS* 9100, inscription, Lambaesis, 3rd C.AD

Lucius Aemilius Cattianus, chief clerk (*cornicularius*), and Titus Flavius Surus, registrar (*actarius*), and also the clerks (*librarii*) and record clerks (*exacti*) of Legion III Augusta, Loyal and Avenging, whose names are recorded below, established the record office of the legion with statues of the divine house, from the very generous pay and benefactions which they confer on them. It has been formally decided that, if anyone takes over the position of a chief clerk of the legion or of a registrar who has been honourably discharged, he should give to the man whom he has replaced a sum of 1,000 *denarii* as an entrance fee; similarly, if anyone takes over the position of any clerk, he should give a sum of 1,000 *denarii* to the members of the *collegium* as an entrance fee; and if anyone from the same *collegium* gains an honourable discharge, he should receive from his colleagues a payment of 800 *denarii*; similarly, if someone takes his leave of his colleagues, he should receive 500 *denarii*.

(On the left pillar) Record clerks: 20 names
(On the right pillar) Clerks: 22 names.

It is interesting that Cattianus and Surus (who also appear in a dedication made by the *optiones* – text no. 233) receive a payment from those taking their place rather than from their *collegium*. However, this payment made by their successors was presumably in lieu of a membership fee for the association of *cornicularii* and *actarii*, if the successor was not a member. The reference to the generosity of pay and benefactions indicates the substantial rises in army pay granted under the Severan dynasty.

233 *CIL* 8. 2554 = *ILS* 2445, inscription, Lambaesis, 3rd C. AD

For the welfare of the Emperors, the *optiones* built their meeting hall along with statues and images of the divine house, and also their protecting deities, from the very generous pay and benefactions which they confer on them, under the supervision of Lucius Egnatius Myron, treasurer; they formally decided that when a fellow member of the asociation sets out to take up his promotion, he should receive 8,000 sesterces, and that veterans too on their discharge should receive on 1 January a payment of 6,000 sesterces each, and the treasurer will see to the distribution of this payment on the appropriate day without delay (64 names follow).

Payments in the *collegium* of *optiones* on promotion and retirement are more than the equivalent sums for the horn-players and clerks (texts nos 231–2).

234 *CIL* 3. 11189, inscription, Carnuntum (Petronell), Upper Pannonia, 3rd C.AD

For the welfare of our lords the Emperors [_ _ _] (names of Maximinus and his son Maximus erased), and the entire divine house, in honour of the association of fellow-veterans, Lucius Cassius Florentinus, veteran of Legion XIV Gemina [Maximiniana], from the post of armourer, officer of the association mentioned above, vowed this to their spirit and majesty.

6 The army, the local community, and the law

SOLDIERS IN LOCAL LIFE

By the late second century, legionary and auxiliary troops were permanently stationed in nineteen provinces, while in many others smaller detachments of auxiliaries were regularly based. Moreover, individual soldiers or detachments were frequently in transit, and sometimes the emperor himself, with an entire army. From the presence of 400,000 soldiers in the provinces there were many potential benefits and also dangers for local communities, especially those situated near main roads.

The location of the army in separate provinces, and often in different bases within one province, meant that there was no overall system of army supply. Markets will have been stimulated, since the soldiers needed grain, foodstuffs, meat, wine, iron, timber, building materials, replacement draught animals and horses, leather, and clothing. The army was not self-sufficient, though soldiers did produce a wide range of manufactured goods and used the legion's *territorium* (an area of land allocated to a legion in the vicinity of its base) for limited growing of crops and pasturing of animals. It has been calculated that 300,000 soldiers would require about 100,000 tonnes of wheat annually, (including an additional allocation for cavalrymen), rising to 150,000 tonnes by the end of the second century with the increase in army numbers (Garnsey and Saller 1987: 88–95). Most bulk supplies would be brought to the camps from the immediate locality or over relatively short distances, and the presence of so many grain consumers should have had an impact on the rather static agricultural set-up of local communities, and may have encouraged the production of more grain, though this is difficult to demonstrate. There was certainly considerable potential for profit since by no means all the grain for army use was in the form of taxes or rents in kind.

Military bases though sometimes set up in sparsely inhabited and under-exploited areas, were often established in locations of strategic importance for communications, and hence also for trade. Everywhere the soldiers brought protection, building activity, technical assistance, and new facilities, which although in the first instance for their own enjoyment, demonstrated a fresh dimension of organized life in an urban environment. Most importantly, soldiers attracted people. The possibility of profit and advancement brought those, both Roman citizens and non-citizens, who provided indispensible services for the troops – traders, craftsmen, innkeepers, and women. Temporary settlements (*canabae*) of a primitive nature grew up in the vicinty of the military camps. As the legions began to acquire semi-permanent or permanent bases, so the *canabae* developed into more sophisticated and permanent structures, which in lay-out were often influenced by the camp itself. Their population included local women who, having formed liaisons with soldiers, often bore their children. Moreover, the settlement of discharged soldiers in colonies seems to have been discontinued after Hadrian. There may have been a preference among veterans to settle close to where they had served among their comrades and families. The result will have been a further influx of Roman citizens into the *canabae* and an enhancement of their status. Smaller settlements (*vici*) also grew up round forts and outposts manned by auxiliary soldiers.

The local military commander could influence how the *canabae* developed, since it was his responsibility to determine whether the civilian settlement should be in close proximity to the camp or some distance away. At Lambaesis, for example, it was situated about one mile from the camp, the two being linked by a wide paved road. By contrast at Rapidum in Mauretania the *canabae* abutted upon the camp. In any case the *canabae* would normally be on the officially designated territory of the legion, and consequently a legionary legate was responsible for jurisdiction over them. In this he would require some assistance and it is understandable that, rather than divert his military tribunes or centurions from their military duties, he turned to the Roman citizens in the *canabae*, particularly perhaps veteran soldiers, to take on the role of *de facto* magistrates. Naturally these men, in order to add to their prestige and authority, assimilated some of the terminology used in self-governing communities; in various settlements people appear styled as 'magistrate', 'aedile', and *decurio*. The way in which these officials describe themselves on inscriptions cannot, however, provide an accurate picture of the administration of the *canabae*, since they did not necessarily understand their exact legal status. It was an essentially informal administration appointed by the legate, under his supervision, and solely responsible to him. There seems to have been no distinction in the *canabae* between veteran soldiers and civilian Roman citizens, but non-citizens would have had no part in the administration. Expansion of the *canabae* sometimes led to the development of an adjacent settlement, perhaps related to an existing native community. The composite civilian settlement then might progress to municipal or even colonial status. Carnuntum was situated on the Danube in a strategically important position where the east–west route along the river met the south–north route from Aquileia. A military camp was first established here by Tiberius, and by the end of Trajan's reign the Legion XIV Gemina formed the garrison, where it was to remain as long as Roman control lasted. After the division of Pannonia into upper and lower provinces, Carnuntum became the chief settlement of Upper Pannonia and the seat of the governor. The *canabae* grew up in an unsystematic fashion on three sides of the military camp, close to which an amphitheatre and forum were built. Then a separate civilian settlement developed to the west of the camp near the modern town of Petronell, with several large buildings including an amphitheatre with a capacity of about 13,000. In AD 124 during his visit to Pannonia, Hadrian granted municipal status to Carnuntum, and in AD 194 Septimius Severus, who as governor of Upper Pannonia had launched his successful attempt on the purple from here, made it the colony Septimia Carnuntum.

At Chester the *canabae* were established close to the legionary camp, with some civilian buildings grouped along the road from the east gate, others on the west side between the defences and the river Dee, and a limited settlement in the southern sector. The amphitheatre outside the camp could accommodate 7,000 spectators and clearly served the legion and most of the civilian population; the civilians also shared the water supply by tapping into the fortress aqueduct. By the end of the first century a sizable settlement had developed and in the first half of the second century there was a significant improvement in living conditions, as timber buildings were gradually replaced by stone, and more elaborate houses were built, some containing private bath suites. But there is no definite evidence that Chester was elevated to municipal or colonial rank (Mason 1987).

The advancement of Carnuntum to municipal rank by Hadrian shows that there was no objection in principle to the development of communities of this status in close proximity to a military establishment. It may be an accident of our evidence (from inscriptions) that such developments appear most commonly in the third century. There is certainly no reason to associate these changes with Septimius Severus; although he permitted soldiers to form legally valid marriages, this does not mean that the government undertook to provide any special facilities for soldiers' families, especially since their liaisons had been widely tolerated before. If Severus was generous in conferring municipal or colonial status, he was perhaps attempting to ensure the loyalty of communities, especially those closely associated with the military camps, during the civil wars.

For the relationship of military camps and local settlements – MacMullen 1967: 119–25; Lengyel and Radan 1980: 239–74; Jones 1984; J. Ch. Balty, *JRS* 1988, 97, 1993; Jones and Mattingly 1990: 153–78.

235 *P. Amherst.* 107 = *SP* 387, papyrus, Egypt, AD 185

To Damarion, *strategus* of the Hermopolite nome, from Antonius Justinus, soldier on double pay, sent by Valerius Frontinus, prefect of the Heraclian *ala* stationed at Coptos. I have had measured out to me by the elders of the village of Terton Epa in the upper Patemite district the quota imposed on their village out of the 20,000 *artabae* (about 1,040,000 litres) of barley which the most distinguished prefect, Longaeus Rufus, ordered to be bought up out of the harvest of the past twenty-fourth year, for the requirements of the above mentioned *ala*, namely one hundred *artabae* (about 5,200 litres) of barley measured out by the public receiving measure on the basis of the measurement stipulated, that is, 100 *artabae* in accordance with the reckoning made by the officials of the nome. I have handed out four copies of this receipt. Year twenty-five of Emperor Caesar Marcus Aurelius Commodus Antoninus Augustus Pius, Conqueror of the Armenians, Conqueror of the Medes, Conqueror of the Parthians, Conqueror of the Sarmatians, Conqueror of the Germans, Greatest Conqueror of the British, Pauni [_ _ _] (Second hand) I, Antonius Justinus, soldier on double pay, have had measured out to me the hundred *artabae* of barley, 100 *artabae*, as signified above.

236 *P. Lond.* 482 = Fink, *RMR* 80, papyrus, Egypt, AD 130

Ala Veterana Gallica, troop (*turma*) of Donacianus, Serenus, procurator, greetings to the contractors of hay. I have received the hay for my comrades in the squadron for the month of June, and I have myself paid the conveyance charge, and thirty cavalrymen are assigned to you. In the consulship of Catullinus and Aper. (Thirty names follow.)

Serenus appears to be a soldier, but the contractors to whom he writes may be either military or civilian, and had perhaps leased out part of the land belonging to the *ala* on the agreement that they provide fodder in appropriate instalments for the cavalrymen of the troops. See MacMullen 1967: 9; more receipts for fodder and foodstuffs – Fink *RMR* 76, 78–79; 81.

237 *ILS* 9103, inscription, Carnuntum (Petronell), Upper Pannonia, AD 205

Sacred to Jupiter Best and Greatest, for the welfare of the Emperors, Gaius Julius Catullinus, soldier of Legion XIV Gemina, Martial and Victorious, who leases the land called Furianus under the contract (?) of Nertius Celerinus, chief centurion, willingly and deservedly paid his vow on 1 October in the consulship of Emperor Antoninus Augustus, for the second time, and Geta Caesar.

The chief centurions seem to have been responsible for allocating leases to soldiers and others for trading on, or cultivation of, the land within the legion's territory. Cf. *ILS* 4222; 9104. For the territory of the legion, see MacMullen 1967: 6–12.

238 Speidel 1981b, papyrus, Fayum, Egypt, 2nd/3rd C.AD

Flavius Silvanus, standard-bearer of the horseguards of the prefect, to the elders of the village of Socnopaios, greetings. I have received from you the spears of palm-wood that were assigned to you, for which I have paid out the agreed fee from public funds.

These villagers in the Fayum may have been supplying spear shafts rather than the complete weapon, possibly for light missiles used in training. Note the fragmentary text from Vindolanda, which seems to refer to a contract for the supply of wooden components to the army (Bowman and Thomas 1987: 140–2).

239 *BGU* 1564 = *SP* 395, papyrus, Egypt, AD 138

Copy of order for payment. Ammonius, son of Polydeuces, Syrion, son of Heras, Heraclides, son of Heraclides, all three collectors of clothing (in requisitions), and Hermes, ex-*agoranomos*, to Heraclides, banker, greetings. Pay to Heraclides, son of Horgias, Heron, freedman of Publius Maevius, and Dioscorus, freedman of the mighty god Serapis, weavers of the village of Philadelphia, for them and the other weavers in the same village on their mutual responsibility, (these sums) as an advance payment of the cost of the clothing which is part of that which his excellency the prefect Avidius Heliodorus ordered to be prepared for the requirements of the soldiers in Cappadocia: one white tunic with belt, 5 feet, 1 inch (3½ cubits) long, 4 feet, 6 inches (3 cubits, 4 *dactuloi*) wide, weight 3 pounds, 6 ounces (3³/⁴ *minae*) – 24 drachmae on account; four white Syrian cloaks, each 8 feet, 8 inches (6 cubits) long, 5 feet, 8 inches (4 cubits) wide, weight 3 pounds, 6 ounces (3³/⁴ *minae*) – 24 drachmae on account for each; total 96 drachmae; combined total 120 drachmae; for the requirements of the hospital in the imperial camp, one plain white blanket, 8 feet, 8 inches (6 cubits) long, 5 feet, 8 inches (4 cubits) wide, weight 3 pounds 9 ounces (4 *minae*) – 28 drachmae on account; total of payment order – 148 silver drachmae; but from the advance of 28 drachmae in respect of the blankets, 6 drachmae were deducted for the imperial treasury. It is agreed that they are to make the clothing of good soft pure white wool without any kind of stain and that it is to be well-woven, firm, with finished hems, satisfactory, without damage, and not in value below the price paid to them in advance for the clothing. If, when it is handed over, any of the clothing is missing or is held to be of inferior value, they shall on their mutual responsibility repay the value of the missing clothing, together with dues and expenses, and the deficit in respect of clothing of inferior value. And they shall deliver them promptly with the established specifications and weights, separate from other public clothing requirements which they owe. The second year of Emperor Caesar Titus Aelius Hadrian Antoninus Augustus Pius, Thoth 12.

240 Tacitus (1st–2nd C.AD), *Histories* 4. 22

In response to these threats of concentrated war, the legionary commanders Munius Lupercus and Numisius Rufus strengthened the rampart and walls. They demolished the buildings which because of the long peace had grown up close to the camp and had assumed virtually the proportions of a town, in case they proved of assistance to the enemy.

This is the legionary camp at Vetera where the *canabae* lay to the south-east (Petrikovits (1958), cols. 1801–34). A civilian settlement which developed about three kilometres north-west of the camp, near Xanten, was made a colony by Trajan.

241 *CIL* 13. 6797 = Smallwood *GN* 430, inscription, Moguntiacum (Mainz), Upper Germany, AD 43–4

To Tiberius Claudius Caesar Augustus Germanicus, chief priest, in the third year of his tribunician power, *imperator* for the fourth time, father of the fatherland, consul for the third time, the Roman citizen businessmen engaged in bag manufacture (set this up) when Gaius Vibius Rufinus was legate with propraetorian power.

Two legions were stationed at Moguntiacum from Augustus to Domitian. Thereafter one legion – the XXII Primigenia – remained until the fourth century. A substantial civilian settlement containing Roman citizens developed between Moguntiacum and the Rhine, becoming the main town in Upper Germany and the seat of the governor; it did not, however, acquire municipal or colonial status (Decker and Seltzer 1976).

242 *ILS* 2472, inscription, Moguntiacum, 2nd C.AD

For the welfare of Marcus Aurelius [Commodus] Antoninus Pius Fortunate, in honour of Fortune the Returner of Legion XXII Primigenia, Loyal and Faithful, Gaius Gentilius Victor, veteran of Legion XXII Primigenia, Loyal and Faithful, honourably discharged, dealer in swords, gave instructions in his will that this should be set up, to the value of 8,000 sesterces.

243 *CIL* 3. 14509 = *ILS* 9105, inscription, Viminacium (Kostolac), Upper Moesia, 3rd C.AD

[The divine ?] Septimius Severus Pertinax Pius Fortunate, Conqueror of the Arabs, Conqueror of the Adiabenici, Greatest [Conqueror of the Parthians], and [Emperor Caesar Marcus] Aurelius Antoninus Pius Fortunate Augustus, restored the *canabae* of Legion VII Claudia Antoniniana, Loyal and Faithful.

The civilian settlement at Viminacium may have achieved municipal status under Hadrian, becoming a colony during the reign of Gordian III (AD 238–44).

244 *CIL* 3. 7474 = *ILS* 2475, inscription, Durostorum (Silistra), Lower Moesia, 2nd C.AD

To Jupiter Best and Greatest, for the welfare of Emperor Caesar Titus Aelius Hadrian Antoninus Augustus Pius and Verus Caesar, Gnaeus Oppius Soterichus and Oppius Severus, his son, constructed at their own expense the shrine and statue on behalf of the Roman citizens and those who dwell in the Aelian *canabae* of Legion XI Claudia. It was dedicated by Tiberius Claudius Saturninus, legate of the Emperor with propraetorian power.

Significantly, the *canabae* at Durostorum were named after Hadrian. This indicates the increasing importance of these communities, even if the use of the emperor's name was originally unofficial.

245 *CIL* 3. 1008 = *ILS* 2476, inscription, Apulum (Alba Iulia), Dacia, 2nd C.AD

Sacred to the Fortune of the Emperor and the *Genius* of the people of the *canabae*, Lucius Silius Maximus, veteran of Legion I Adiutrix, Loyal and Faithful, the first to act as an official in the *canabae*, and Silia Januaria and Silius Firminus bestowed this as a gift.

246 *ILS* 9106, inscription, Apulum, 2nd C.AD

To Marcus Ulpius Apollinaris, prefect of the camp of Legion XIII Gemina, the councillors and Roman citizens dwelling in the *canabae* of the same legion, (set this up) from public funds.

Inscriptions record *decuriones* of the *canabae* at Apulum and a guardian of the temple of Roman citizens (*CIL* 3. 1093; 1100; 1158). The camp at Apulum was the base of the Legion XIII Gemina which remained here from the conquest to the withdrawal under Aurelian. After Hadrian's reorganization of the province Apulum was the headquarters of the governor of Upper Dacia, and after further changes by Marcus Aurelius, it became the seat of the governor of the three Dacias. The *canabae* developed to the south of the military establishment. In Marcus Aurelius' reign this settlement received municipal status (*Municipium Aurelium Apulense*), and then colonial status perhaps under Commodus (*CIL* 3. 7773). It seems that Septimius Severus established a second *municipium* in proximity to the colony, with which it coexisted.

247 *CIL* 3. 6166 = *ILS* 2474, inscription, Troesmis, Lower Moesia, 2nd C.AD

For the welfare of Emperor Caesar Trajan Hadrian Augustus, Gaius Valerius Pudens, veteran of Legion V Macedonica, and Marcus Ulpius Leontius, official of the inhabitants of the *canabae*, and Tuccius Aelianus, aedile, bestowed this as a gift for the veterans and Roman citizens dwelling in the *canabae* of Legion V Macedonica.

Canabae, and also a separate settlement, developed close to the base of Legion V Macedonica on the south bank of the lower Danube, and the latter was established as a *municipium* in the reign of Marcus Aurelius.

248 *CIL* 8. 20834 = *ILS* 6885, inscription, Rapidum (Sour Djouab), Mauretania Caesariensis, AD 167–9

To Emperors Caesars Augusti Marcus Aurelius Antoninus, Conqueror of the Armenians, Greatest Conqueror of the Parthians, Conqueror of the Medes, in the [_ _ _] year of his tribunician power, consul for the third time, and Lucius Verus, Conqueror of the Armenians, Greatest Conqueror of the Parthians, Conqueror of the Medes, in the twelfth (an error) year of his tribunician power, consul for the third time, the veterans and civilians dwelling in Rapidum built the wall from its foundations with squared stones, at their own expense and entirely from their own resources, that is of the veterans [and civilians] living within the same wall, with the help and direction of Baius Pudens, [outstanding man], procurator of the Emperors, excellent governor, who also [dedicated it].

This inscription from the west gate of the town is identical to one at the east gate. Rapidum was established as an auxiliary fort by Hadrian in 122, and the civilian settlement, which was built within a few feet of the southern wall of the camp, and also approached close to the western wall (see Figure 5), was itself protected by the construction of ramparts described in the inscription; it acquired municipal status in the third century, before being destroyed *c.* 270; after this only a part of the town was reoccupied (Laporte 1989).

249 *CIL* 3. 6580 = *ILS* 2304, inscription, near Alexandria, Egypt, AD 194

To Emperor Caesar Lucius Septimius Severus Pertinax Augustus, chief priest, in the second year of his tribunician power, acclaimed *imperator* for the third time, consul for the second time, proconsul, father of the fatherland, the veterans of Legion II Traiana Brave, who have been honourably discharged and who began their military service in the consulship of Apronianus and Paulus (AD 168) [_ _ _]

(On the front and sides the names of 46 soldiers remain, including:)

Second Cohort

Century of Faustinus

[_ _ _] Valerianus, son of Lucius, of the tribe Collina, from Antioch, trumpeter
[_ _ _] Alexander, son of Titus, of the tribe Pollia in the camp
[_ _ _] Rufus, son of Marcus, of the tribe Collina, from Nicomedia
[_ _ _] Isidorus, son of Publius, of the tribe Pollia, from Thebes

[_ _ _] Century of Aemilius Ammonius

[_ _ _] Priscillianus, son of Gaius, of the tribe Collina, from Caesarea, standard-bearer

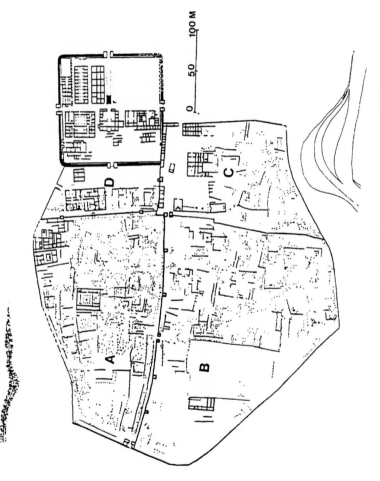

Figure 5 Rapidum (Sour Djouab) in Mauretania. Camp built in AD 122

[_ _ _] Century of Aurelius Antigonus

[_ _ _] Capitolinus, son of Marcus, of the tribe Pollia, clerk of the prefect of the camp
[_ _ _] Sarapammon, son of Marcus, of the tribe Pollia, from Tanis

[_ _ _] Century of Paternus

[_ _ _] Dionysius, son of Lucius, of the tribe Pollia, in the camp

[Century of _ _ _]

_ _ _] Dioscorus, son of Gaius, of the tribe Pollia, in the camp

[Century of _ _ _] Lucianus

[_ _ _] Ischyrion, son of Lucius, of the tribe Pollia, in the camp
. . .

Fifth Cohort

Century of Celer

Marcus Gabinius Ammonianus, son of Marcus, in the camp

Century of Flavius Philippianus

Titus Aurelius Chaeremonianus, son of Titus, of the tribe Pollia, in the camp
Gaius Valerius Apollinaris, son of Gaius, of the tribe Collina, from Hierapolis

Century of Severus

Marcus Aurelius Isidorus, of the tribe Pollia, from Alexandria
Gaius Pompeius Serenus, son of Gaius, of the tribe Pollia, in the camp

Century of Servilius Pudens

Publius Aurelius Proclion, of the tribe Pollia, from Alexandria
Gaius Julius Gemellinus, son of Gaius, of the tribe Pollia, in the camp
Publius Aelius Hermias, son of Publius, of the tribe Collina, in the camp
Titus Aurelius Sarapammon, son of Titus, of the tribe Pollia, in the camp

Titus Flavius Apollinaris, son of Titus, of the tribe Pollia, in the camp
Marcus Furfanius Longus, son of Marcus, of the tribe Collina, from Paraetonium

Century of Marinus

Marcus Aurelius Herodes, son of Marcus, of the tribe Pollia, in the camp

Of the forty-one soldiers whose origins are mentioned, thirty-two come from Egypt, and twenty-four of these state the military camp (*castris*) as their birthplace, all but one having the tribe Pollia. These men obviously had no *municipium* or colony to cite as their birthplace, and it is likely that most of them were illegitimate sons born to soldiers from women living in the *canabae*; those who were non-citizens (see pp. 153–60) could be attracted into the army by the offer of citizenship on enlistment, a practice that should be linked with the development of local recruiting. For example, around AD 161–192 about 25 per cent of the known soldiers of the III Augusta in Africa were recruited from the town of Lambaesis or *castris*, rising to 39 per cent in the Severan era (Le Bohec 1989b: 491–530).

250 Salway, 1965: no. 26, inscription, Carriden, Britain, 2nd/3rd (?) C.AD

To Jupiter Best and Greatest, the people of the *vicus* dwelling at the fort of Velunia (?), happily, willingly, and deservedly paid their vow, under the direction of Aelius Mansuetus.

Vici (the inhabitants are *vicani*) grew up along the approach roads to smaller forts, and contained workshops and dwellings and related farmland and cemeteries. Note the development near the fort on the river Phasis, described by Arrian (text no. 146). *Vici* were distinguished from *canabae* by their size and also by the fact that there were probably fewer Roman citizens in them. There is some confusion in terminology in that *vicus* retained its basic meaning of a 'subdivision' of a larger entity, so large *canabae* were sometimes subdivided into *vici* (Salway 1965: 9–13; Jones and Mattingly 1990: 158–61).

SOLDIERS, MARRIAGE, AND FAMILY LIFE

A rule that almost certainly originated with Augustus forbade Roman soldiers to marry during service. In a long-service, professional army it was of course impossible to prevent them from forming liaisons with local women and from begetting children, but by denying them the consequences of a legally valid marriage the government could hope to discourage such unions. Certainly there was no obligation on it to make provision for the accommodation of wives and children or to take account of them in the transfer of legions to new bases. Although many soldiers doubtless remained unmarried, many others did form unions and regarded themselves as married men. This will have become more common as the legions settled into permanent bases, while soldiers' families lived in nearby *canabae* or other settlements. Therefore the status of a soldier's 'wife' and children, and rights concerning the acquisition and leaving of property, assumed greater importance. Emperors tended to deal with the problem of military marriages in a piecemeal fashion as individual difficulties were brought to their attention, and there was no decisive action until Septimius Severus swept away the prohibition, probably in AD 197. By then its relevance had been undermined by concessions made to soldiers in respect of making a will and inheritance rights. Severus, however, after his violent usurpation of power, wished to cement the army's loyalty by a dramatic gesture of goodwill (Campbell 1978).

251 *CIL* 3. 3271, inscription, Teutoburgium (Dalj), Pannonia, 1st C.AD

To Tiberius Claudius Valerius, son of Brittus, decurion of the second *ala* of Aravaci, from Spain, fifty years of age, thirty years of military service, and to Claudia Januaria, his wife, and to Claudia Hispanilla, his daughter, both still living, in accordance with his will, Flaccus, decurion, his brother, and Hispanilla, his daughter, heirs, had this erected.

252 *ILS* 2389, inscription, Lugdunum (Lyon), Lugdunensis

To the spirits of the departed and the everlasting memory of Celerinius Fidelis, a citizen from Batavia, soldier of Legion XXX (Ulpia Victrix), clerk of the procurator of the province of Lugdunensis, who lived forty years, and when he died left three surviving children. Celerinius Augendus, outstanding man, holder of the equestrian military offices, and Maturinia Pia, arranged for the erection of this (monument) to a dutiful brother and a beloved husband, and made the dedication while it was still under construction.

253 *CIL* 7. 229 = *RIB* 594, inscription, Bremetenacum (Ribchester), Britain

Covered by this earth is she who once was Aelia Matrona and lived twenty-eight years, two months, eight days, and Marcus Julius Maximus, her son, who lived six years, three months, twenty days, and Campania Dubitata, her mother, who lived fifty years. Julius Maximus, senior treasurer (?) of the *ala* of Sarmatians, her husband, erected this memorial to his incomparable wife, and to his son who was extremely devoted to his father, and to his most resolute mother-in-law.

These funeral inscriptions are cited to show the desire among ordinary soldiers for female companionship and normal family life, although only text no. 251 is securely dated to the period before the marriage ban was removed.

254 Bowman and Thomas 1987: 137–40, tablet, Vindolanda, Britain, *c.* AD 100–105

Claudia Severa to her Lepidina, greetings.

I cordially invite you, sister, to make sure that you come to us on 11 September for the day of the celebration of my birthday, since if you come you will make the day more pleasant for me by your arrival.

Pass on my best wishes to your Cerialis. My Aelius and my little son send [you (?)] their greetings.

(Second hand) I shall expect you, sister. Be well, sister, my dearest love, and so may I be, and hail.

(On the back, third hand ?) To Sulpicia Lepidina, (wife) of Flavius Cerialis, from Severa.

The author of the letter, Claudia Severa, was married to Aelius Bocchus who is likely to have been the commander of a military unit in north Britain; Lepidina was probably the wife of Flavius Cerialis, who was the prefect of one of the cohorts stationed at Vindolanda (Bowman and Thomas 1987: 129–30). There was no restriction on the marriage of equestrian officers in the army, and this letter is good evidence for the presence of wives and children in army quarters, and the nature of camp life in Britain some sixty years after the conquest.

255 Dio (2nd–3rd C.AD), 60. 24

He (Claudius) granted the privileges of married men to the soldiers (AD 44), since they were not legally permitted to have wives.

Claudius was presumably granting not the privileges accorded to married men with children, which were inappropriate, but formal exemption from the penalties imposed by Augustus' legislation on the unmarried and childless; it was an anomaly if these had been applied to soldiers who were forbidden to marry.

256 *BGU* 1690 = *FIRA* 3. 5, papyrus, Philadelphia, Egypt, AD 131

Epimachus, son of Longinus, soldier of the second cohort of Thebans, century of Octavius Alexander [affirmed _ _ _] that a daughter,

Longinia, had been born to him on 26 December just past, from Arsus, daughter of Lucius, his concubine. Therefore he said that he had made this declaration because of the restriction imposed by military service. Carried out at Philadelphia in the winter quarters of the second cohort of Thebans on 26 December, in the consulship of S[ergius Octavius] Laenas Pontianus and Marcus Antonius Rufinus, in the sixteenth year of Emperor Caesar Trajan Hadrian Augustus, on the thirtieth day of the month Choiak.

(In Greek) I, Epimachus, son of Longinus, the soldier mentioned above, have affirmed that my daughter, Longinia, was born, just as is written above.

Since soldiers were not permitted to contract a legal marriage, the children of their unofficial unions were illegitimate and could not be entered on the record of births. Soldiers therefore tended to make unofficial declarations of birth before witnesses to establish the child's identity, which might help in any claims on their father's property.

257 Mitteis and Wilcken 1912: II.2 no. 372, and *FIRA* 3. 19, papyrus, Egypt, AD 114–42 (extracts)

(i) Year 20 of the divine Trajan 10 Tybi (5 January 117). When Lucia Macrina had made a statement through her advocate, Phanius, that she was seeking a monetary deposit from the estate of the soldier Antonius Germanus, now deceased, Lupus (Marcus Rutilius Rufus, prefect of Egypt, 113–17) said: 'We know that deposits of this kind are dowries. For cases like this I do not grant a judge. For a soldier is not permitted to marry. If you claim a dowry and I grant a judge, it will seem that I have been persuaded that the marriage is legal.'

This papyrus contains a collection of decisions made by prefects of Egypt in respect of soldiers' families.

A woman could not claim back her dowry from the estate of a soldier since she was not recognized as being legally married (Campbell 1978: 154).

(ii) Year 18 of Trajan, 27 Phaophi (24 October, 114)

Longinus Hy[_ _ _] declared that he, a Roman citizen, had served in the first cohort of Thebans under Severus, and had while in military service lived with a Roman woman by whom he had begotten Longinus Apollinarius and Longinus Pomponius, and he asked that these be certified (as Roman citizens). Lupus, having talked with his legal advisers, stated: 'The boys will be [certified] since they have been born of a Roman woman. You also wish to establish them as [legitimate (?)], but I cannot make you their legal father.'

If both parents were Roman citizens, then even though they lacked the right to contract a legal marriage (*conubium*), their children would be citizens, but illegitimate. Illegitimate children who were citizens could be instituted as heirs and receive a legacy, but might be subject to inheritance tax if they were held not to be near relatives.

(iii) Year 18 of Trajan, 10 Payni (4 June 115).

Chrotis made a statement through her advocate Philoxenus that she, a citizen of Alexandria, had married Isidorus, also a citizen of Alexandria, and that afterwards when he was serving in a cohort, bore him a son, Theodorus, in whose name she now petitioned, arguing that, {although she had omitted to make a declaration of his birth}, it was nevertheless clear that he was the son of that man (Isidorus), from the will which he made, in which he left the child as heir of all his property. When the will of Julius Martialis (the Roman name given to Isidorus when he joined up), soldier of the first cohort of Thebans, was read out, Lupus consulted with his legal advisers and declared: 'Martialis could not have a legitimate son while he was serving in the army, but he made him his heir legally'.

Under local law, two Alexandrian citizens could legally marry, but the marriage was held to be dissolved for the duration of military service. It is not clear if Isidorus became a Roman citizen on enlistment; Roman citizens could not normally institute a non-Roman as heir, but concessions possibly made by Trajan extended this privilege to soldiers (see text no. 259). Chrotis was presumably worried that the failure to register her son would count against him, since acquisition of an estate required proof that the beneficiary was the lawful son. Another interpretation at {} – 'that the inheritance tax should be remitted if it had been overlooked' – refers to the fact that, if Theodorus were judged not to be a close relative, he would be subject to the inheritance tax.

(iv) Year 5 of our lord Antoninus (142), third extra day. When Octavius Valens and Cassia Secunda, whose case had been adjourned from yesterday, came into court, Eudaemon (Valerius Eudaemon, prefect of Egypt, 142–3), having consulted with his legal advisers, declared: 'Yesterday, when the memorandum of that splendid man, Heliodorus, was read out, there was a clear reason for an adjournment, namely, in order that judgment should be reached in the case of those who are forbidden (i.e. to marry), in the presence of the mother of this boy. Today, having considered the relevant circumstances, I confirm the opinion I gave yesterday. Whether this man served in a legion, a cohort, or an *ala*, the child born to him could not be his legitimate son; moreover, since he is not the legitimate son of his father, who is an Alexandrian citizen, he cannot be an Alexandrian citizen. Therefore this boy, who was born to Valens while he was serving in a cohort, is his illegitimate son and cannot be admitted to Alexandrian citizenship'. And he added: 'You said yesterday that you had other sons; what ages are they, when were they born?' Octavius Valens replied: 'One recently, the other is older'. Eudaemon said: 'Where were you serving when the older boy was born?' Valens replied: 'In the cohort, and the little one too'. Eudaemon said: 'You must know that they are in the same situation as this one. There are some things which cannot be changed.' Valens said: 'Now, if I manage to go abroad you yourself could sign my petition, so that I may obtain my rights through a legal representative. What wrong have the children committed?' Eudaemon said: 'I have been foolish in explaining in detail what I could have said in a few words; what you are attempting is impossible, and neither this boy nor your other sons are citizens of Alexandria'.

This case illustrates the problems caused by the ambivalent attitude of the government which tolerated the unofficial unions of soldiers but compelled its officials to enforce the legal consequences. There was a conflict between the duty of the prefect and the feelings of the soldier, who genuinely believed that he was married. Even if the children in question were Roman citizens, possession of Alexandrian citizenship would be desirable in that it conferred certain privileges.

258 Pliny (1st–2nd C.AD), *Letters* 10. 106–7

Pliny to Emperor Trajan. Since I was asked, sir, by Publius Accius Aquila, a centurion of the sixth part-mounted cohort, to forward to you a petition in which he entreats you to show your benevolence in respect of the citizen status of his daughter, I thought that it would be harsh to deny his request since I know how willingly and sympathetically you respond to appeals from the soldiers.

Trajan to Pliny. I have read the petition you forwarded on behalf of Publius Accius Aquila, centurion of the sixth part-mounted cohort. I have been moved by his appeal and have granted Roman citizenship to his daughter. I have sent to you his petition duly annotated which you can give to him.

Trajan is here conceding a privilege normally granted to auxiliary soldiers after twenty-five years' service, or on discharge (see p. 193); this is particularly

striking if Aquila's daughter had been born from an unofficial liaison during
military service.

259 Gaius (2nd C.AD), *Institutes* 2. 109-10

But this strict observance of legal formalities in the drawing up of wills
has been relaxed through imperial decisions in respect of soldiers
because of their extreme ignorance. For even though they do not employ
the established number of witnesses, or transfer their property, or
formally announce their wills, nevertheless their testamentary dispositions are valid. Moreover, they are permitted to institute as heirs
both non-Romans and Latins or to leave them legacies, although as a
general rule non-Romans are prohibited from taking an inherititance or
legacies by the process of civil law, and Latins by the Junian law.

Soldiers will usually have formed liaisons with local women who were not
Roman citizens, and any children will therefore have been non-Romans. The
concession described by Gaius, which was not extended to civilians, enabled
soldiers to institute their 'wives' or children as heirs or legatees. Gaius thought
that this was one of a series of measures taken by emperors to alleviate the
problems of soldiers. It was presumably introduced earlier than the reign of
Marcus Aurelius when Gaius probably finished the *Institutes* and perhaps
should be ascribed to Trajan, who is known to have confirmed and extended the
legal privileges that soldiers enjoyed in making a will (text no. 263).

260 *BGU* 140 = Smallwood *NH* 333, papyrus, Egypt, AD 119

Copy of a letter [of the emperor] translated [into Greek, which] was
displayed in [year] three of Trajan Hadrian Augustus during the
consulship of Publius Aelius (Hadrian) for the third time and Rusticus,
in [_ _ _], in the winter camp of Legion III Cyrenaica and Legion
XXII Deioteriana, on 4 August, which is 11 Mesore, at the headquarters building:

I know, my dear Rammius (Quintus Rammius Martialis, prefect of
Egypt, AD 117–19), that children whom their parents accepted as their
offspring during their military service, have been prevented from
succeeding to their father's property, and that this was not considered
severe since they had acted contrary to military discipline. Personally I
am very happy to establish principles by which I may interpret more
benevolently the rather harsh ruling of the emperors before me.
Therefore, despite the fact that those children who were acknowledged
during military service are not the legitimate heirs of their fathers,
nevertheless I decide that they too are able to claim possession of the

property in accordance with that part of the edict that allows a claim to relatives by birth. It will be your duty to make this benefaction of mine known both to my soldiers and to the veterans, not in order that I may appear to be extolled among them, but so that they may make use of this if they do not know about it.

This letter deals with intestate succession, in which illegitimate children normally had no claim. The munificent tone of the letter suggests that Hadrian was referring to all children of soldiers, not merely those who were Roman citizens. However there were legal limitations to the concession in that it was associated with the edict's provision for claims by blood relatives; therefore the claims of illegitimate children would be preceded by those of legitimate children and agnates (i.e. people descended through the male line, for example, a brother or father). Nevertheless, Hadrian's letter was a further move towards the recognition of military marriages, and its tone emphasizes his personal responsibility and good will towards his soldiers, which he takes as sufficient reason to condone a breach of military regulations.

261 *CJ* 9. 9. 15, AD 242

The same Emperor (Gordian) to Hilarianus, soldier. If your former wife left the province before she could be accused of adultery, an accusation cannot be brought in her absence, and it is not legally proper to demand that she be brought back to that province in which you are serving as a soldier. But you will certainly be able to bring a formal accusation against her when your military duties permit. For the time which you have given to your military obligations should not deprive you of the retribution which you demand for the grief inflicted on you as a husband. Published on 12 March, in the consulship of Atticus and Praetextatus.

This rescript illustrates the legally valid marriage of soldiers after the Severan era, since adultery can occur only in the context of a *iustum matrimonium* (Campbell 1978: 159–66). This story of a failed personal relationship reminds us that soldiers lived in the same world as civilians and indeed faced additional problems because of their military duties. The emperor is sympathetic while upholding the normal legal process.

262 *FIRA* 3. 47, papyrus, Egypt, AD 142

Antonius Silvanus, cavalryman of the first Mauretanian *ala* of Thracians, aide (*stator*) of the prefect, troop of Valerius, made his will. Let my son, Marcus Antonius Satrianus, be the sole heir of all my property, both military and civilian. Let all others be disinherited. And let him formally accept my inheritance within the first hundred days (after my death). If he does not formally accept it, let him be disinherited. Then in the second rank let [_ _ _] Antonius [_ _ _], my brother, be my heir, and let him formally accept my inheritance within the next sixty days. And to him, if he does not become my heir, I grant and bequeath seven hundred and fifty silver *denarii*. As steward of my military property with the purpose of collecting my assets and handing them over to Antonia Thermutha, mother of my above-mentioned heir, I appoint Hierax, son of Behex, soldier on double pay of the same *ala*, troop of Aebutius. And she is to keep the property until my son and heir is free from guardianship (i.e. until he comes of age) and receives it from her. To him (Hierax) I grant and bequeath fifty silver *denarii*. I grant and bequeath to Antonia Thermutha, mother of my above-mentioned heir, five hundred silver *denarii*. I grant and bequeath to my prefect fifty silver *denarii*. In respect of my slave Cronio after my death, if he has handled everything properly and handed it over to my above-mentioned heir or steward, then I wish him to be set free and I wish the five per cent tax (for manumissions) to be paid on his behalf out of my estate.

Let all fraud and deceit be absent from this will.

Nemonius, soldier on double pay, troop of Marius, purchased the estate and its assets for the purpose of making the will; Marcus Julius Tiberinus, soldier on pay and a half, troop of Valerius, held the scales, Turbinius, standard-bearer of the troop of Proculus, acted as a witness (?).

The will was made at Alexandria in Egypt in the Augustan camp, winter quarters of Legion II Traiana Brave and the Mauretanian *ala*, on 27 March, in the consulship of Rufinus and Quadratus.

(Second hand, in Greek) I, Antonius Silvanus, the above-mentioned, have examined my will written out above, and it has been read through and it satisfies me as it stands above.

(Various other hands) I, Nemonius [_ _ _], soldier on double pay, troop of Marius, signed (?).
Julius Tiberinus, soldier on pay and a half, troop of Valerius.
Turbinius, cavalryman, standard-bearer of the troop of Proculus.
Valerius [_ _ _] Rufus, cavalryman, standard-bearer [_ _ _]
I, Maximus, soldier on double pay [_ _ _] signed.
[_ _ _]
(In Greek) I, Antonius Silvanus [signed].

In a Roman will the heir was responsible for the entire estate like a modern executor. This will was made during military service but conforms with normal legal practice. The soldier, and probably his family, are Roman citizens, but he cannot be legally married. He does not therefore refer to Antonia Thermutha as 'wife', but as 'mother of my heir', since to use the term 'wife' might invalidate the will. His son, although illegitimate, can be legally instituted as his heir, and Antonia can receive a legacy in the will. Note that Silvanus has in addition to his camp property civilian assets, which suggests that he had set up a household for his family. Cf. text no. 375 – will of a veteran sailor; for soldiers' legal privileges, pp. 160–70.

SOLDIERS BEFORE THE LAW

The privileged treatment of soldiers before the law may be explained partly in terms of the special role and circumstances of a professional army in which soldiers were absent for long periods and unable to defend their rights, lacked professional legal advice, and were of differing background and legal status. But soldiers' privileges in making wills and in acquiring and disposing of property, went much further and indeed attracted the attention of social commentators like Juvenal. There was doubtless an idea that military duties took precedence over civilian legal requirements, and also a need to encourage volunteers; but above all, emperors wished to cement the personal loyalty and affection of their troops by displaying a personal interest in their welfare. What is more, each soldier had a direct avenue of approach to his commander-in-chief by presenting a petition. Soldiers were also husbands and fathers, and closely connected with the hopes, fears, and lifestyle of the lower classes, where they had family connections and friends. Their petitions to the emperor help to illustrate their daily life and the position of the army in a non-military context. Petitioning the emperor was available to all Roman citizens, and soldiers would not necessarily be advantaged by this process, but in time of political crisis or during military campaigns, emperors might find it more difficult to reject petitions from soldiers, who were already objects of special attention before the law. The emperor's position was crucial; he needed to keep the troops contented, but his decisions influenced the development of the law, which affected all citizens (see also texts nos 258–61; Campbell 1978; 1984: 254–99; Vendrand-Voyer 1983).

263 *D* 29. 1. 1–2

(Ulpian (3rd C.AD), **Book XLV On the Edict**)

The divine Julius Caesar was the first to grant to soldiers the right to make a will free from formal legal requirements. However that concession was for a limited period only. The divine Titus was the first after this to extend the right, and then Domitian. Subsequently the divine Nerva granted the most extensive indulgence to the troops.

Trajan followed this, and from that time onwards the following section began to be inserted in the instructions to governors; section from the instructions: 'It has been brought to my attention that wills made by my fellow-soldiers are frequently being produced which would be the subject of dispute if the full rigour of the law were to be strictly applied to them. Therefore in response to the justness of my feelings for my excellent and outstandingly loyal fellow-soldiers, I have decided that due consideration must be given to their simple-minded ignorance, so that, regardless of the way in which their wills have been drawn up, their wishes are to be considered valid. So, they may draw up their wills in whatever way they wish, and in whatever way they can, and the mere wish of the testator is to be sufficient for the division of his property.' Now the word 'soldier' is said to have been derived from *militia*, that is the hardship (*duritia*) which they endure on our account, or from the word 'multitude', or from the evil from which soldiers customarily protect us, or from the number of one thousand men . . .

(Gaius (2nd C.AD), **Book XV On the Provincial Edict**)

The proconsul issues a separate edict in respect of the wills of soldiers, because he knows very well that in accordance with the decisions of the emperors, unique and extraordinary regulations are applied to their wills.

Trajan's remarkably expansive language will certainly have persuaded governors to take a special interest in testamentary cases involving soldiers, and gave the troops privileges not enjoyed by other Roman citizens, no matter how socially distinguished. These passages also reveal what may have been the official explanation of military privileges – the soldiers endured hardships on behalf of the state and had a simple-minded ignorance of legal technicalities. Later, Trajan found that he had gone too far.

264 *D* 29. 1. 24

(Florentinus (3rd C.AD), **Book X The Institutes**)

The divine Trajan stated in a rescript to Statilius Severus: 'The privilege conferred on soldiers, which renders their wills valid regardless of how they have been executed, should be interpreted as follows. The first point to be ascertained is that the will was executed, and that can be done without putting the will in writing and also applies to those who are not soldiers. Therefore, if a soldier, in respect of whose property the case before you is concerned, called together persons to witness his will, and specifically declared whom he wished to be his heir and on which slave he wished to confer liberty, then you may conclude that he did make his will in this way without putting it in writing, and that his wishes should be honoured. But if, as often happens in casual conversation, the soldier said to some one: "I make you my heir", or "I leave you my property", this should not be regarded as a valid will. It benefits no one more than the soldiers to whom this privilege was given, that cases like this should not be allowed. For otherwise it would not be difficult for witnesses to appear after the death of a soldier and declare that they had heard him say that he was leaving his property to some one whom they wanted to benefit, and in this way the true wishes of the soldier would be frustrated.'

265 *Titles from Ulpian* 23. 10

The wills of soldiers are valid regardless of how they have been executed, that is, even if they lack strict legal form. For soldiers have been permitted by the decisions of emperors to make a will in whatever way they wish and in whatever way they can. But a will executed by a soldier in contravention of strict legal form is valid only if he died while in service or within a year following his discharge.

In making a will soldiers were privileged in three main areas; first, the execution of the will did not have to conform to normal legal rules, so that even an unfinished will or one completed without witnesses was valid; this was important since Roman testamentary procedure was strict. Second, soldiers were free from many constraints concerning those to whom they could leave property (see text no. 259) and were permitted to disinherit by passing over in silence (normally an act of specific disherison was necessary). Third, since for a soldier a mere expression of wish was a will, (*D* 29. 1. 34. 2), he could alter his testament with a minimum of formality. These privileges were granted to all soldiers, not merely those involved in campaigns, and were valid during service and for one year after; more senior officers, such as prefects and military tribunes, apparently had the right to make a military will, but it was restricted to the duration of their service (*D* 29. 1. 21; *CJ* 6. 21. 4). The special testamentary privileges of soldiers developed unsystematically through the decisions of emperors and the benevolent attitude of jurists, who were influenced by imperial goodwill. In legal practice there was a clear distinction between civilians (*pagani*) and soldiers (*milites*), which may also be significant for attitudes to soldiers in court (nos. 275–8). The importance of the testamentary privileges of the army can also be seen from the long chapter in the *Digest* (29. 1) on this theme, and the number of petitions directed to emperors seeking explanation or confirmation (*CJ* 6. 21).

266 *CJ* 6. 21. 2, AD 213

The same Emperor (Antoninus) to Septimus, soldier. If a soldier instituted his comrade as heir to his camp property alone, then it is legally right for his mother to take possession of the rest of his property on the grounds that he died intestate. But if he instituted an outsider as his heir and that person has accepted the inheritance, your wish to have his property transferred to you is not legally justifiable.

Published on 19 February, in the consulship of Antoninus for the fourth time, and Balbinus.

The point of difficulty here is that a soldier, in contravention of normal law, could make a will for part of his property and be intestate for the rest, or institute separate heirs for different parts of his property. For camp property, see texts nos. 269–73.

267 *CJ* 6. 21. 5, AD 224

The same Emperor (Alexander) to Sozomenus. In the will of a soldier, whether he was still in service or had died within a year of an honourable discharge, the inheritance and legacies are due to those to whom they have been bequeathed, since among the other privileges granted to soldiers, they also have an unrestricted right to bequeath their property by their wills to whomever they wish, unless the law specifically prohibits them.

Published on 16 January, in the consulship of Julianus and Crispinus.

268 *CJ* 6. 21. 7, AD 229

The same Emperor (Alexander) to Fortunatus. You cannot claim freedom for yourself on account of these words: 'I grant and bequeath to my freedman Fortunatus', if it is the will of a civilian (*paganus*) which is being cited. But, since you state that the testator was a soldier, if he did not mistakenly believe that you were his freedman but had the intention of conferring freedom upon you, then you are indeed entitled to your freedom directly, and also to the right to claim the legacy through the special privilege associated with military service.

Published on 20 June, in the consulship of Alexander Augustus for the third time, and Dio.

269 *Titles from Ulpian* 20. 10

A son under his father's control cannot execute a will since he possesses nothing of his own which he could dispose of in a will. But the divine Augustus decided that a son under his father's control who is a serving soldier may execute a will in respect of property (*peculium*) that he acquired in military service.

164   *The Roman Army*

In Roman law every family member was in the power of the oldest surviving made ascendant (*pater familias*). Therefore, during the lifetime of his father, a son (*filius familias*), no matter how distinguished, remained under his legal control, could own no property and consequently could not make a will (Campbell 1984: 229–30). Augustus' decision brought a concession to soldiers not enjoyed even by upper-class Romans still in the power of their fathers, but managed to avoid a complete upset in the normal legal process, since if the son died intestate, the camp property reverted to the father as if it had never left his control.

270 *D* 49. 17. 11

(Macer (3rd C.AD), **Book II On Military Matters**)

Camp property (*castrense peculium*) is defined as whatever was given by his parents or relatives to a man who is serving in the army, or whatever a son under his father's control himself acquired during military service, and which he would not have acquired if had he not been a soldier. For whatever he might have acquired without being a soldier does not constitute part of his camp property.

271 Justinian (6th C.AD), *Institutes* 2. 12

Not all persons, however, are permitted to make a will, since, in the first place, those who are under the legal control of another do not have the right of making a will; to such a degree, indeed, that even if their fathers have granted them permission, they nevertheless cannot legally make a will. Excepted from this rule are those whom we have mentioned previously, and especially soldiers who are under the control of their fathers and to whom has been granted by the decisions of emperors the right to execute a will in respect of property that they may have acquired while in military service. Originally this right was granted only to serving soldiers by the authority of the divine Augustus, and by that of Nerva, and then also by that of the excellent Emperor Trajan. Later, by a written reply of the divine Hadrian, the right was granted to soldiers who had been discharged from service, that is, to veterans. Therefore if they have made a will in respect of their property acquired in military service, it will belong to the person whom they have instituted as heir. But if they should die without making a will, with no surviving children or brothers, the property will belong to their parents by the usual legal rules. From this we can conclude that whatever a soldier who is under his father's power may have acquired in military service cannot be appropriated by his father nor sold nor otherwise interfered with by his father's creditors, nor in the event of his father's death does it become the common property of his brothers, but whatever he acquired in military service belongs entirely to the soldier . . .

272 *CJ* 12. 36(37). 3, AD 224

The same Emperor (Alexander) to Felicianus, soldier. The man who told you that you were freed from the ties of your father's control by taking the military oath, is in error. Soldiers too still remain in the control of their fathers, but they have the property acquired in military service as their own and the father has no rights over this.

Published on 13 October in the consulship of Julianus and Crispinus.

273 *CJ* 12. 36(37). 4

Emperor Gordian Augustus to Gallus, soldier. Since you claim that you were instituted as heir by your brother, who is serving with you in the same camp, your request that this inheritance should be included in your camp property rather than pass to the father in whose control you still are, seems entirely reasonable. For I am compelled to believe that your toils away from home, and the company of your joint military service, and the fellowship in carrying out your duties together, must certainly have added considerably to your brotherly love, and indeed rendered you both more affectionate to one another.

Jurists were in doubt whether a soldier's inheritance from a near relative who was also soldier could belong to the *castrense peculium*. It was important to consider if the will was drawn up before or after the shared military service. It is notable that Gordian and his advisers benevolently support this soldier without further enquiry.

274 *CJ* 2. 50(51). 2, AD 222

The same Emperor (Alexander) to Petronius, centurion. If those who are absent in the interests of the state have suffered any loss in respect of their property, or if anyone has been released from an action which could have been brought against him (by those absent in the interests of the state), within one year of their return from public business complete restitution may be granted to them, without limit of time.

Published on 19 October, in the consulship of Emperor Alexander.

Soldiers, in common with others who were absent on behalf of the state, were entitled through the praetor's edict to the assistance of the law if they had suffered loss through inability to defend their interests while detained away from home. Soldiers clearly formed the largest group of those who served away from home, and the praetorians were also included in this category, as Antoninus Pius confirmed, although normally those who served the state in Rome were not classified as absent on public business (*D* 4. 6. 5. 1; 6. 35. 4).

275 Juvenal (1st–2nd C.AD), *Satires* 16

Gallius, who can count up the benefits of a successful career in the army? If military service is profitable, I hope that the gate of the camp will welcome me, a terrified recruit, under a lucky star. For one moment of good fortune brings more benefit than a letter of recommendation to Mars from Venus (line 5) or from his mother Juno who delights in the shore of Samos.

Let us discuss first the benefits shared by all soldiers, of which not the least is that no civilian would dare to beat you up, and if he gets a thrashing he will conceal it and will not dare to show the praetor his teeth which have been knocked out (line 10), and the black lumps and swelling bruises on his face, and his one remaining eye for which the doctor holds out little hope. If a man seeks to gain redress for this, he is granted a military judge in hobnailed boots and hefty jurors sitting on mighty benches, in accordance with the ancient law of the military camps and the practice of Camillus (line 15), that a soldier may not be involved in litigation outside the wall of the camp and far from the military standards. Of course the judgment of the centurions in the case of soldiers is extremely just, and I am certain to obtain retribution if I lodge a legitimate complaint! But the whole unit is against you, and all the soldiers (line 20) unite in complete agreement to make sure that your retribution is something that needs medical treatment and is worse than the original offence. So, it would be an act of incredible stupidity, since you have two legs, to provoke so many boots and thousands of hobnails. Besides, what witness would dare to come so far from the city? (line 25) Who is such a faithful friend that he would come inside the wall of the military camp? Therefore dry your tears at once and do not bother your friends who are going to make excuses anyway. When the judge says: 'Produce a witness', let somebody or other who witnessed the assault declare: 'I saw it' (line 30), and I shall believe him worthy of our bearded and long-haired ancestors. You can more easily find a dishonest witness who will speak out against a civilian, than one prepared to tell the truth against the interests and honour of a soldier.

Let us now examine other benefits and emoluments (line 35) of taking the military oath. If a dishonest neighbour steals from me a valley or meadow which is part of my ancestral land, and digs up from the middle of the boundary the sacred boundary stone to which I offer every year a broad cake and porridge, or if a debtor refuses to pay back the money which he borrowed from me (line 40), claiming that his signature was forged and the receipt is worthless, my case will have to wait for the legal session which initiates the litigation of the entire people. But then too I shall have to put up with a thousand irritations, a thousand delays. Often the benches of the courtroom are made ready, one lawyer has taken his cloak off (line 45), another has gone for a pee, then there is an adjournment. In the legal arena we fight a slow battle. But those who put on armour and wear a sword belt have their cases heard on whatever date suits them, and their property is not worn away by the brake of a long lawsuit (line 50).

Moreover to soldiers alone is given the right of executing a will while their father is still alive. For it was decided that whatever was acquired through the toil of military service should not be included in the body of property all control of which resides in the father. Therefore an ageing father hunts a legacy from his soldier son who is earning military pay (line 55). Well-earned approval brings promotion and confers the right rewards on distinguished service. It is indeed in the interests of the commander to ensure that brave men are also the most satisfied, that they are all happy with with their military decorations and medals, all (line 60) [_ _ _

The text breaks off at line 60. Presumably it was unfinished or the end of the manuscript has been lost. It is interesting that Juvenal thought that the privileged position of the soldiers in Roman society was one of the themes likely to gain a responsive audience among the upper classes. Soldiers can get away with abusive and violent conduct, and it is very difficult to pursue them in court; as plaintiffs soldiers are better off than civilians, and in the right of *castrense peculium* they are uniquely privileged.

276 *D* 49. 16. 4. 8

(Menander (3rd C.AD), **Book I On Military Affairs**)

Not everyone who is involved in a law suit and for that reason joined the army should be ordered to be discharged from the army, but only the person who joined up with the intention of making himself, under the protection of military service, more formidable to his opponent. The person who was involved in litigation before he enlisted in the army should not be lightly exonerated; but he should be exonerated if he gives up the case.

277 *CJ* 12. 33(34). 1

Emperors Severus and Antoninus Augusti, greetings to their Antonius. If you wish to put your name forward for military service, present yourselves to those who have the right to check recruits. But you should not be unaware that those who seek to enlist because they are involved in litigation, are normally dismissed from the service on the demand of their opponents.

278 *D* 22. 5. 3 .6

(Callistratus (3rd C.AD), **Book IV On Judicial Enquiries**)

Witnesses should not be summoned without good reason to travel a long distance, and still less should soldiers be summoned from the standards and their duties for the purpose of giving evidence; the divine Hadrian established this point in a rescript.

279 *D* 49. 16. 3. 1

(Modestinus (3rd C.AD), **Book IV On Punishments**)

Military punishments are of the following types: reprimand, fines, imposition of fatigues, transfer to another branch of the army, reduction in rank, dishonourable discharge. For soldiers are not condemned to the mines or to hard labour, and are not subjected to torture.

Veterans and sons of veterans were also immune from certain punishments (*D* 49. 18. 3).

  The legal texts show that Roman law, which normally served the interests of the upper classes, gave a privileged position to soldiers, who, being generally from a poor background, lacked the usual criterion for special treatment – social eminence. This demonstrates the importance of the part they played in life and society in the Roman world and in the nexus of imperial politics, since their loyalty was critical for emperors. The jurists recognized that soldiers were likely to have a superiority in court, and we may see this point in certain other restrictions on the legal activities of soldiers – on accepting as gifts items involved in litigation (*D* 4. 7. 11), on acting as agent for a third party (*CJ* 2. 12. 7), on purchasing land in the province where they served (*D* 49. 16. 9 pref.). It is difficult to define how soldiers were 'more formidable' in court and to what extent Juvenal, with a satirist's licence, was exaggerating the problem. For civilian plaintiffs it was doubtless difficult to pursue through the usual legal process soldiers who could exploit official unwillingness to have them taken away from the camp. It was a principle of Roman law that a suit should be brought in the *forum* of the defendant, i.e., where he lived. That might mean a trial in the military camp, perhaps with a military judge delegated by the army commander, and few civilians can have been confident about receiving fair treatment, given the usually benevolent attitude of the emperor and his officials to the army (Campbell 1984: 254–63).

280 *CJ* 5. 16. 2, AD 213

The same Emperor (Antoninus) to Marcus, soldier. If you prove to the governor of the province that the female slave was bought with your money and that the receipt of purchase was written in the name of your concubine in order to make her a gift, he will order that she be returned to you. For although a gift may be valid where there is not a formal marriage, nevertheless I do not wish my soldiers to be robbed in this way by their concubines through deceitful displays of affection.

Published on 18 February in the consulship of Antoninus Augustus for the fourth time, and Balbinus.

Caracalla in benevolent and effusive manner sweeps aside legal technicalities to help a soldier who had changed his mind about a gift made to his mistress.

281 *CJ* 3. 44. 5, AD 224

The same Emperor (Alexander) to Cassius, soldier. The wishes of a soldier which he expressed in his will with reference to the erection of a monument in his honour, should not be neglected by his father and mother, his heirs. For although the right of bringing a complaint on these grounds has been abolished by previous decisions, nevertheless they cannot avoid ill will and the consciousness of guilt that surrounds their failure to carry out a last duty of this nature and their contempt for the final wishes of the deceased.

Published on 24 April, in the consulship of Julianus and Crispinus.

The emperor looks benevolently on the soldier's concern for his comrade's last wishes, but cannot alter the law.

282 *CJ* 9. 23. 5, AD 225

The same Emperor (Alexander) to Gallicanus, soldier. Since you were asked to write out your comrade's will and on his instructions assigned a slave to yourself, the slave is considered as not bequeathed and therefore you cannot take up the legacy. But in line with my usual benevolence, in your case I remit the penalty of the Cornelian law, whose precepts you have infringed more through inadvertence, in my opinion, that with fraudulent intent.

Published on 15 June, in the consulship of Fuscus for the second time, and Dexter.

It is interesting that in a similar case involving a civilian petitioner, Severus Alexander did not accept ignorance of the law as a mitigating factor (*CJ* 9. 23. 3).

283 *CJ* 1. 18. 1, AD 212

Emperor Antoninus Augustus to Maximus, soldier. Although when you were conducting your case, through ignorance of the law on account of the simple-minded ignorance of those in military service, you omitted to make appropriate representations, nevertheless if you have not yet made reparation, I grant that you may use the evidence for your defence, if an action is now being brought against you in accordance with the judgment.

Given on 25 April, in the consulship of Asper and Asper.

Permission for the soldier to reopen his defence at this late stage will have made life difficult for the plaintiff; ignorance of the law was not usually an acceptable explanation for failure to observe proper procedure.

SOLDIERS AND CIVILIANS

In their ideal role the troops, in the words of Dio of Prusa (Speeches 1. 28), were like shepherds who, with the emperor, guarded the flock of the empire. And some communities did indeed benefit from the proximity of army units or through the influence of fellow-citizens who were soldiers. But the dominating theme is the brutal oppression of civilians by soldiers, whom emperors were apparently unable or unwilling to restrain. Soldiers were distinguished by special privileges and treatment in court; they were comrades of the emperor; they were armed; they were often in contact with local people, sometimes in a police capacity; in certain areas their officers were the only available source of legal jurisdiction. It is not surprising that in these circumstances soldiers exploited their status, prestige, and physical might to oppress civilians, sometimes on their own initiative, sometimes on the orders of higher officials, since the system of provincial administration made demands (in the form of requisitions) on local communities, which were difficult to monitor and control. Inscriptions and papyri containing the complaints of provincial communities preserve an authentic record of serious, widespread, and persistent abuse, and indicate that in any analysis of the failings of Roman provincial administration, soldiers appear as the most intransigent culprits.

The population of Rome can hardly have escaped unscathed from the presence of the praetorians. Juvenal vividly depicts how the unfortunate pedestrian might have his foot squashed by a soldier's hobnailed boot in the crush of the streets. But he also spoke of beatings and intimidation for which redress was difficult (text no. 275). Hostile relations between plebs and soldiers were exacerbated by the fights and disturbances at games and chariot races where soldiers were detailed to keep order (provincial maladministration – Brunt 1961; role of soldiers – Mac-Mullen 1967; Campbell 1984: 246–54; Isaac 1992: 269–310).

284 *ILS* 6099 = *EJ* 354, inscription, near Brixia, probably AD 28

In the consulship of Lucius Silanus, priest of Mars and Gaius Vellaeus Tutor, on 5 December, the senate and people of Siagu made a guest-friendship agreement with Gaius Silius Aviola, son of Gaius, of the tribe Fabia, military tribune of Legion III Augusta, prefect of engineers, and have chosen both him and his descendants as patron to them and their descendants. Gaius Silius Aviola, son of Gaius, of the tribe Fabia, has received them and their descendants into his good faith and clientship. Arranged by Celer, son of Imilcho Gulalsa, suffete.

Aviola contracted patronage agrements with two other small towns in Africa – Apisa Maius and Themetra (Chott Mariem) (*ILS* 6099a; 6100). Aviola, who apparently lived near Brixia in northern Italy, must have made these arrangements through his service with the III Augusta in Africa.

285 *ILS* 5950, inscription, Dalmatia, AD 37–41

Lucius Arruntius Camillus Scribonianus, legate with propraetorian power of Gaius Caesar Augustus Germanicus, appointed Marcus Coelius, centurion of the seventh legion, as ajudicator between the Sapuates and the [La]matini, in order to establish boundaries and set up markers.

Cf. text no. 206. Senior officers could delegate the resolution of minor disputes among soldiers to experienced centurions, who in turn sought advice from other centurions or decurions acting as a *consilium* (*FIRA* 3. 64 – a disputed inheritance). From this limited beginning it was doubtless convenient on occasion to employ centurions to deal with specific problems outside the military sphere. Gradually they acquired more general responsibilities of a quasi-legal kind. Since the soldiers under a centurion's command often had to arrest suspected law-breakers, the centurion was left to sort things out among civilian litigants and on a formal level refer the matter to a responsible official for further action; informally, however, the centurion's decision often brought an effective legal solution, because the litigants were happy with an immediate decision, or because no other official was readily available, or because other officials were glad to have some of the burden of jurisdiction removed. Eventually, the centurion would be seen by the local inhabitants as a source of *de facto* legal authority and a means of redress. This was not a deliberate advance in militarism; the government was simply using in an unplanned way some better-educated soldiers to supplement existing officials in a minor role. The danger was that the army was being more closely insinuated into local life and that verdicts of centurions would be dictated by overriding military requirements. The development of the judicial role of centurions is illustrated by many papyri from Egypt, but the situation in other provinces is likely to have been similar (Campbell 1984: 431–5; Davies 1989: 175–85).

286 *P. Oxy.* 2234, papyrus, Oxyrhynchus, Egypt, AD 31

To Quintus Gaius Passer, centurion, from Hermon, son of Demetrius. Near the village of Teïs in the toparchy of Thmoisepho of the Oxyrhynchite nome, I own a plot of land inherited from my paternal grandfather, called 'of the Woodland', in which there is a public dyke and a cistern, which is situated in the middle of my land, along with cubic measures (?) and other things. For all of these I pay the appropriate public taxes. But I am being attacked and plundered by the fishermen Pausis, Papsious and his brother, and Cales, Melas, Attinus, Pasoïs, and their accomplices, not few in number. They also brought along Titius the soldier, and approaching my cistern with many fishing lines and scaling knives, they fished with gaffs and pulled out fish worth one silver talent. Moreover, when I remonstrated with them, they came up to me apparently intending to [_ _ _] me. Since they are using force against me in many ways, I am taking recourse to you, and I request, if you agree, that you have the accused brought before you so that they may pay me back for the value of the fish, as was mentioned above, and so that in future they may keep away from my property, in order that I may be assisted. Farewell. Year 17 of Tiberius Caesar Augustus, 17 Pachon.

287 *P. Ryl.* 2. 141 = Daris, *Documenti* 76, papyrus, Euhemeria, Egypt, AD 37

To Gaius Trebius Justus, centurion, from Petermuthis, son of Heracleus, resident of Euhemeria, farmer of state lands and public tax collector, farmer of the estate of Antonia, wife of Drusus. On the second of the current month, Pachon, in the first year of Emperor Gaius Caesar, while I was remonstrating with Papontos, son of Orsenuphis, and Apion, also called Capareis, shepherds, about damages they owed to me because of their flocks grazing over my land, they gave me a severe beating and abusively stated that they would not pay. And I lost forty silver *drachmae* which I had with me from the sale of opium, and a belt. Therefore I ask that I may receive redress so that the state should suffer no loss. Farewell.

288 *P. Mich.* 175 = Daris, *Documenti* 77, papyrus, Socnopaiou Nesos, AD 193

To Ammonius Paternus, centurion, from Melas, son of Horion, from the village of Socnopaiou Nesos, priest of the god who is in the village. In the same village there belongs to me and my cousins Phanesis and Harpagathes, in common and with equal shares, as an inheritance from our maternal grandfather, a vacant piece of ground, surrounded by a wall, where we deposit every year the hay which we have. Then recently one cousin, Harpagathes, died and although his share was inherited equally by both of us, yesterday, which was the twenty-second, when I was depositing our hay in this place, Phanesis attacked me boldly and insolently, took my hay, and did not allow me to deposit it in our share but tried to push me out of this and to claim for himself alone what belongs to me; in addition to this he treated me with the most disgraceful viciousness. Therefore I request that you order him to be brought before you so that I may obtain the fair decision that is in your power. Farewell.

(Second hand) Year 1 of Publius Helvius Pertinax Augustus, 23 Pharmuthi.

In a more serious case recorded in a papyrus dated 27 May AD 243, a woman, Bathsabbatha Arsinoe from the village of Magdala, probably between Resapha and the Euphrates in Syria, petitions a centurion about the murder of her brother and the appropriation of his property. A soldier from the Legion XVI Flavia Firma at Appadana and a veteran appeared before the centurion to give evidence (Feissel and Gascou, 1989: 558). The involvement of a centurion in local affairs also appears in *P. Yadin* 11; in AD 124 a centurion in the camp at En Gedi in Judaea made a large short-term loan at 12 per cent interest to a Jew named Judah, who owned a neighbouring palm grove (Yadin 1989).

289 Bowman and Thomas 1983: no. 22, tablet, *c.* AD 95–105

[_ _ _]ius Karus to his Cerialis, greetings. [_ _ _] Brigionus has asked me, sir, to commend him to you. Therefore I ask, sir, that if he has requested anything from you, you agree to give him your approval. I ask

that you should think it appropriate to commend him to Annius Equester, centurion responsible for the region, at Luguvalium (Carlisle). [By doing this] you will place me in your debt [both in his] name and [in mine]. I hope that you are having the best of fortune and are well.
(Second hand) Farewell, brother.
(Back) To Cerialis, prefect.

This is the earliest evidence we have for a centurion of a district, though there is no indication of what kind of jurisdiction, if any, he exercised. There are other examples from Bath (text no. 211) and Ribchester in Britain, Egypt, Galatia, Lugdunensis, Noricum, and Pannonia.

Many ostraca from Mons Claudianus in Egypt show that a centurion of this fort was responsible for issuing passes for travellers on the road which descended from Mons Claudianus towards the valley of the Nile; they were addressed to *stationarii*, who were responsible for supervision of the roads leading to the fort and the mines in the area – 'Antoninus, centurion, to the *stationarii*, greetings. Allow to pass a woman and two children. 10 Phaophi' (2nd C. AD; see Bingen *et al.* 1992: 57–74, especially no. 58).

290 Petronius (1st (?) C.AD), *Satyricon* 82

(Encolpius rushes into the street with his hand on his sword hilt) Then a soldier spotted me; he was probably a deserter or a nocturnal cut-throat; 'Hey, comrade', he said, 'what legion or whose century do you belong to?' I lied boldly about my legion and century, but he said: 'Well then, in your army do the soldiers walk about wearing white slippers?' Since my expression and my trembling gave away that I had been lying, he ordered me to hand over my sword and to watch out for myself. So, I was robbed. . .

Petronius is writing a novel in which his hero, Encolpius, is at large in southern Italy, perhaps near Puteoli; the author imagines that an encounter with a soldier could be frightening and violent, and that soldiers could be casual thieves; he must have expected this to be credible to his audience. Apuleius, in his novel *The Golden Ass*, imagines the same kind of incident in a provincial setting.

291 Apuleius (2nd C.AD), *The Golden Ass* 9. 39; 42; 10. 1; 13 (extracts)

(The hero has been turned into an ass and is in the service of a gardener) But our return was not free from trouble. For we encountered a tall legionary soldier, as his dress and appearance indicated, who arrogantly and abusively demanded where he (the gardener) was taking the unladen ass. But my master, who was still rather perplexed, and ignorant of Latin, passed on without saying anything. The soldier, unable to contain his usual insolence and outraged at his silence as if it were an insult, struck him with the vine-wood staff he was holding and shoved him off my back. Then the gardener replied humbly that he could not make out what he had said because he did not understand his language. Then the soldier interjected in Greek: 'Where are you taking this ass?' The gardener said that he was making for the next town. The soldier said: 'But I need its help, for I have to bring our governor's belongings from the nearby fort with the other baggage animals', and he seized me by the rein and began to take me away by force . . . (The gardener succeeds in overpowering the soldier and escapes to the neighbouring town where he hides with the ass in a friend's house; eventually the soldier's comrades come looking for the miscreant and put pressure on the local authorities to find him.) (Section 42) Then there developed a violent argument between the two sides, the soldiers swearing in the name of the emperor himself that we were definitely inside, the shopkeeper constantly swearing by the gods that we were not . . . (The ass is spotted as he looks out of an upstairs window.) Immediately a tremendous uproar broke out and some of the soldiers rushed up the stairs, grabbed me and dragged me down like a captive. Then with no further hesitation they searched every part more carefully, and when they opened up the chest they discovered the poor gardener, dragged him out, and pushed him in front of the magistrates; he was led away to jail where he was destined to pay with his life . . .

(Book 10, Section 1) . . . The soldier led me away from my stall with no one to prevent him and in his billet (so it seemed to me) loaded me with all his baggage and decked me out in a military fashion and then led me out onto the road. For on my back I was carrying a glittering helmet, a shield whose polished surface gleamed afar, and an exceptionally long spear in a conspicuous position. He had deliberately arranged things like this with a great heap of equipment like an army on the move, not because of military procedure, but in order to terrorize unfortunate travellers. When we had completed our journey over a plain along a good road, we came to a small community where we put up, not in an inn, but in the house of a town councillor . . .

(Section 13) But at that moment I was immersed in the waves of fortune. The soldier, who had got me with no seller involved and had appropriated me without paying any money, was to set off to Rome in the course of his duty on the orders of his superior officer to carry some letters addressed to the mighty emperor, and first sold me for eleven *denarii* to two of his neighbours, who were brothers and slaves.

The reference to the soldier's vine-wood staff suggests that Apuleius had a centurion in mind (though see Millar 1981: 67, n. 25). In this scene set in Thessaly, Apuleius imagines how ordinary people went in fear of approaching soldiers, who were likely to be brutal and arrogant, inadequately supervised, using the name of the provincial governor or emperor to cover their wrongdoing, and difficult to bring to a fair trial; in Apuleius' novel it is a joke on the theme of a reversal of fortune that the soldier gets beaten up, but for the gardener, with no hope of legal redress, this was probably the only way out. In the end the soldier profits from what was an act of open robbery. The dividing line between what soldiers could legally demand for transport and accommodation (note that the soldier is able to stay in the house of a town-councillor), and the unjust exploitation of this, was probably often blurred. Cf. *New Testament*, Matthew 5. 41 for compulsion on people to provide services (*angareuein*); see also text no. 298.

292 *D* 1. 18. 6. 5–7

(Ulpian (3rd C.AD), **Book I Opinions**)

The governor of the province must ensure that persons of humble means are not subjected to injustice by having their solitary light or meagre furniture taken away for the use of others, under the pretext of the arrival of officials or soldiers. The governor of the province should ensure that nothing is done in the name of the soldiers by certain individuals unjustly claiming advantage for themselves, which does not relate to the communal benefit of the army as a whole.

It is important that this formal judgment of a governor's responsibilities by an experienced Roman offical assumes not only that Roman administration might be inequitable but also that soldiers were frequently to blame.

293 *P.S.I.* 446 = *SP* 221, papyrus, Egypt, AD 133–7

Marcus Petronius Mamertinus, prefect of Egypt, declares: I have been informed that many of the soldiers, while travelling through the country, without a certificate requisition boats, animals, and persons beyond what is proper, on some occasions appropriating them by force, on others getting them from the *strategoi* by exercise of favour or deference. Because of this private persons are subjected to arrogance and abuse and the army has come to be censored for greed and injustice. I therefore order the *strategoi* and royal secretaries to furnish to absolutely no one any travel facilities at all without a certificate, whether he is travelling by river or by land, on the understanding that I shall punish severely anyone who, after this edict, is caught giving or taking any of the things mentioned above. [Year ?] of the lord Hadrian Caesar, 8 Thoth.

Mamertinus' frank admission of hostile criticism of the army's behaviour, and the series of edicts issued by Prefects of Egypt about these matters, are a further indication of the government's inability over a long period to deal with the problem of illegal and excessive requisitions, for which soldiers had a major responsibility.

294 Pliny (1st–2nd C.AD), *Letters* 10. 77–8

Pliny to Emperor Trajan. You have acted with great wisdom, sir, in issuing instructions to Calpurnius Macer, distinguished man, to send a legionary centurion to Byzantium. Consider if you think that we ought to look after the interests of the people of Juliopolis in the same way. This community, although very small, bears extremely heavy burdens and suffers more severe injustices precisely because of its comparative weakness. Whatever help you give to the people of Juliopolis will be of benefit to the whole province. For they are situated at the head of the route into Bithynia and put up with countless people travelling through the town.

Trajan to Pliny. Such is the situation of Byzantium with a huge crowd of travellers converging on it from all sides, that in accordance with the precedent established earlier, I decided that it was necessary to assist its government with the protection of a legionary centurion. If I decide to help the people of Juliopolis in the same way, I shall burden myself with a precedent, for many other cities, particularly the weaker ones, will seek the same kind of assistance. I have sufficient confidence in your abilities to think that you will take every precaution to ensure that they are not exposed to injustice. However, if anyone has acted contrary to my rules of conduct, they should be brought to book at once; but, if their offences are too serious for adequate punishment to be exacted on the spot, then if they are soldiers, you should inform their commanding officers what you have discovered, or, if they are persons passing through on their way back to Rome, you may write to me.

An important road from Nicaea ran along the northern bank of the river Sangarius through south-east Bithynia to Juliopolis, thence to Galatia and the army camps in Cappadocia. Communities situated near major roads probably suffered more than most, because of the passage of officials and soldiers. It is significant that Trajan assumes that soldiers may be the main culprits in making improper demands on the local population for travel facilities. This problem had existed from the time of Augustus, and we find Libuscidianus, the governor of Galatia at the start of Tiberius' reign, lamenting that he has to tighten up with his own edict the regulations of Augustus and Tiberius on the requisition of animals and carts by officials and soldiers journeying past Sagalassus, which was responsible for transport over a substantial territory in Pisidia (see Mitchell, *JRS* 1976: 106–31; and texts nos 298–301).

295 *New Testament*, Luke, 3. 14

Moreover serving soldiers asked him (John the Baptist): 'And what shall we do?' He replied to them: 'Do not extort money from anyone, do not use blackmail, be satisfied with your pay'.

The Greek word translated here by 'extort' is *diaseiein*, which literally means 'to shake down' (see texts nos 296–7). This passage may refer to the troops of king Herod, but its relevance is certainly more general, and other passages in the *New Testament* indicate the bad reputation of Roman soldiers in the east (Acts, 10. 1–36; Matthew, 8. 5–10; 27. 27–32; John, 19. 23–24).

296 *P. Oxy.* 240 = *EJ* 117, papyrus, Egypt, AD 37

[_ _ _] village secretary [son of _ _ _] Eremus. [I swear by Tiberius Cae]sar the new Augustus, Emperor, son of [divine Zeus the Liberator] Augustus, that I know nothing of anyone being subjected to extortion (*diaseiein*) in the vicinity of the above-mentioned villages by the soldier [_ _ _] and his associates. [If I swear truthfully] may things go well for me, but if untruthfully, the opposite. Year 23 of Tiberius Caesar Augustus, 17 Mecheir.

297 *SB* 9207, papyrus, 2nd C.AD

To the soldier on guard duty (*stationarius*)	2 drachmae, 1 obol
Gift	240 drachmae
Suckling pig	24 drachmae
To the guard	20 drachmae
For extortion (*diaseismos*)	2200 drachmae
To two police agents	100 drachmae
To Hermias, police agent	100 drachmae
To the [_ _ _]	2574 drachmae, 3 obols

Second half-year: Pha[menoth]

To the soldier at his demand	500 drachmae
Currency exchange	12 drachmae
8 jars of wine at 10 drachmae $^{1/8}$ obol	[_ _ _]

To the police chief	[_ _ _]
Dyke tax	1 drachma
Cattle tax (?)	1 drachma
To the soldier at his demand	400 drachmae
Currency exchange	15 drachmae

It is extraordinary that in a private account entries are made so casually for payments to soldiers and for extortion; as it stands, with one exception, these are by far the most expensive items on the account and it looks as if the owner has quietly written off these sums without any hope of redress. Payments to the police agents, the chief of police, and the *stationarius* (a junior officer or soldier holding a post which ensured the security of an area or a road) must also be viewed as suspicious. This is a vivid example of how commonplace were theft and blackmail at the hands of soldiers.

298 Epictetus (1st C.AD), *Discourses* 4. 1. 79

If a requisition is taking place and a soldier takes (your mule), let it go, do not hold on to it, and do not complain. For if you do, you will get a beating and lose your mule all the same.

299 *OGIS* 609 = *AJ* 113, inscription, Phaenae, Syria, AD 185–6

Julius Saturninus (governor of Syria) to the people of Phaenae, chief village of the district of Trachonitis, greetings. If any soldier or private person establishes a billet for himself by force in your houses, contact me and you will receive redress. For you are not obliged to provide any joint contribution for visitors, nor, since you have a public hostel, can you be compelled to receive visitors into your homes. Publish this letter of mine in a conspicuous location in your chief village, so that no one can argue that he did not know of it.

Phaenae was situated on the north-west corner of the Trachonitis, on the road running from Bostra to Damascus. Security for the roads in southern Syria was provided by legionary troops and there is some evidence that in the second half of the second century a garrison may have been stationed at Phaenae (Isaac 1992: 135–6, 298). The public hostel had presumably been built to protect the inhabitants from requests for billets by soldiers passing along the road, and the idea of such hostels was apparently common in southern Syria.

300 Columella (1st C.AD), *On Agriculture* 1. 5. 6–7

The buildings (of an estate) should not be close to a marshy area or on a military road ... A road is a plague to an estate because of the depredations of passing travellers and the endless hospitality required for those who turn aside from it. Therefore I think that in order to avoid problems of this kind, an estate should not be situated on a road. . .

301 *CIL* 3. 12336 = *AJ* 139, inscription, Scaptopara, Thrace, AD 238 (extract)

To Emperor Caesar Marcus Antonius Gordian Pius Fortunate Augustus, petition from the villagers of Scaptopara and of Griseia . . . We live and have our property in the village mentioned above which is exposed to harm because it has the advantage of hot springs and is located between two of the army camps which are in your (province of) Thrace. Previously, as long as the inhabitants remained undisturbed and free from oppression, they reliably paid their tribute and met their other obligations. But when at times some persons started to become insolent and to use force, then the village started to decline. A famous festival is held two miles from our village, and those persons who stay there for fifteen days for the festival do not remain in the vicinity of the festival itself, but leave it and come down on our village, forcing us to provide them with hospitality and purvey many other items for their enjoyment without payment. In addition to these persons, soldiers too, who have been despatched somewhere else, leave their proper routes and come to us, and similarly intimidate us into furnishing them with hospitality and provisions, and pay no money. Moreover, the governors of the province and indeed your procurators, are regular visitors here to use the hot springs. We unceasingly receive those in authority, as we are required to do, but being unable to put up with the others, we have repeatedly approached the governors of Thrace, who in accordance with the letters of the divine emperors, have ordered that we are to remain undisturbed. For we made clear that we could no longer put up with it but intended to leave our ancestral homes because of the violence of those who descend on us . . .

Although emperors and their officials were usually willing to help those who had been oppressed by soldiers and others, the response was not sufficiently strong or effective to make a lasting difference; hence measures often had to be repeated; in this case the emperor merely instructs the villagers to approach the provincial governor. However they had been assisted by one of their number, Pyrrhus, who served in the praetorian guard and had presumably used his position there to present the petition.

7   The army in politics

Ancient commentators, even well-connected senators like Tacitus and
Dio, experienced in administration and government, tended to examine
imperial politics in terms of events and personalities rather than by
analysis of long-term trends or political institutions, and there is no
adequate discussion of the role of the army in politics. It was of course
difficult for historians living under an autocratic monarchy to discuss
sensitive political issues which might constitute what Tacitus called the
'secrets of ruling', about which Sallustius Crispus, imperial confidant,
advised Livia: 'the accounts of empire will not add up unless the
emperor is the only auditor'(*Annals*, 1. 6).

Augustus the military leader was the paymaster and benefactor of
his troops, who were discreetly but effectively encouraged to identify
with his family. But having acquired power and respectability, he
intended that his political dependence on the army should never
formally be recognized. In the *Res Gestae* there is no mention of this.
Instead he chose to emphasize his accumulation of military honours as
his armies defeated foreign peoples and fulfilled the imperial destiny
of Rome. Although he was represented at times with the military
attributes of a Roman *imperator*, he could not permanently assume the
status and demeanour of a war lord. Augustus set a pattern for his
successors by winning consent for his rule among the privileged
classes through a display of traditional virtues in both the civil and
military spheres, and by strictly controlling the army. Upper-class
military commanders represented the point of contact between army
and emperor, and would have been offended by signs of indiscipline
and social upheaval. The soldiers, who in any case lacked serious
political consciousness, were entitled to pay and other emoluments in
return for their quiescence, and their loyalty was conspicuously
rewarded at the accession of an emperor and at other times crucial to
the dynasty.

The Roman emperor held his powers by virtue of a law on the vote of the people, though in practice a decree of the senate determined this. But that was a formality and the senate had no right to choose and make emperors. Nor had the army, which, along with the senate and people, was the other permanent institution in the Roman state. For the law made no mention of the emperor's command of the army. Moreover, although the troops might be loyal to a dynasty there was no rule of dynastic succession, since at the start Augustus at least in public was not establishing a monarchy. An emperor emerged, therefore, through a number of factors – connection to the previous emperor by birth or adoption, the goodwill of senate and people, a demonstration of support by the praetorians under the direction of the influential praetorian prefects, and the acquiescence of governors and soldiers in the provinces. So, in certain circumstances the support of the praetorians or the legions could be decisive, and in a sense soldiers could informally 'make' an emperor. The events of AD 68/69 openly demonstrated the potential importance of provincial army commanders, but the practices and ambiguities of the Augustan principate worked well, and in the next 125 years there were only two attempts (by Saturninus in AD 89 and Avidius Cassius in AD 175) to follow this example.

After the violent usurpation of power by Septimius Severus in AD 193, in a period of just over forty years, four emperors in succession met violent deaths, three of them as a result of military rebellion. The balance between the various roles that an emperor had to play had shifted. The army's position in political life was increasingly important and also more visible; the soldiers now looked for greater financial rewards and were more insistent in opposition if they did not get what they wanted. The emperor, who had all the trappings of a commander-in-chief, was under increasing pressure to spend more time with his troops, and to show himself a good comrade and competent military leader, and indeed to assume the attitudes and demeanour of a war lord. Capacity to rule was dangerously associated with ability to control and direct an army. Maximinus, who overthrew Severus Alexander, became the first Roman emperor personally to fight in battle (Campbell 1984: 365–414; the emperor as commander-in-chief – chapter 3).

The following extracts, set out in chronological order by the period to which they refer, are intended to illustrate some of the ways in which ancient writers thought in general terms about the army and its developing role in politics, its part in the making and removing of emperors, and the dangers of civil war.

302 Appian (2nd C.AD), *Civil Wars* 5. 17

... the soldiers did not serve the interests of the state, but only of those who had recruited them; and they gave their support to these people not because of the compulsion of the law, but because of personal inducements; and they fought not against enemies of Rome but against private adversaries, not against foreigners, but against fellow-citizens, men just like themselves. All these factors contributed to a breakdown of military discipline; the soldiers believed that they were not so much serving in an army as helping out, through their personal decision and favour, leaders who found their assistance essential for private ends.

Appian is here describing the consequences of the civil wars of 44–31 BC and the development of a personal rapport between commanders and soldiers which in his view had serious implications for future political events.

303 Dio (2nd–3rd C.AD), 53. 11

Immediately he arranged for those men who were to form his bodyguard to be voted twice the pay granted to the other soldiers, to ensure that he was efficiently protected. By doing this he showed that his true intention was to establish a monarchy.

In 27 BC Augustus in a speech to the senate claimed that he wished to give up his dominant position, but in response to senatorial objections then withdrew this suggestion and eventually was granted a portion of the provinces to administer as his direct responsibility. Dio is sarcastic, arguing that the occasion was set up by Augustus who wanted it to seem that he was reluctantly compelled by the weight of popular opinion to take on certain responsibilities on behalf of the state; it was a way of suggesting that his position in the state was compatible with the institutions of the republic. In Dio's view the maintenance of the privileged praetorian guard and the fact that the provinces controlled directly by Augustus contained most of the troops, demonstrated the dichotomy between appearance and reality in imperial politics, since real power depended on control of the army.

304 Tacitus (1st–2nd C.AD), *Annals* 6. 3

But he (Tiberius) severely rebuked Junius Gallio, who had proposed that praetorian guardsmen who had been discharged should have the right of sitting in the first fourteen rows of the theatre reserved for equestrians, asking him as if he were present in person what business *he* had to do with the soldiers, who were entitled to receive their commands and their rewards from no one but the emperor. He had certainly discovered something which the divine Augustus had not foreseen. Or was he an agent of Sejanus seeking to encourage dissension and rebellion by inducing inexperienced minds to overturn military discipline by the offer of privileges?

Sejanus was Tiberius' powerful praetorian prefect, executed in AD 31. Although Tiberius encouraged the senators to play their part in discussing affairs of state (in AD 14 he had stated that the soldiers belonged not to him but the state – Dio 57. 2), it was wise for them to avoid the politically sensitive area of the emperor's relationship with his troops. It is significant that Augustus had written out in his own hand a memorandum for Tiberius, which included the numbers of legions and auxilia in the army, naval units, information on the provinces and client kingdoms, and details of taxation and income (*Annals*, 1. 11).

305 (a) *BMC* 1, p. 165, no. 5 = Smallwood *GN* 36(a), *aureus*, Rome, AD 41–2 (see Plate 12)

Obverse. Head of Claudius, laureate.

TIBERIUS CLAUDIUS CAESAR AUGUSTUS, CHIEF PRIEST, TRIBUNICIAN POWER.

Reverse. The praetorian camp, depicted by a wall with battlements, arched entrances, and two columns supporting a pediment, with a soldier standing on guard.

THE EMPEROR WELCOMED.

305 (b) *BMC* 1, p. 166, no. 8 = Smallwood *GN* 36(b), *aureus*, Rome, AD 41–2

Obverse. As (a)

Reverse. Claudius, clad in toga, shaking hands with a praetorian.

THE PRAETORIANS WELCOMED.

After Gaius had been murdered on 24 January AD 41, the senate met but could not agree what to do next. Those who had plotted against Gaius had different motives; a few perhaps wanted a republic, many more will have favoured the choice of a new emperor from outside the Julio-Claudian family, others will have supported the claims of Gaius' uncle, Claudius. But Claudius had been conveyed to the praetorian barracks where he negotiated for the crucial support of the guardsmen. After he had received an ineffectual deputation from the senate, Claudius addressed the praetorians, promised a donative, and was saluted as *imperator*. At a second meeting the senate now acquiesced in a situation that it could not change. The soldiers probably reckoned that a member of the Julio-Claudian family was best for their interests since that family was well-known to them, had ensured their pay and benefits, and would be certain to keep the guard in existence. Although it is an over-simplification to say that the praetorians made Claudius emperor, it is true that their support was more obviously important than before. The donative he paid was enormous, probably 15,000 sesterces each, with a payment to the legionaries in proportion, and the first coins minted with the type illustrated above may well have been used in this donative. They are so unusual, with their clear emphasis on comradely spirit and mutual support of emperor and soldier, that Claudius himself may have been directly responsible for their design. They celebrate an association between emperor and soldiers that Augustus had been at pains to conceal (for Claudius' accession, see Levick 1990: 29–39; donatives – Campbell 1984: 165–72; 182–90).

306 Dio, 60. 15

(The aftermath of the collapse of the revolt of Scribonianus, governor of Dalmatia.) Then he (Claudius) rewarded the soldiers in various ways, and in particular arranged for the citizen troops, legions seven and eleven, to be voted by the senate the titles: Claudian, Faithful, and Loyal.

For the grant of honorary titles to legions, see Campbell 1984: 88–93; from the reign of Caracalla, who especially emphasized his relationship with the troops, all units took the name of the reigning emperor.

307 Tacitus, *Annals* 12. 69

Then, at midday on 13 October, the gates of the palace were suddenly opened and Nero accompanied by Burrus emerged to the cohort of the praetorians which according to military practice was on guard duty. At a word from the commanding officer he was greeted with a welcoming cheer and placed in a litter. It is reported that some men, looking round and hesitating, asked where Britannicus (Claudius' son) was; but since no one raised any objections, they accepted what was offered to them. Nero was conveyed into the camp, said a few words that suited the occasion, promised a donative on the scale of his father's generosity, and was saluted as emperor. The decision of the soldiers was followed by a decree of the senate, and there was no hesitation in the provinces.

The support of the troops, or of those whose strength could immediately be brought to bear, was more important than the approval of the senate, and could influence other troops and their leaders. A man who could not command the undivided support of the praetorians could hardly inspire confidence in his capacity to rule. It became more difficult to arrange things so that this was done discreetly, since the accessions of Claudius and Nero highlighted the practical, overwhelming power of the army. But the support of the senate, expressed in its decree, was not negligible, and later Nero could speak of the 'authority of the senators' and the 'agreement of the soldiers' (*Annals*, 13. 4).

308 Tacitus, *Histories* 1. 4

The death of Nero had been greeted at first with a wave of delight, but it had also stirred up different emotions not only in Rome among the senators, the people, and the soldiers in the capital, but also among all the legions and their commanders, since a secret of empire had been revealed – an emperor could be created outside Rome.

The civil wars of AD 68–69 brought an abrupt end to the long-established Julio-Claudian dynasty. For nearly one hundred years the succession had been regulated inside the imperial family with the help of the praetorian guard. The success of the governor of Spain, Sulpicius Galba, in seizing power in 68, brought the legionaries in the provinces dramatically to the forefront, demonstrated the helplessness of the senate and the inadequacy of the praetorians as a defence against an invasion of Italy by a provincial army, and substantially reduced the influence of the guard until the reign of Commodus. The example set by Galba was immediately followed by Vitellius, and then by Vespasian, who was to place the day of his assumption of power on 1 July AD 69, the day on which he had been acclaimed by the troops in Egypt, rather than on the day in late December AD 69, when his powers were formally voted by the senate (for the civil wars and the role of the army, see Campbell 1984: 365–74).

309 Dio, 64. 9

People hated him (Otho) especially because he had revealed that the position of emperor could be bought, and had put Rome in thrall to the most audacious men; moreover, he placed no value on the senate and people and had indeed persuaded the soldiers that they could both kill and create an emperor.

310 *SB* 10295, with Bowman 1970, papyrus, Oxyrhynchus, AD 175 (?)

Alexandrians [_ _ _] you carry goodwill towards me [_ _ _] in your hearts and remain steadfast in your opinions. I am [therefore] coming to you with good fortune, since having been chosen emperor by the most noble soldiers, it is among you that I shall auspiciously take up my rule,

and starting from you most of all to use my power to grant benefits, as far as is right to make provision for my native city, I [have made provision _ _ _] year, 1 Pharmuthi.
(Rear) To Apolinarios, councillor and ambassador (?)

Bowman argues that this fragmentary text is part of a letter written by Avidius Cassius, who, as governor of Syria, raised a rebellion against Marcus Aurelius in 175. The mention of Alexandria as his native city will then refer to the fact that his father had been prefect of Egypt. Whoever is the author, it is significant that he mentions his choice by the soldiers first, seemingly as the most important and possibly the only justification for his rule (for this interpretation, see Campbell 1984: 375–6).

An emperor under threat from revolt had to rally his troops and allay their fears and suspicions. One way to do this was to speak to the soldiers at hand in a formal *adlocutio*, which according to literary re-creations followed a general pattern: inform the troops of the situation; criticize the motives and character of the rebels; depreciate opposing military forces; adopt the moral high ground by representing the struggle to be on behalf of the whole Roman empire (Campbell 1984: 85–8).

311 Dio, 74. 11

When the news of Pertinax's fate had been spread abroad, some people ran to their houses, others to the soldiers' barracks, all of them looking out for their own safety. But Sulpicianus (father-in-law of Pertinax), since he happened to have been sent by Pertinax to the praetorian barracks to calm things down there, remained in it and intrigued for his proclamation as emperor. Meanwhile Didius Julianus, a greedy money-maker and extravagant spendthrift, who was always eager for political disorder and consequently had been exiled by Commodus to his home community of Milan, hearing about the death of Pertinax, hurried to the barracks, and standing at the gates of the wall, called out bids to the soldiers for the right to rule over the Romans. There then occurred a shameful incident that dishonoured Rome. For both the city and all its empire were auctioned off just as if they were in a market place or some auction-room. The dealers were men who had murdered their own emperor, the buyers were Sulpicianus and Julianus, who bid against each other, one from inside, the other from outside. They went on gradually raising their bids to 20,000 sesterces per man. Some soldiers would give the message to Julianus: 'Sulpicianus is offering so much. How much more are you going to add to this?' And to Sulpicianus some would say: 'Julianus is bidding so much. What do you promise in addition?' Sulpicianus would have won since he was inside and was also prefect of the city, and furthermore was the first to name a figure of twenty thousand sesterces, if Julianus had not stopped raising his bids by a small amount but instead offered 5,000 sesterces extra, shouting the amount out in a loud voice and also indicating it with his fingers. The soldiers, won over by the excessive size of this bid and also worried in case Sulpicianus might intend to avenge Pertinax, an idea which Julianus had planted in their minds, received Julianus into the barracks and proclaimed him emperor.

Cf. Herodian, 2. 6. Pertinax had won the support of the senate but he was deeply unpopular with the praetorians because, having restrained their behaviour in Rome, he had fraudulently claimed to have given them as large a donative as Marcus Aurelius. On 28 March 193 he was murdered by the praetorians, the first emperor to be overthrown because of purely military discontent because he could not satisfy the demands of his troops. Dio was clearly outraged by the sequel, the 'auction' of the empire, which does indeed show a want of discipline and respect among the praetorians, who had been excessively indulged by Commodus. But it was the willingness of two senators to bid for the purple which made this scene possible. The rule of Julianus had little chance of stability, based as it was upon such open bribery of a praetorian guard which was now thoroughly discredited, and the fate of the empire was to be decided by the commanders of the armies in the provinces.

312 Dio, 75. 2

But he himself (Septimius Severus) was the first to break this law (not to execute senators) and he did not maintain it, executing many. Indeed Julius Solon, the very man who, on his instructions, had drawn up this decree, was executed not long afterwards. Severus did many things which did not win our approval, and he was blamed for making Rome unpleasant because of the large numbers of soldiers in it, for burdening the state with excessive financial expenditure, and most importantly, for basing hopes for his security on the strength of his army rather than on the support of those around him. Some people particularly criticized him because he ended the practice of recruiting the praetorians exclusively from Italy, Spain, Macedonia, and Noricum, which produced men of more respectable appearance and reasonably decent character, and ordered that any vacancies should be filled from all the legions equally. His intention was in this way to have bodyguards who were more skilled in the military arts, and moreover to grant a kind of prize for those who distinguished themselves in war. In reality, the facts clearly show that he incidentally ruined the young men of Italy by turning them towards brigandage and a gladiatorial career rather than the military service which they had engaged in before. Furthermore, he filled the city with a mixed mob of soldiers who were ferocious to look at, terrifying to hear, and coarse in conversation.

In AD 193 Septimius Severus, the governor of Upper Pannonia, marched on Rome with his army (the first such successful coup for almost 125 years), and in a bitter civil war defeated Pescennius Niger, governor of Syria. Soon afterwards conflict was renewed, this time against Clodius Albinus, governor of Britain, and not until AD 197 was Severus in unchallenged control. Dio's judgement of these events is especially important since he was a contemporary who lived almost to the end of the dynasty. Although Dio is critical of Severus, he admits that he had some good qualities and does not present him as an exponent of military absolutism (for Dio's history of Septimius Severus, see Millar 1964: 138–50). Significantly, he believed that because of the circumstances of his accession Severus was forced to rely more openly on his army and therefore paid less attention to the other groups on which to some extent imperial government depended, in particular the senate and individual senators. These events were changing the principle established by Augustus that the military leader should not appear to be at the mercy of his troops.

Severus invaded Italy in AD 193 with the support initially of the legions in Pannonia. After seizing Rome he disbanded the praetorian guard; it had been disloyal, betraying and murdering two emperors, and he needed to set an example; he also needed to reward his own troops – most of the new guard was recruited from the Danubian legions (see texts nos 64–66). Indeed, before he could leave Rome, his legionaries demanded 10,000 sesterces, the sum paid to his troops by Octavian in 43 BC (Dio, 46. 46). In the event they were satisfied with 1,000 sesterces as a down payment. This was part of the price of the army's support in his bid for political supremacy, although Dio's comments reflect the exaggerated reaction of senators who disliked Severus for other reasons, and also his dislike of the ordinary soldiers (the Severan dynasty – Campbell 1984: 401–14; texts nos 313–17).

313 Dio, 76. 15

At any rate, before he (Septimius Severus) died, he is reported to have made the following comments to his sons, and I give his exact words with no adornment: 'Stick together, make the soldiers rich, despise all the rest'.

314 Herodian (2nd-3rd C.AD), 2. 6

Then for the first time (after the murder of Pertinax in AD 193) the character of the soldiers was corrupted and they learned to have a disgraceful and unbounded craving for money, while despising any feelings of respect for their emperors. Since there was no one to take any action against the soldiers who had cold-bloodedly murdered an emperor, or to prevent the outrageous auction and sale of the imperial power, this was a major reason for the disgraceful state of disobedience that was to persist in the years to come. The soldiers' steadily increasing lust for money and contempt for their leaders had culminated in the shedding of blood.

Herodian was probably writing in the first half of the third century AD, and had held some public offices, though it is not clear if he was of senatorial or equestrian rank. He is incorrect in asserting that this was the first time the soldiers were bribed, since in a sense this had been true since the time of Augustus, and of course Claudius had paid a huge donative to the praetorians. But he is right to emphasize that to induce soldiers to break their military oath created a bad example and made it more difficult to guard against military anarchy.

315 Petrus Patricius, *Exc. Vat.* 152 (excerpt from Dio's history – Loeb Dio, vol. 9, p. 470)

The False Antoninus (Elagabalus – AD 218–22) was despised and killed by the soldiers. For when people, especially if armed, have got used to despising their rulers, they place no limit on their power to do whatever they like, but keep their weapons to use against the very person who gave them this power.

316 Dio, 80. 2

Ulpian (praetorian prefect) corrected many of the wrongs perpetrated by Sardanapalus (another name for Elagabalus), but after he had killed Flavianus and Chrestus so that he could succeed to their position, he himself was murdered not long afterwards by the praetorians, who attacked him during the night, even though he fled to the palace and took refuge with the emperor himself (Severus Alexander) and his mother. Indeed, even while he was alive, there was a substantial disturbance between the people and the praetorians which arose from some small cause and which resulted in a battle between them lasting three days with many dead on both sides. Since the soldiers were coming off worse, they turned their attention to setting fire to buildings, and for this reason the people, fearing that the entire city might be destroyed, reluctantly came to an agreement with them. In addition to these incidents, Epagathus, who was considered to be mainly responsible for the murder of Ulpian, was sent to Egypt, to all appearances as governor but in reality to avoid any disturbance in Rome if he were to be punished there; he was then removed from Egypt to Crete where he was executed.

There is alarming evidence that Severus Alexander failed to establish discipline and respect in the army during his reign. After the incident described above the praetorian guard was ready to attack Dio himself because he had reportedly enforced strict discipline in Pannonia; the emperor had to request him to spend his second consulship outside Rome. Moreover, revolts and low morale persisted in the provincial armies. Severus Alexander, who had become emperor through military coup, failed to master the problems caused by soldiers who expected more from their emperor than ever before, in respect both of financial rewards, and also of effective military leadership. So, when Maximinus plotted against Alexander, he could appeal to his own tough military bearing in contrast to the emperor's incapacity as a leader of the army, as well as his parsimony.

317 Herodian, 6. 9

(Severus Alexander tries to rally his men) But some demanded the execution of the military prefect and Alexander's confidants, arguing that they had been responsible for the retreat. Others criticized his mother for her greed and miserliness; because of this parsimony and a reluctance to distribute donatives, Alexander was detested. So, the soldiers stayed where they were for a time shouting out different complaints. But the army of Maximinus was already in sight, and the young recruits called out to their comrades to desert a miserly little sissy and cowardly little boy who was a slave of his mother, and join a man who was courageous and moderate, always their fellow-soldier in battle, and devoted to the military arts. The soldiers were won over, abandoned Alexander and went over to Maximinus, who was acclaimed emperor by everyone.

318 Epictetus (1st-2nd C.AD), *Discourses* 4. 13. 5

Moreover, we think that we can safely trust the person who has already confided his business to us. For we feel that he would never reveal our business because of a fear that we would reveal his. This is how reckless people are caught by soldiers in Rome. A soldier in civilian dress sits down next to you and starts to revile the emperor; then since you have a kind of security from him of his good faith since he began the abuse, you speak your mind and are immediately hauled off to prison.

This is the view of one contemporary source (Epictetus was probably referring to circumstances in Rome in the time of Domitian) that the army was inextricably linked with the political well-being of the emperor, and although this is the only explicit reference to the use of soldiers in this sinister way, we may compare the case of Votienus Montanus, prosecuted in 25 for speaking abusively of Tiberius, where a soldier was one of the witnesses (Tac., *Annals* 4. 42).

319 *CIL* 5. 938 = *ILS* 2905, inscription, near Aquileia

Lucius Trebius, son of Titus, father   Lucius Trebius Ruso, son of Lucius, ordered this to be set up

I was born in the depths of poverty, then I served as a sailor in the fleet by the side of the Emperor (Augustus) for seventeen years without causing any ill-feeling or giving any offence, and was honourably discharged.

This place is sixteen feet square.

The army's political role was based on the personal association of troops and emperor, and here in the case of one ordinary sailor (whose sentiments are unlikely to be different from those of many soldiers), we get a simple and very illuminating view of that relationship. Starr (1960: 28, n. 37) argues that 'Augustus' mentioned here refers specifically to Augustus himself.

8 Veterans

DISCHARGE AND BENEFITS

By decision of Augustus the Roman state had accepted responsibility for veterans' superannuation, paid either in cash or as a plot of land, which might be allocated individually or as part of an organized military colony. It seems unlikely that these rewards can have been confined to praetorians and legionaries, as the number and significance of the auxiliaries increased. In any event, all veterans could look forward to a relatively privileged status in comparison with the rest of the lower classes, since they were exempt from certain taxes and personal services and immune from some punishments. Furthermore, there were benefits that came with long and satisfactory service and eventually with honourable discharge itself. Auxiliaries and sailors received citizenship for themselves and existing children, and also the right of marriage (*conubium*) with one woman, even if non-Roman, which, although it did not make the wife a citizen, meant that future children would be citizens. Praetorians also received the right of *conubium*; for discussion of other difficulties in the position of praetorians and legionaries, see texts nos 328–9 and 341.

The evidence for much of this is contained on small bronze folding tablets, described by modern scholars as diplomas or diplomata, which from the second century onwards contained a copy of the imperial authorization of the discharge of soldiers from various auxiliary units in a province, stating: the name of the emperor, the military units concerned, their location, their commanding officer, a definition of the privileges conferred, the date, the name of the individual soldier, the location of the master copy in Rome, and a list of witnesses to the diploma's accurate transcription.

Diplomas were first issued probably by Claudius to individual auxiliaries to show that they had been granted the benefit of citizenship (a traditional prize for those who provided sterling military service for Rome) even though they were still serving in the army. Later, diplomas were issued both to serving soldiers and to veterans, and from Trajan's reign onwards only to veterans since all soldiers now received their benefits only on the completion of service (unless they performed particularly creditably – text no. 326). However, although diplomas were issued to praetorians and urban soldiers at least from Vespasian's reign, the evidence suggests that legionaries did not normally receive them (text no. 329), and it is possible that not all praetorian and auxiliary veterans received them, but only those who made a specific request or had a special need, and that they had to pay for their issue themselves. Perhaps they intended to settle in an area distant from the base of their original unit and needed clear proof of their status; or, in the case of praetorians, veterans requiring a diploma may have intended to settle where they were likely to marry a non-Roman woman.

Diplomas provide important evidence not only for the record of individual soldiers but also for the organization of the Roman army, recruitment and settlement patterns, the history and location of auxiliary units, and the tenure of provincial governorships (*CIL* 16 and supplement; Mann 1972; Mann and Roxan 1988; Roxan 1978; 1981; 1985; 1986; Eck and Wolff 1986).

320 Augustus, *Res Gestae* 3. 3

There were about five hundred thousand Roman citizens who swore the military oath to me. Rather more than three hundred thousand of these I settled in colonies or sent them back to their home towns when they had completed their service, and to all of them I allocated land or granted money as a reward for their military service.

See also texts nos 18–19 for Augustan expenditure on discharged soldiers, and the establishment of the military treasury.

321 *ILS* 9060, with Mann and Roxan 1988, tablet, Fayum, Egypt, AD 122

In the consulship of Manius (?) Acilius Aviola and Pansa, on 4 January, Titus Haterius Nepos, prefect of Egypt, granted honourable discharge on the completion of his military service to Lucius Valerius Noster, cavalryman óf the *ala* of Vocontians, troop of Gavius.

(Second hand) I have read everything written above, and I have granted honourable discharge, 4 January.

This wooden tablet was perhaps intended as a simple statement of discharge, enabling a soldier to prove that he was a *bona fide* veteran; or it may have been a temporary proof of veteran status until Noster received a bronze diploma. It is difficult to speculate further since we cannot know if any special circumstances attached to this case. Cf. texts nos. 329–30.

322 *ILS* 1986 = Smallwood *GN* 295, diploma, Stabiae, AD 52

Tiberius Claudius Caesar Augustus Germanicus, chief priest, in the twelfth year of his tribunician power, acclaimed *imperator* twenty-seven times, father of the fatherland, censor, consul for the fifth time, has granted to the trierarchs and oarsmen who served in the fleet which is at Misenum under the command of Tiberius Julius Optatus, freedman of the Emperor, and who were honourably discharged, and whose names are written below, to them, their children, and their posterity, citizenship and the right of marriage (*conubium*) with the wives they had when citizenship was granted to them, or, if they were unmarried, with those whom they married afterwards, limited to one wife for each man.

11 December in the consulship of Faustus Cornelius Sulla Felix and Lucius Salvidienus Rufus Salvianus.

To the common sailor Sparticus Dipscurtus, son of Diuzenus, a Bessian.

Recorded and authenticated from the bronze plaque which has been affixed at Rome on the Capitoline, on the righthand side of the temple of the Faith of the Roman people.

(Witnesses) Lucius Mestius Priscus, son of Lucius, of the tribe Aemilia, from Dyrrhachium, Lucius Nutrius Venustus, from Dyrrhachium, Gaius Durrachinus Anthus, from Dyrrhachium, Gaius Sabinius Nedymus, from Dyrrhachium, Gaius Cornelius Ampliatus, from Dyrrhachium, Titus Pomponius Epaphroditus, from Dyrrhachium, Numerius Minius Hylas, from Thessalonice.

This diploma, which refers to sailors of the fleet, who had the same kind of benefits as auxiliaries, is the earliest known example. Claudius, who had a reputation for generosity in extending citizenship, probably turned what had been a concession to individuals or small groups, into a regular part of the conditions of military service.

323 Dušanić, 1978 = Roxan 1985: 79, diploma, Negoslavci, Pannonia, AD 65 (Plates 13 and 14)

Nero Claudius Caesar Augustus Germanicus, son of the divine Claudius, grandson of Germanicus Caesar, great-grandson of Tiberius Caesar Augustus, great-great grandson of the divine Augustus, chief priest, in the eleventh year of his tribuncian power, acclaimed *imperator* nine times, father of the fatherland, consul for the fourth time, has granted to the infantrymen and cavalrymen who are serving in the three cohorts which are called (1) first and (2) second Thracians and (3) seventh Breucians, and are in Germany under the command of Publius Sulpicius Scribonius Proculus, and who have served twenty-five or more years, and whose names are written below, to them, their children, and their posterity, citizenship and the right of marriage (*conubium*) with the wives they had when citizenship was given to them, or, if they were unmarried, with those whom they married afterwards, limited to one wife for each man.

17 June in the consulship of Aulus Licinius Nerva Silianus and Publius Pasidienus Firmus.

To infantryman of the seventh cohort of Breucians which is commanded by Gaius Numisius Maximus, son of Gaius, of the tribe Velina, Liccaius, son of Liccaius, a Breucian.

Recorded and authenticated from the bronze plaque which is affixed at Rome on the Capitoline in front of the military treasury on the base of the monument of the Claudii Marcelli.

(Witnesses) Gaius Marcius Nobilis, from Emona, Sextus Teius Niceros, from Aquileia, Gaius Caecina Hermes, from Aquileia, Titus Picatius Carpus, from Aquileia, Lucius Hostilius Blaesus, from Emona, Marcus Trebonius Hyginus, from Aquileia, Lucius Annius Potens, from Aquileia.

The wording of this diploma shows that these soldiers were still in service when they received their rewards (cf. text no. 324).

324 *ILS* 9054 = Smallwood *NH* 343, diploma, Siscia, Upper Pannonia, AD 100

Emperor Caesar Nerva Trajan Augustus, Conqueror of the Germans, son of the divine Nerva, chief priest, in the fourth year of his tribunician power, father of the fatherland, consul for the third time, has granted to the cavalrymen and infantrymen who are serving in the three *alae* and twenty-one cohorts, which are called (1) first praetorian, and (2) first Claudian New, and (3) second Pannonians; and (1) first Flavian Bessians, and (2) first Thracians, Roman citizens, and (3) first Flavian milliary Spanish, and (4) first Antiochenses, and (5) first Lusitanians, and (6) first Montani, Roman citizens, and (7) first Cisipadians, and (8) first Cretans, and (9) first milliary Vindelici, Roman citizens, and (10) first Syrian Thracians, and (11) first Cilicians, and (12) second Spanish, and (13) second Macedonian Gauls, and (14) second milliary Britons, Roman citizens, Loyal and Faithful, and (15) second Flavian Commagenians, and (16) third Britons, and (17) fourth Raetians, and (18) fifth Gauls, and (19) fifth Spanish, and (20) sixth Thracians, and (21) seventh Breucians, Roman citizens, which are in Upper Moesia under the command of Gaius Cilnius Proculus, and who have been honourably discharged having completed twenty-five or more years' service, and whose names are written below, to them, their children, and their posterity, citizenship and the right of marriage (*conubium*) with the wives they had when citizenship was given to them, or, if they were unmarried, with those whom they married afterwards, limited to one wife for each man.

8 May, in the consulship of Titus Pomponius Mamilianus and Lucius Herennius Saturninus.

Of the first cohort of Antiochenses which is commanded by Marcus Calpurnius Sabinus, to infantryman Sapia Anazarbus, son of Sarmosus.

Recorded and authenticated from the bronze plaque which is affixed at Rome on the wall behind the temple of the divine Augustus at the statue (?) of Minerva.

(Witnesses) Quintus Pompeius Homerus, Aulus Ampius Epaphroditus, Tiberius Claudius Vitalis, Gaius Julius Aprilis, Gaius Vettienus Modestus, Lucius Pullius Verecundus, Lucius Pullius Speratus.

325 Roxan 1985: 102, diploma, Lussonium (Dunakömlöd), Lower Pannonia, AD 157 (Plates 15, 16, 17 and 18)

Emperor Caesar Titus Aelius Hadrian Antoninus Augustus Pius, son of the divine Hadrian, grandson of the divine Trajan, Conqueror of the Parthians, great-grandson of the divine Nerva, chief priest, in the nineteenth year of his tribunician power, acclaimed *imperator* twice, consul for the fourth time, father of the fatherland, has given to the cavalrymen and infantrymen who served in five *alae*, which are called (1) first Thracian veteran archers, and (2) first Roman citizens, and (3) first praetorian, Roman citizens, and (4) first Flavian Augustan milliary British, and (5) first Augustan Ituraeans; and thirteen cohorts, (1) first Alpine part-mounted, and (2) third Batavians, and (3) first German Thracians, and (4) first Alpine infantry, and (5) first Noricans, and (6) third Lusitanians, and (7) second Asturians and Callaeci, and (8) seventh Breucians, and (9) first Lusitanians, and (10) second Augustan Thracians, and (11) first Montani, and (12) first Campanian volunteers, and (13) first Thracians, Roman citizens, which are in Lower Pannonia under the command of Iallius Bassus, legate, and who have been honourably discharged having completed twenty-five years' service, and also members of the fleet who have completed twenty-six years' service, and whose names are written below, the Roman citizenship for those of them who did not have it, and the right of marriage (*conubium*) with the wives they had when citizenship was given to them, or, with those whom they married afterwards, limited to one wife for each man.

8 February in the consulship of Marcus Civica Barbarus and Marcus Metilius Regulus.

Of the first German cohort of Thracians which is commanded by Gaius Turpilius Verecundus, from among the infantrymen, to Monnus, son of Tessimarus, from the Eravisci, and to Nicia, daughter of Tricanus, his wife, from Canac[_ _ _]

Recorded and authenticated from the bronze plaque which is affixed at Rome on the wall behind the temple of the divine Augustus at the statue (?) of Minerva.

(Witnesses) Marcus Servilius Geta, Lucius Pullius Chresimus, Marcus Sentilius Jasus, Tiberius Julius Felix, Gaius Bellius Urbanus, Gaius Pomponius Statianus, Publius Ocilius Priscus.

This diploma illustrates the change in formula which was introduced around November–December 140 and which restricted the discharge benefits of the auxilia so that only children born after military service were granted citizenship, that is, the grant ceased to apply retrospectively to existing children, as provided for in texts nos. 322–24. The motive for this has been much debated but remains obscure. It may be that the government wished to bring the auxilia into line with the citizen troops, who, it is usually argued, did not receive retrospective citizenship for existing children. Since more citizens now were choosing to serve in auxiliary units, this anomaly was more obvious. It is by no means certain that the citizen troops were less privileged in this respect (see below, text no. 341). But even if this is true, it does not explain why the problem was resolved by a restriction in benefits. The purpose may have been to encourage more sons of soldiers to enlist in the army in the expectation of gaining Roman citizenship. A further suggestion is that the concessions made to soldiers by Trajan and Hadrian (above p. 157) in respect of the liaisons they formed during service, were likely to have encouraged cohabitation and the production of illegitimate offspring with their troublesome legal consequences. Antoninus Pius could have decided to legalize military marriages, but that perhaps seemed too extreme at this stage, and instead he attempted to discourage such liaisons. No similar restrictions were placed on sailors, who were less numerous, though by 166 the formula on their diplomas had been altered and now referred to a grant of citizenship to them, and their children born to women whom they proved to have lived with them in accordance with 'the permitted custom'

(*CIL* 16. 122 – AD 166). This phrase cannot mean legal marriage and must refer to the practice by which the government turned a blind eye to liaisons formed by soldiers during service, while denying them the consequences of a legal marriage. These diplomas were now worded more explicitly possibly because questions had been raised about the status of children of veterans of the fleet as a conseqence of the restriction placed on similar benefits for auxiliaries (Campbell 1978: 163–5; 1984: 439–45; Roxan 1986; Link 1989).

326 *CIL* 16. 160 = Smallwood *NH* 344, diploma, Porolissum, Dacia, AD 106

Emperor Caesar Nerva Trajan Augustus, Conqueror of the Germans, Conqueror of the Dacians, son of the divine Nerva, chief priest, in the fourteenth year of his tribunician power, acclaimed *imperator* six times, consul for the fifth time, father of the fatherland, has granted Roman citizenship before they have completed military service to the infantry-men and cavalrymen who are serving in the first milliary Ulpian Decorated Loyal and Faithful cohort of Britons, Roman citizens, which is in Dacia under the command of Decimus Terentius Scaurianus, and whose names are written below, because they performed dutifully and loyally in the Dacian campaign.

11 August, at Darnithithis, in the consulship of Lucius Minicius Natalis and Quintus Silvanus Granianus.

To infantryman Marcus Ulpius Novantico, son of Adcobrovatus, from Leicester (Ratae).

Recorded and authenticated from the bronze plaque which is affixed at Rome on the wall behind the temple of the divine Augustus near the statue (?) of Minerva.

(Witnesses) Publius Cornelius Alexander, Lucius Pullius Verecundus, Publius Atinius Amerimnus, Gaius Tuticanius Saturninus, Lucius Pullius Trophimus, Gaius Julius Paratus, Marcus Junius Eutychus.

This soldier was granted the privilege of citizenship before the completion of service because of his distinguished service in the Dacian War. Novantico apparently settled where he had been serving in Dacia, the findspot of the diploma. Mann (1972: 237), points out that although citizenship was granted in 106, the diploma was not issued until 110.

327 *ILS* 1993 = *MW* 400, diploma, Tomi (Constanţa), Lower Moesia, AD 76

I, Emperor Caesar Vespasian Augustus, chief priest, in the eighth year of my tribunician power, acclaimed *imperator* eighteen times, father of the fatherland, censor, consul for the seventh time, designated for an eighth, have appended the names of the special bodyguards (*speculatores*) who served in my praetorian guard, and also of the soldiers who served in the nine praetorian and four urban cohorts, to whom, as they have courageously and loyally performed their military service, I grant the right of marriage (*conubium*), with one wife and the first one only, so that, even if they unite in marriage with women of non-Roman status, they may raise their children just as if they have been born from two Roman citizens.

2 December in the consulship of Galeo Tettienus Petronianus and Marcus Fulvius Gillo.

Sixth praetorian cohort: to Lucius Ennius Ferox, son of Lucius, of the tribe Tromentina, from Aquae Statiellae (Acqui in Liguria).

Recorded and authenticated from the bronze plaque, which is affixed at Rome on the Capitoline on the base of the statue of Jupiter of Africa.

The wording of praetorian diplomas is significantly different from the others. First, the emperor is in personal charge; there is no mention of the praetorian prefects or any other subordinate officer. Second, he uses the first person throughout in contrast to other diplomas, where the third person is employed. Third, an honorific phrase referring to courageous and loyal service is added. Emperors found it expedient to emphasize their especially close personal association with their bodyguard.

328 Roxan 1985: 132, diploma, Butovo, near Nicopolis ad Istrum, Lower Moesia, AD 228

I, Emperor Caesar Marcus Aurellius Severus Alexander Pius Fortunate Augustus, son of the divine Antoninus Magnus Pius, grandson of the divine Severus Pius, chief priest, in the seventh year of my tribunician power, consul for the second time, father of the fatherland, in respect of the soldiers whose names are listed who served in the ten Severan praetorian cohorts, I, II, III, IV, V, VI, VII, VIII, VIIII, X, Loyal and Avenging, and who have courageously and loyally performed their military service, grant the right of marriage (*conubium*) with one wife and the first one only, so that, even if they unite in marriage with women of non-Roman status, they may raise their children just as if they have been born from two Roman citizens.

7 January in the consulship of Quintus Aiacius Modestus for the second time and Marcus Maecius Probus.

First Severan praetorian cohort Loyal and Avenging: to Marcus Aurelius Secundus, son of Marcus, of the tribe Ulpia, from Nicopolis.

Recorded and authenticated from the bronze plaque which is affixed at Rome on the wall behind the temple of the divine Augustus at the statue (?) of Minerva.

After discharge Secundus returned to his home town, Nicopolis ad Istrum, founded by Trajan, which explains his irregular tribe name, Ulpia. This town originally was part of Thrace but around AD 197 had been transferred by Septimius Severus to Lower Moesia for administrative purposes.

All praetorians were of course Roman citizens and therefore did not require a grant of citizenship. The diplomas appear to suggest, however, that they were less privileged than veterans of the fleet and the auxilia, in that they received citizenship only for children born after discharge. Yet this seems improbable since the praetorian guard was the most privileged section of the army, and emperors were especially keen to keep its goodwill. Now, it is unlikely that there was any attempt at one moment to work out systematically all the rules of discharge and benefits. Therefore at the start the government perhaps assumed that most praetorians would associate with Italian women, who were likely to be Roman citizens (especially when the guard was stationed in small Italian towns), and that children of such unions would be citizens, even if not legitimate. This attitude was then modified as problems arose, and in my view an ambiguous form of wording was employed on the diplomas, which could be taken as meaning that all children of praetorians were to be Roman citizens. So, in my translation 'tollant' in the original is expressed as 'raise' rather than 'beget', since the latter would make explicit that only children born after discharge could be citizens (Campbell 1984: 439–45; exhaustive discussion in Link 1989).

329 *P.S.I.* 1026 = Smallwood *NH* 330, papyrus, Caesarea, Syria Palaestina, AD 150

Recorded and authenticated from the petition published along with others in the portico of Junia [_ _ _], in which was written the text which is written out below.

To Vilius Cadus, legate of the Emperor with propraetorian power, from twenty-two veterans of Legion X Fretensis who began their military service in the consulship of Glabrio and Torquatus or in the consulship of Paulinus and Aquilinus (AD 124 and 125), and whose names are listed below. Since, sir, we served in the praetorian fleet at Misenum and then, after transfer to the Fretensis Legion through the generosity of the divine Hadrian, conducted ourselves over twenty [years] in every respect as good soldiers should, now indeed in these most felicitous times we have been discharged from our military oath and, as we are about to return to Egypt, to our native city of Alexandria, we ask and request that you should think it appropriate to affirm for us that we have been discharged by you, in order that it may be obvious from your affirmation that we have been discharged from this very legion, not from the fleet, so that your endorsement (*subscriptio* – a response to the petition written at the end) may serve us as written evidence (*instrumentum*) if circumstances demand, and so that we may be eternally grateful to your compassion.

(The names and centuries of twenty-two veterans follow.)

I, Lucius Petronius Saturninus, presented (this petition) on behalf of myself and my fellow-veterans. I, Pomponius, wrote it. Endorsement: Veterans from the legions do not usually receive a written document (*instrumentum*). However you wish it to be made known to the prefect of Egypt that you have been discharged from you military oath by me on the orders of our emperor. I shall give you your bonus and a written document. [Publish this?]. Executed in the First Flavian Colony of Caesarea, 22 January, in the consulship of Squilla Gallicanus and Carminius Vetus.

These Egyptian soldiers had begun service as non-citizen sailors in the fleet at Misenum; at some date between AD 125 and 138 they were transferred to the X Fretensis, based at Jerusalem, which had presumably suffered heavy casualties during the Jewish revolt. At this point they will have become citizens. They were anxious, therefore, to confirm their citizenship through their status as legionary veterans. It is clear from this text that legionaries did not normally receive diplomata or official certificates of discharge, even if they asked for them (see Mann and Roxan 1988; text no. 321 above). Cadus grants only an informal *instrumentum*, in the sense of a simple statement that he was discharging these legionaries and making this known to the Prefect of Egypt. Of course it need not follow that legionaries were denied privileges of citizenship for their children similar to those granted to other troops. It is indeed unclear how emperors could give fewer privileges to legionaries than to auxiliaries, since the situation was bound to be obvious to the troops. In the early period the government perhaps reckoned that no concessions were needed for legionaries since they were already citizens and, being forbidden to marry, should not have had children. So, diplomata were not available to them. This rule was not applied to auxiliaries, who were more informally organized and in any event might require proof of grants of personal citizenship. In the case of praetorians who needed proof of their privileges, diplomata were granted largely as a mark of honour. Subsequently, citizenship may have been informally granted to legionaries' children (see text no. 341), even though no diplomata were issued.

330 *P. Hamb.* 31 = Daris, *Documenti* 90, papyrus, Fayum, Egypt, AD 103

Extract from the volume of certifications of status (*epikrisis*) by the then prefect, Vibius Maximus. Certifications of status by Vibius Maximus in

year 7 of the divine Trajan, month Hathyr, [through] the tribune [_ _ _
son of] Proclus. [_ _ _] page twenty-seven: Lucius Cornelius [Antas]
who wishes to live in the Arsinoite nome, with his [wife] and children,
Heraclides – years, Crispina – years, and Ammonarion – years. The
above-mentioned Antas displayed a bronze tablet, a copy of which is set
out here, by means of which he demonstrated that he had been
registered along with his children and his wife, as follows: Lucius
Cornelius Antas, son of Heraclides, born in the military camp, soldier
on double pay of the Augustan *ala* of which Messius Julianus is the
prefect, Antonia, daughter of Crispus, his wife, Heraclides his son,
Crispina his daughter, Ammonarion his daughter. He also brought
forward a copy of the records in the (temple) of Castor and Pollux which
included the statement that he had served for twenty-six years and had
been honourably discharged; and he produced three witnesses to his
identity: Claudius [_ _ _], Egnatius Niger, Julius [_ _ _]
(Back) Copy of the certification of status of Cornelius Antas.

In this document the spaces left for the children's ages were not filled in. In
Egypt the *epikrisis* examined the status of individuals to establish who was
liable to tax, especially the poll tax. Since veterans were exempt from the tax, if
they chose to settle in a particular district (nome) it was necessary to keep
accurate records of tax-payers and non tax-payers. Soldiers presented their
diplomas (if they had them) or other documentation to the official delegated by
the prefect, as proof of honourable discharge and entitlement to benefits.
Veterans who appear 'without bronze tablets' can readily be explained as those
who at the *epikrisis* presented a document other than a diploma. In one case a
veteran produced a letter from his commanding officer stating that he had been
honourably discharged from his unit (Daris *Documenti*: 97; cf. text no. 329).

331 *D* 49. 16. 13. 3

(Macer (3rd C.AD), **Book II On Military Affairs**)

In general there are three kinds of discharge: honourable, medical,
dishonourable. An honourable discharge is that which is granted when
the full period of military service has been completed; a medical
discharge is when some one is pronounced to be unsuitable for military
service through mental or physical infirmity; a dishonourable discharge
is when someone is dismissed from the service because he has
committed an offence. A man who has been dishonourably discharged
may not live in Rome or be in the imperial entourage.

An honourable discharge was the key to all a veteran's *praemia*; soldiers who
were dismissed from the service for medical reasons were in practice held to be

honourably discharged and received their benefits in accordance with a time scale based on the duration of their completed military service (Modestinus – 27. 1. 8. 2–5). The rules about discharge from the army were clearly of great importance to soldiers since there are several imperial rescripts about the details (Campbell 1984: 311–14).

332 *CJ* 5. 65. 1, AD 213

Emperor Antoninus Augustus to Saturninus. Men who are released from their military oath on medical grounds after twenty years' service, both keep an unblemished reputation and are entitled to the official privileges granted to veteran soldiers.

Published on 7 August in the consulship of Antoninus Augustus for the fourth time and Balbinus.

333 *CJ* 12. 35(36). 6

The same Emperor (Gordian) to Brutus, soldier. Once soldiers have been discharged for medical reasons, it is not usual to grant reinstatement on the grounds that they have recovered good health, since soldiers are not lightly discharged and only after doctors have declared that they have contracted an infirmity and this has been rigorously investigated by a suitable judge.

334 *CJ* 12. 35(36). 3

The same Emperor (Antoninus) to Julianus. Since soldiers who have been dishonourably discharged are designated with a mark of ill-repute, they may not have access to any of the privileges normally granted to men of unblemished record. They do however have the right of staying wherever they wish, with the exception of those places from which they are specifically excluded.

335 *CJ* 12. 35(36). 7

The same Emperor (Gordian) to Domnus, veteran soldier. Your fears are groundless that a blemish on your record because of an offence against military law should be held to have damaged your good name now that you are a veteran. This is especially true since it has been decided that soldiers who were censured for an offence that could also be committed by a civilian, should not be branded with infamy after their discharge.

336 *D* 49. 18. 1–5

(Arrius Menander (3rd C.AD), **Book III On Military Affairs**)

Among other privileges of veterans they have special rights even when they have committed an offence, in that they are distinguished from other people in respect of the punishments they suffer. For a veteran is not sent to the wild beasts nor beaten with rods.

(Ulpian (3rd C.AD), **Book III Opinions**)

The immunity bestowed on soldiers who have been honourably discharged is also valid in those communities in which they reside, and it is not undermined if any of them voluntarily undertakes a public office or duty. It is right that they should all pay taxes and normal charges relating to inherited property.

(Marcianus (3rd C.AD), **Book II Rules**)

The same distinction is extended to veterans and the children of veterans as to town councillors, and therefore they are not to be condemned to the mines or to public works or to the beasts, and are not to be beaten with rods.

(Ulpian, **Book IV On the Duties of a Proconsul**)

It was laid down in a rescript to Julius Sossianus, veteran soldier, that veterans are not exempt from contributing to the cost of repairing roads. Furthermore, it is clear that veterans are not exempt from taxes levied on their property. In addition, it was laid down in a rescript to Aelius Firmus and Antonius Clarus, veterans, that their ships can be requisitioned.

(Paul (3rd C.AD), **Book on Judicial Enquiries**)

The divine Great Antoninus with his father stated in a rescript that veterans are exempt from the charges associated with the building of ships. Moreover, they have exemption from the collection of taxes, that is, they may not be appointed as tax collectors. But veterans who have allowed themselves to be elected as members of local government, must perform their obligations.

337 *FIRA* 3. 171 = Smallwood *GN* 297, papyrus, Egypt, AD 63

(a) Copy of the register

Year 10 of Emperor Nero Claudius Caesar Augustus Germanicus, seventh of the month Augustus, in the great hall on the tribunal, there were present in the council Norbanus Ptolemy, judicial administrator and official of the Idios Logos, Aquillius Quadratus and Tennius Vetus [_ _ _] Atticus, Papirius Pastor and Baebius Juncinus, [tribunes], Julius Lysimachus, Claudius Heracleides, officer in charge of finance, Claudius Euctemon and Claudius Secundus.

With reference to discharged soldiers, in respect of citizenship; [Tuscus]: I told you before that the situation of each of you is neither similar nor identical. For some of you are veterans from the legions, others from *alae*, others from cohorts, others from the fleet, with the result that your legal rights are not the same. I shall deal with this matter, and I have written to the *strategoi* in each nome to ensure that the rewards of [each] person are completely guaranteed, according to the legal rights of each person. (Another hand) [_ _ _] I wrote [_ _ _]

(b) Copy of a hearing

The legionaries came forward on the camp road at the temple of Isis. Tuscus the prefect replied to us: Do not create an ungodly uproar. No one is causing you any problem. Write out on tablets where each one of you lives and I shall write to the *strategoi* to ensure that no one causes you any trouble.

On the fourth of the month of Augustus we gave him the tablets at his headquarters in the camp, and he said to us: Have you handed them over separately, (completely) separately? And the legionaries replied to him: We have handed them over separately.

On the fifth of the same month we greeted him near the Paliurus, and he greeted us in turn. And on the [seventh] of the same month we greeted him in the Hall as he sat on the tribunal. Tuscus said to us: I have spoken to you in the camp and now I say the same thing. Legionaries are treated in one way, members of cohorts in another way, and members of the fleet in another way. Each of you should return to his own affairs and not be idle.

The first papyrus (a) refers to a decision of the prefect of Egypt assisted by his advisory council. Some veterans were not satisfied with their privileges or perhaps had encountered difficulties in persuading local officials that they were entitled to exemptions. The prefect emphasizes the differences in status between veterans from different arms of the service (cf. text no. 329). It may be that the privileges in text no. 336 were restricted to legionary and praetorian veterans, or perhaps there were special arrangements in Egypt (see text no. 339). The second papyrus (b) seems to be a record kept by the soldiers of several meetings with the prefect in respect of their petitions; the last encounter probably refers to the meeting described by papyrus (a). It is obscure how the veterans had organized themselves for this joint petition, but significant that they were able to approach the prefect directly and apparently wait in the camp for a reply.

338 *SB* 12508, papyrus, Egypt, AD 149

Copy. Aurelius Petronius [_ _ _] to Diophantus, royal scribe of the [Arsinoite nome, Heracleides district], greetings. Achillas, son of Harpocrates, cavalryman of the *ala* of Vocontians – before his military service his name was Oronnous son of Rapalios (?) and Tamestremphi – residing in the village of Syngna, is recorded as having served in the army for more than twenty-five years. It is proper therefore to write to you that in accordance with the grant of our mighty Emperor he has been released from payment of the poll tax. Farewell.

(Second hand) I pray that you are well.

(Third hand) Year 13 of Emperor Caesar Titus Aelius Hadrian Antoninus Augustus Pius, on 4 Phaophi.

339 *SP* 285 = Daris, *Documenti* 105, papyrus, Arsinoite nome, Egypt, AD 172

[_ _ _] from Gaius Julius Apollinarius, veteran, landholder in the village of Karanis. It has been laid down, sir, that veterans after their discharge have a period of five years' respite (from compulsory public services). In contravention of this ruling I was threatened after two years of my respite and was arbitrarily chosen for compulsory public service, and up until the present moment I have been continuously performing compulsory public service without a break. Treatment like this is entirely forbidden even in the case of the native population, and the rule ought to be much more strictly observed in my case since I have served for such a long time in the army. Therefore I have been forced to have recourse to you with my just petition, and I request that you secure for me an equivalent period of respite in accordance with the rules about this, so that I may be able to look after my own property, since I am now an old man on my own, and that I may be thankful to your fortune for ever. Farewell.

(Second hand) I, Gaius Apollinarius have presented this (petition).

(Third hand) Year 12, 29 Mecheir.

(Fourth hand) (Subscript) Present your case to the *strategus* and he will take appropriate action.

(Fifth hand) Deliver.

There is no mention in the legal texts of a restriction on veterans' exemptions to a five-year period after discharge, and it may have been a special regulation applied only in Egypt. Sometimes even veterans, like most of the civilian population, had difficulties in escaping from the clutches of officials.

340 *BGU* 628 = *FIRA* 1. 56, papyrus, Egypt, late 1st C.BC

_ _ _] when Manius Valens, veteran, [tax-collector?], read out the part of the edict which is quoted below:

Imperator Caesar, son of a god, triumvir for the second time for the settlement of the state, declares: I have decided to proclaim that all veterans shall be granted [exemption from] tribute [_ _ _], to bestow on them, their parents and children, and the wives they have or shall have, exemption in every respect, and so that they may be Roman citizens with every proper legal right, they are to be exempt (from taxation), free from military service, and excused from the performance of compulsory public services. Moreover, the above-mentioned are to have the right of registering their vote and being enrolled in the census in any tribe they wish, and if they wish to be enrolled in absence, that will be granted in respect of those who have been mentioned above, the veterans themselves, their parents, wives, and children. Moreover, just as I wished veterans to be exempt in respect of the points mentioned, I grant that they may be permitted to have, use, and enjoy whatever priesthoods, offices, rewards, benefits, and emoluments they possessed. I have decided that they are not to be appointed against their will to other magistracies or as ambassador or superintendent or tax-farmer; moreover, I have decided that no one is to be billeted in their homes in order to lodge or spend the winter there (?).

Octavian's triumviral powers (first voted up to 31 December, 38 BC) were renewed for five years in the autumn of 37 and therefore formally expired at the end of 33 if they ran retroactively, or at the end of 32. After the defeat of Antony he did not call himself triumvir (Tac., *Annals* 1. 2). This edict then should be dated to the period just before the battle of Actium, and must represent an attempt to cement the loyalty of his army in his bid for control of the Roman world. The language emphasizes the military leader's generosity to his troops and their families, and his concern for their welfare. It is likely, however, that the grant of these privileges to all the family of a veteran was exceptional (perhaps it had been targeted at particular groups of soldiers) and did not survive the settlement of conditions of service in 13 BC. But the regular benefits of military life could at any time be supplemented by the generosity of the emperor.

It is obscure why Valens cited the edict. Perhaps some imposition had been placed on him or his home; or if the restoration 'tax-collector' is correct, he may have been trying to give up this post which he had accepted earlier, presumably in the expectation that it would be profitable. Tax farmers bought from the state the right to collect certain taxes and then tried to recoup their outlay and make a profit.

341 *ILS* 9059 = *FIRA* 1. 76, tablet, Arsinoite nome, Egypt, AD 94

(Exterior face, names of nine witnesses in the margin)

In the consulship of Lucius Nonius Calpurnius Torquatus Asprenas and Titus Sextius Magius Lateranus (AD 94), 2 July, year 13 of Emperor Caesar Domitian Augustus, Conqueror of the Germans, month of Epeiph, the eighth day, at Alexandria in Egypt: Marcus Valerius Quadratus, son of Marcus, of the tribe Pollia, veteran, honourably discharged from Legion X Fretensis, declared that he had had a copy made and authenticated from the bronze plaque, which is affixed in the Great Caesareum, as you climb the second flight of steps beneath the portico on the right, beside the temple of the marble Venus, on the wall, on which is written the text which is set out below:

Emperor Caesar Domitian Augustus, Conqueror of the Germans, son of the divine Vespasian, chief priest, in the eighth year of his tribunician power (AD 88–89), acclaimed *imperator* sixteen times, censor in perpetuity, father of the fatherland, declares: I have decided to proclaim by edict that the veterans among all of you (i.e. soldiers) should be free and exempt from all public taxes and toll dues, that they themselves, the wives who married them, their children, and their parents, should be Roman citizens with every proper legal right, that they should be free and immune with total exemption, and their parents and children mentioned above should have the same legal rights and the same status in respect of total exemption, and that their land, houses, and shops shall not [_ _ _] against their will and without payment (?) [_ _ _

(Interior face)

[_ _ _] of veterans with their wives and children mentioned above (whose names) have been inscribed in bronze, or if they were un-married, with those whom they married afterwards, limited to one wife for each man, and who served at Jerusalem in Legion X Fretensis and were honourably discharged when their service was completed by Sextus Hermetidius Campanus, legate of the Emperor with proprae-torian power, on 28 December, in the consulship of Sextus Pompeius Collega and Quintus Peducaeus Priscinus (AD 93), and who began their military service in the consulship of Publius Galerius Trachalus and Tiberius Catius (AD 68), and in the consulship of Titus Flavius and Gnaeus Arulenus (AD 69).

(Copied?) on the authorization of Marcus Junius Rufus, prefect of Egypt, in the consulship of Lucius Nonius Calpurnius Torquatus Asprenas and Titus Sextius Magius Lateranus, on 1 July, year 13 of Emperor Caesar Domitian Augustus, Conqueror of the Germans, month of Epeiph, the seventh day.

At that place (where the original inscription was displayed) Marcus Valerius Quadratus, son of Marcus, of the tribe Pollia, in the presence of those men who were to act as witnesses, declared and swore by Jupiter Best and Greatest and the *Genius* of the most revered Emperor Caesar Domitian Augustus, Conqueror of the Germans, that Lucius Valerius Valens and Valeria Heraclus and Valeria Artemis, the three children mentioned above, were all born to him during his military service, that they had been inscribed on the original bronze record, and that they had acquired Roman citizenship through the benevolence of the same splendid emperor.

This wooden tablet is part of a diptych and is inscribed on the outer and inner faces in a way similar to the bronze diplomas certifying military privileges. In AD 94 Valerius Quadratus copied down Domitian's edict and then the certification of discharge of veterans of the X Fretensis; finally he made a declaration before witnesses of the birth of his three children, who received Roman citizenship through Domitian's edict. The damaged text of the interior face seems to suggest that legionaries of X Fretensis were receiving a statement of benefits and privileges at this time, but this may have been confined to a special category, i.e, only those who had joined up in 68 and 69 (Campbell 1984: 443–4).

In any event, the language of Domitian's edict, like that of Octavian, illustrates his expansive generosity to veterans and their families. If it is true that since Augustus' time legionary veterans had received on an *ad hoc* basis citizenship for children born in service, Domitian's edict could have established this formally as a military privilege. Domitian came to rely more openly on the goodwill and loyalty of his troops, especially since he found it difficult to trust the senatorial class, and this edict may have been issued in the aftermath of the revolt in 89 of Saturninus, governor of Upper Germany.

VETERAN COLONIES

In 47–44 Caesar sought to accommodate about 15,000 of his veterans on lands in Italy, although he avoided confiscation, and they were settled in relatively small groups without disruption of the status of existing communities. After Philippi in 41, a large amount of land from eighteen cities in Italy was expropriated by Octavian to satisfy about 46,000 veterans, and further settlements in Italy and Gaul for about 20,000 men were made after the defeat of Sextus Pompey at Naulochus in 36. After his victory at Actium in 31, Augustus, who stood as the bringer of peace and order, could not repeat the upheavals of these years which had caused much bad feeling. He boasted in the *Res Gestae* that he had paid for all the land given to his soldiers. It is likely that many veterans at this time preferred to receive land rather than monetary *praemia*, and this suited Augustus because there was much land available by conquest outside Italy, and because compensation for land which had to be bought in Italy was cheaper than cash payments.

Augustus paid great attention to the details of the foundation of his colonies, as we know from the works of the Roman land surveyors (*Agrimensores*). He formulated the basic law of land division – 'as far as the scythe and plough shall go' and laid down what sort of land and pasture each settler should get. He also defined those destined for specially favoured treatment, and insisted on careful demarcation of each land division scheme, specifying the erection of wooden posts to designate individual allocations; in addition, he was responsible for the meticulous compilation and lodging of records of the settlement details, and the establishment of a legal framework controlling each settlement's relationship with neighbouring communities. Most veteran colonies survived into the late empire although there is no way of testing in detail Augustus' boast (text no. 344) about the twenty-eight colonies he founded in Italy. But his concern for their prosperity can be seen in his financial benefactions, in his personal assocation with his veterans, and in his title, known from three colonies, 'Parent' or 'Parent of the Colony'.

The foundation of colonies consisting mainly or exclusively of soldiers continued up to the time of Hadrian, though the settlement of legionary veterans in Italy was largely discontinued after the Flavian era. Military colonies in the provinces were founded in more remote areas on the periphery of Roman territory, sometimes on the site of a disused legionary base or on recently conquered land. But at any one time probably more soldiers received monetary *praemia*. In total less than fifty colonies are known for the period AD 14–117, yet it has been calculated that about three hundred would have been required to cope with the likely number of discharged veterans in this period (see text no. 360). The practice of veteran settlement was neither systematic nor coherent and there is certainly no sign of an attempt to disseminate the principles of Roman civilization and government by means of such colonies, or deliberately to establish recruiting areas; in the main, colonies were *ad hoc* arrangements made when it suited the government.

Emperors gradually stopped founding colonies as new land became more difficult and expensive to obtain. More importantly, veterans preferred to settle close to where they had served, not in an organized colony situated elsewhere. There had indeed been problems over this even in the first century AD. By the second century local recruitment was the norm and military units tended to be permanently stationed in one location, with the result that soldiers and their families were more closely tied to this area.

The evidence for veteran colonies is fragmentary: scattered allusions in literary sources, archaeological remains of colonies, inscriptions from the sites confirming colonial status and showing the veterans who were settled there and their legions, and the texts of the land surveyors. In their discussions of land division and allocation, in which they had a crucial role, surveyors not only provide useful general observations, but also cite many examples, which seem in the main to be accurate, and provide evidence of unparalleled detail on the mechanism and problems of colonial foundations (Keppie 1983; 1984b; Mann 1983; land survey – Dilke 1971; Hinrichs 1974).

342 Hyginus Gromaticus (1st–2nd? C.AD), *The Establishment of 'Limites'* (Thulin 1913: 140–2)

When the struggles of the great wars had been brought to an end, distinguished Romans founded cities to enlarge the Roman state, assigning them either to the victorious citizens of the Roman people or to discharged soldiers, and called them colonies since these lands were newly given over to agriculture (*colo*; *cultura*). Colonies were allocated to these victorious men who had taken up arms in an emergency. For the Roman people did not have enough soldiers to keep pace with the expansion of the state. At that time land was a prize and was considered a reward for completion of service. It happened that many legionaries luckily survived the wars and from their first rank in military service passed to a hard-working life of peace and quiet in cultivating the fields. Now, when they were being settled along with their standards, eagle, centurions, and tribunes, land was allocated in proportion to the rank they had held . . . The divine Julius Caesar . . . kept his soldiers on after they had served their time, and when the veterans baulked at this, dismissed them. But soon when these very soldiers asked to be allowed to share his military service again, he took them back and after several wars, when peace had been established, settled them in colonies.

Similarly, the divine Augustus, when peace had been imposed throughout the world, settled as colonists the soldiers who had served in the armies of Antony and Lepidus along with men of his own legions, either in Italy, or in the provinces. For some of these he founded new cities after enemy settlements had been wiped out; in other cases he settled soldiers in old towns and called them colonists. Moreover, cities which had been founded by kings or dictators and which the civil wars had drained of manpower, he re-founded as colonies and increased their population, and sometimes their territory.

Hyginus Gromaticus traces the history of colonial foundations; in the earlier type Julius Caesar settled legions in their existing military framework (cf. Appian, *Civil Wars* 2. 139–41); under Augustus, certainly after 27 BC, whole legions were no longer discharged simultaneously, and smaller groups of men were settled, often in existing communities. This is a rare explicit comment by an ancient writer on the sometimes complex motives for Augustus' colonial foundations. Veterans of Antony and Lepidus who received land from Augustus were probably settled in the provinces.

343 Siculus Flaccus (2nd? C.AD), *On the Status of Land* (Thulin 1913: 126–7)

Furthermore, there is the term 'bronze tablet with double entries'. This originated as follows. Men settled as colonists by the divine Julius Caesar took up military service again under Augustus. When the wars were over they returned victorious to reclaim their lands; however others received land in place of those soldiers who had died. Consequently, in these *centuriae* there may be found the names both of those who had been originally settled as colonists and of those who afterwards took their place.

344 Augustus, *Res Gestae*, 28

I founded colonies of soldiers in Africa, Sicily, Macedonia, both Spanish provinces, Achaea, Asia, Syria, Narbonese Gaul, and Pisidia. In addition Italy has twenty-eight colonies founded under my authority which in my lifetime were very distinguished and populous.

For Augustus' expenditure on colonies founded in 31 and 14 BC, see texts nos 18–19. After Actium he may have discharged between 40,000 and 50,000 men from his own legions (discussion in Brunt 1971: 332–42; Keppie 1983: 73–86). The twenty-eight colonies mentioned by Augustus cannot include all those which had been founded or reinforced between 41 BC and AD 14; it is likely that he means those founded immediately after Actium and perhaps later in his reign.

Augustus himself linked the settlements of 14 BC with those of 31 BC, and soldiers recruited after Actium will have been ready for discharge in 14 BC, perhaps about 30–35,000 men.

345 Dio (2nd–3rd C.AD), 53. 25

(Marcus Terentius Varro Murena attacked the Salassi in 25 BC) When he had compelled them to come to terms he demanded a fixed sum of money, as if he were intending to inflict no other punishment. Then he sent soldiers to all areas of the country apparently to collect the money, but in fact he arrested all those of military age and sold them into slavery on the understanding that none of them should be set free within twenty years. Furthermore, the best of their land was granted to some of the praetorians, and on it the city called Augusta Praetoria was established.

Augusta Praetoria Salassorum (modern Aosta), was founded probably in 25 BC with 3,000 veterans on the site of Varro's encampment. The layout of the town, square in outline and divided into sixteen large blocks by two avenues running east-west and north-south, and several smaller streets all intersecting at right angles, resembles that of a Roman military camp, and it may suggest the close relationship of military and town planning manuals in the early empire (Keppie 1983: 205–7).

346 Hyginus (1st-2nd C.AD), *Categories of Land* (Thulin 1913: 82–3)

Indeed the following situation, which I have found in several places, will need to be examined; namely, when the founder (of a colony) had taken lands from the territory of another community for the purpose of allocation (to the colonists), he naturally conferred ownership rights on each person to whom he allocated land, but did not remove rights of jurisdiction from the territory within which he was making allocations. There are also several edicts of the divine Augustus in which he makes clear that whenever he had taken land away from the territory of another community and had allocated it to veteran soldiers, nothing except whatever was granted and allocated to the veterans should belong to the jurisdiction of the colony.

When a colony was being established, the lands available in the existing community were sometimes insufficient for the colonists and additional land was confiscated from a neighbouring community. Confiscated land that was divided up and allocated to colonists came under the jurisdiction of the new colony. But any other land such as unusable areas (*subseciva*), or small towns, remained under the jurisdiction of the community from which the land had been confiscated. Augustus obviously intended to keep to a minimum the disruption caused in rural communities by his land distributions.

347 *EJ* 347a, inscription, Dalmatia, AD 14 (?)

Dedicated to the divine Augustus and Tiberius Caesar Augustus, son of Augustus, the veterans of the Scunasticus district, to whom the colony of Narona gave lands.

The civilian colony of Narona had been founded at the end of Caesar's dictatorship. This settlement by Tiberius of veterans, probably from the seventh legion, was on land presumably purchased from the colony's territory; it is an example of an attempt to strengthen an existing community by the addition of soldier-settlers.

348 Tacitus (1st–2nd C.AD), *Annals* 14. 27

Veteran soldiers were drafted into the settlements at Tarentum and Antium but did not relieve the under-population of these areas since many of them drifted away to the provinces where they had served, leaving their homes deserted and bereft of children, because they were unused to taking a wife and rearing a family. In the past entire legions were settled with their tribunes and centurions and soldiers each in his own rank, so that they created a community based on mutual agreement and respect. But now soldiers who did not know one another, from different units, without any leader, with no feeling of mutual comradeship, were suddenly brought together in one place just like a collection of individuals of different races rather than a colony.

These communities at Tarentum and Antium, which were founded by Nero in AD 60, were in Tacitus' view populated mainly by legionary veterans, although Suetonius mentions the establishment of some praetorians at Antium (*Nero* 9). The evidence of inscriptions found at Tarentum shows the settlement of men who had served in legions based in Moesia and Syria. Tacitus' criticism of the settlement of small groups rather than entire legions is misplaced since the method of discharge in the imperial period was organized so that single legions were no longer discharged at one moment.

Part of the government's purpose was to strengthen places in Italy suffering from depopulation (cf. text no. 342), and Nero also added veterans to the colonies at Capua and Nuceria (Tacitus, *Annals* 13. 31). But even in the first century there was a reluctance among legionaries to be settled in colonies in Italy, and a determination to return to the areas where they had served.

349 *CIL* 16. 13 = *MW* 398, inscription, Dalgodeltzi, Upper Moesia, AD 71

Emperor Caesar Vespasian Augustus, chief priest, in the second year of his tribunician power, acclaimed *imperator* six times, father of the fatherland, consul for the third time, has granted to the veterans who served in the fleet at Misenum under the command of Sextus Lucilius Bassus, and have completed twenty-six years' service or more, and have been settled at Paestum, whose names are listed below, to them, their children, and their posterity, citizenship and the right of marriage (*conubium*) with the wives they had when citizenship was granted to them, or, if they were unmarried, with those whom they married afterwards, limited to one wife for each man.

9 February, in the consulship of Emperor Caesar Vespasian Augustus for the third time and Marcus Cocceius Nerva.

To Tutio, son of Butius, Dacian. Tablet 1, page 5, line 11.

Recorded and authenticated from the bronze plaque which is affixed at Rome on the Capitoline on the outer part of the base of the altar of the Julian Family opposite the statue of Father Liber.

AE 1975. 251 refers to an equestrian sent 'to divide up the land for the veterans who were settled in the first Flavian colony at Paestum'. This colony was founded in AD 71 (see Keppie 1984b: 98–104). Tutio returned from Paestum to his home in Moesia, where the diploma was found. Another settler returned to Macedonia, and two others moved elsewhere in Italy, one to Pompeii, one to Corsica (Mann 1983: 58). This confirms the view that increasingly veterans preferred to settle either where they had served or near their home community, generally, therefore, in the provinces.

350 *ILS* 2460 = *MW* 378, inscription, Reate, 1st C.AD

To the spirits of the departed, in honour of Gaius Julius Longinus, son of Gaius, of the tribe Voltinia in his home at Philippi in Macedonia, veteran of Legion VIII Augusta, settled by the divine Augustus Vespasian in Reate, (then) of the tribe Quirina, who had this made during his lifetime for himself and Julia Helpis, freedwoman of Gaius, his wife, and Gaius Julius Felix, freedman of Gaius; and he set it up for his [children] and posterity, and for Gaius Julius December, freedman of Gaius, and Julia Veneria, freedwoman of Gaius, and Gaius Julius Prosdoxus, freedman of Gaius.

Reate was Vespasian's home town and veterans from legions in Upper Germany and Britain and also praetorians are known to have been settled here. Further settlements of veterans in Italy by Vespasian are recorded in Samnium (text no. 351), at Panormus, Abella, and Nola (see Blume *et al.* 1848: 211, 230. 236).

351 Hyginus, *Types of Disputes* (Thulin 1913: 94–5)

We should also watch out for the following point: if in the case of two landholders there is a measure of conformity with the area which is stated in the bronze record and in the map notations, even though one owner has sold some part (of his land). Indeed I discovered this in Samnium, where the lands which the divine Vespasian had allocated to veterans were still occupied by the people to whom they had been allocated, but in a different way. For some had bought certain places and added them to their own land, making a boundary by means of a road, or a river, or in some other way. But neither those who sold part of their holdings, nor those who bought and added something to theirs, worked out a definite area. Instead they sold or bought on the basis of defining each area as best it could be in some way or other, as I pointed out, either by a road, or a river, or by some other method.

Hyginus' comments are based on personal observation and indicate that at least these veterans settled by Vespasian remained on their holdings.

352 Hyginus Gromaticus, *The Establishment of 'Limites'* (Thulin 1913: 144)

In some colonies which were established later, for example, Ammaedara in Africa, the *decumanus maximus* and the *kardo maximus* start from the town and are drawn through the four gates just like a military camp, the *limites* making wide roads. This is the most attractive system of establishing *limites*. The colony embraces all four areas of allocated land, is convenient for the farmers on every side, and all the inhabitants have equal access to the forum from all directions. Similarly, in military camps the *groma* (a surveying instrument) is set up at the crossroads where men can assemble, as if to a forum.

For land survey methods, see p. 126. Ammaedara (Haïdra in Tunisia) was a Flavian veteran colony (as can be seen from the title – *colonia Flavia Augusta Emerita Ammaedara*), founded on the site of the legionary camp vacated by the III Augusta, which by Vespasian's time at the latest had been moved to Thevestis. Archaeology of the site confirms that two roads intersected at right angles in the centre of the settlement, though the adjacent land division has a different orientation. The comparison with a Roman military camp should not be pressed too far, since, although a camp had a gate in each of its four sides, its main roads did not intersect in the middle, which was usually occupied by the headquarters of the commanding officer.

353 *ILS* 6105 = *MW* 486, inscription, Rome, AD 82

In the consulship of Domitian [Augustus for the eighth time] and Titus Flavius Sabinus, on 13 June (or 15 July), in the Flavian colony of Peace Deultum, in [the council chamber? _ _ _] and Gaius Occeius Niger, Members of the Board of Two, spoke about the desirability of [offering the patronage] of our colony to [_ _ _ Avi]dius Quietus, legate of the Emperor, most distinguished man, and what they thought ought to be done in respect of this matter, [they came to the following decision on this matter]:

Since we have served in Legion VIII Augusta, and after completion of our [twenty-five years] of service [have been settled] by the most revered emperor in the colony of Deultum, we should petition him (Quietus) that through his outstanding kindness [he should deign] to undertake the patronage of our colony, and that he should permit [a plaque with a record of this matter] to be placed in his house, [so that he may himself delight] in his own kindness and so that his own [good offices] in the enhancement [of our status] may be known. There were present at the inscribing of the decree (a list of names follows).

Since the text is damaged, the date may be either the ides of June or July. Deultum in Thrace was a Flavian veteran settlement founded before AD 79. Veterans of the VIII Augusta are mentioned, but that legion had left the adjoining province of Moesia in 69 and was stationed in Germany after the civil wars. The building of the colony, which was probably planned before 69, may have been delayed by the civil wars, and veterans of the VIII Augusta who had been intended as the original settlers were then brought back to establish it (Mann 1983: 36–7). Or it may be that the veterans were simply sent to a familiar area close to their former legionary station. 'Peace' in the colony's title presumably celebrates the end of the civil wars.

354 *CIL* 3. 1443 = Smallwood *NH* 479, inscription, Sarmizegetusa, Dacia, 2nd C.AD

[On the authority] of Emperor Caesar Trajan Augustus, son of the divine Nerva, the Dacian colony was founded by [Legion] V M(acedonica); Scaurianus, his [legate] with propraetorian power [gave this as a gift.]

The original stone has been lost. This translation follows the restorations accepted by Smallwood; another version produces: . . . founded through [Decimus Terenti]us Scaurianus, his [legate] with propraetorian power.

Eventually called *Ulpia Traiana Augusta Dacica Sarmizegetusa*, this was one of two veteran settlements founded by Trajan in Dacia (the other is Dierna). Its probable date is 110. Terentius Scaurianus was the first governor of the province of Dacia (C. Daicoviciu, *RE* Suppl. 14 (1974) *s.v.* Sarmizegetusa, cols. 610–55).

355 Hyginus, *Categories of Land* (Thulin 1913: 84)

Recently when a reservist of the emperor, a man of military training and also very proficient in our skills (of surveying), was allocating lands in Pannonia to veteran soldiers according to the wishes and generosity of Emperor Trajan Augustus, Conqueror of the Germans, he wrote down or noted on bronze, that is on the maps, not only the quantity of land which he was allocating, but also at the end of the boundary line relating to each settler (i.e. on the map) included the area in the following way: when the measurement for the allocation was completed, he wrote down the area of land listing its length and breadth. Because of this no disputes and litigation about these lands could arise among the veterans.

The bronze map and register recorded the total area of the settlement, the name of each landholder, the location of his holding, and the quantity in *iugera* of individual allocations. The procedure adopted in Pannonia shows the care taken by emperors over the settlement of veterans. This incident probably relates to the foundation of Poetovio (text no. 356).

356 *CIL* 3. 4057 = *ILS* 2462, inscription, Poetovio (Ptuj), Upper Pannonia, early 2nd C.AD

Gaius Cornelius Verus, son of Gaius, of the tribe Pomptina, from Dertona, veteran of Legion II Adiutrix, was settled in the colony Ulpia Traiana Poetovio with double (?) allocation of land on discharge, served as clerk of the governor, fifty years old, lies buried here; he ordered in his will that this should be set up; his heir, Gaius Billienus Vitalis, had this done.

Poetovio was founded by Trajan soon after the Dacian wars or possibly before the end of 102 (if Hyginus in text no. 355 is referring to the foundation of Poetovio, he does not ascribe the title *Dacicus* to Trajan, which was bestowed at the end of 102). The phrase 'double allocation of land' – '*mission(e) agr(aria) II*' is explained on the hypothesis that Verus as a *beneficiarius* was on double pay and hence received a double portion of land. It has also been suggested, however, that Verus was part of a second group of settlers who reinforced the existing community.

357 *ILS* 9085, inscription, near Poetovio, early 2nd C.AD

To the spirits of the departed, Lucius Gargilius Felix, son of Lucius, of the tribe Quirina, from Tacape (in Africa), veteran of Legion I Adiutrix Loyal and Faithful, discharged with a cash discharge grant, [_ _ _] years

Cf. *AE* 1934. 226. Felix, having received his cash *praemium*, may have settled at Poetovio of his own accord. Mann (1983: 33) conjectures that he had been discharged in Dacia and had chosen to make his home in Poetovio because I Adiutrix had been stationed here immediately before its despatch to Dacia and the establishment of the colony. But it is possible that two groups of colonists were settled in Poetovio, one with land, one with money.

358 *SEG* 17. 584 = Smallwood *NH* 313, inscription, Attaleia, Asia, 2nd C.AD

In honour of Lucius Gavius Fronto, son of Lucius Gavius Fronto, chief centurion of Legion III Cyrenaica and camp prefect of Legion XV Apollinaris, the first and only member of his native community (to hold these ranks), father of Lucius Gavius Aelianus, quaestor with pro-praetorian power of the Roman people, grandfather of Lucius Gavius Clarus of the broad purple stripe (i.e. a senator), honoured with the grant of a public horse by the Emperor, and with military decorations, entrusted by the divine Trajan with three thousand legionary veterans to found a colony at Cyrene, the first to promise a permanent tenure of the office of gymnasiarch in his fifth year (holding that office), chief priest of all the Emperors for four years and director of the dramatic and athletic games at his own expense,
Lucius Gavius Seleucus to his patron and benefactor.

The veteran colony at Cyrene was established in the aftermath of the Jewish revolt in 115 and may have been completed by Hadrian.

359 Hyginus Gromaticus, *The Establishment of 'Limites'* (Thulin 1913: 165–6)

We should make a ledger recording all unused land (*subseciva*) so that whenever the emperor wishes he can find out how many men can be settled in that area. . . We shall place in the emperor's record office the bronze registers and ground plan of the entire area which has been divided up, with the lines drawn in according to its established boundaries, and a note of the immediate neighbours. And if anything has been granted or allocated to a colony as an act of munificence, either close by or separated by several other communities, we shall record it in the book dealing with benefactions (*beneficia*). As regards anything else that is relevant to the documentation used by surveyors, not only the colony but also the imperial record office ought to hold a copy signed by the founder.

We have here a rare explicit statement of the circumstances in which an emperor might consult his archives before making a decision. It is clear that the officials charged with carrying out the foundation of veteran colonies, which were established exclusively on an emperor's initiative, showed meticulous attention to detailed planning and the careful recording, not just in the colony but also in Rome, of all transactions.

360 *CIL* 3. 8110 = *ILS* 2302, inscription, Viminacium (Kostolac), Upper Moesia, AD 160 (?)

For the welfare of Emperor Caesar Titus Aelius [Antoninus] Augustus Pius [and Verus] Caesar, [the veterans] of Legion VII [Claudia, Loyal and Faithful], enlisted in the consulship of Servianus and [Varus (AD 134) and of Po]ntianus and [Atticus] (AD 135), [honourably discharged] by Cur[tius Jus]tus, [legate of the Emperor] with pro-praetorian power, and by the legate of the legion, who number 239. (There follows a list of names).

The 239 veterans listed specifically by this inscription were presumably all those discharged on one occasion, probably in AD 160, and represented the men recruited over two successive years (i.e. about 120 were discharged from each year's intake). Mann (1983: 59–60) uses this inscription, supported by other scattered evidence, as a basis for his calculation of about one hundred veterans discharged annually from each legion (25–33 legions = 2,500–3,300 veterans). If the average size of colonial foundations was about 1,000, around 300 colonies will have been needed to accommodate veterans discharged from AD 14–117. Naturally, this kind of calculation can give only an order of magnitude and is very problematic. Other inscriptions show the discharge on a single occasion of a much larger number of veterans who had been recruited on one occasion. This might be explained on the hypothesis that these inscriptions represent an usually large number of recruits because of special circumstances. On the other hand, the inscription from Viminacium may be untypical for reasons we cannot recover.

VETERANS IN LOCAL LIFE

Inevitably there was tension between soldier-settlers and the existing inhabitants, especially when some had been dispossessed without compensation. In 41 BC there were outbreaks of violence in the streets, and Vergil in *Eclogues* 1 and 9 expresses the distress of farming communities disrupted by the arrival of veteran soldiers as the new owners. Moreover, since not all the previous landholders were removed from their land, and since others had their property returned, the veterans had to work side by side with the old inhabitants. This practice was so common that, among their mapping definitions, the *Agrimensores* include 'returned to the original owner'. In some Sullan and Caesarean colonies these divisions are reflected in the nomenclature adopted – 'old' and 'new' inhabitants – and the two groups remained distinct for a time. But there is no clear evidence that these distinctions persisted in a significant way in the administration of a colony, and eventually the two groups will have coalesced. It might be expected that individual veterans would be to the fore in local life and government in colonies and other communities where they settled, by holding office and by conferring benefactions. But of ordinary veterans settled in Italy between 47 and 14 BC, only five are known to have taken part in local government, and of officers, seven ex-tribunes and centurions, who are likely to have been greatly enriched by military service and wealthy enough to meet the entrance requirements for office holding. Indeed, up to the end of the second century AD there is scant indication of a substantial impact by ex-soldiers on the development of local communities. However, the evidence for the role of veterans depends mainly on memorial inscriptions, and there was no uniform practice in the erection of these; such evidence may underplay the less well-off, who may none the less have made a significant contribution to a community, but did not necessarily celebrate their careers in this way. Furthermore, inscriptions can reveal only what offices a man held or how generous he was, not the circumstances of his wealth or the origins of his status in a community.

Many veterans, we may conjecture, were solid and unadventurous, consorting in the main with other veterans. Doubtless some failed as farmers. Whereas in the late Republic there is no reason to suppose that veteran soldiers would have been incompetent farmers, this is not so clear in the imperial period, since men recuited young can have had little farming experience when they were discharged after twenty-five years' service. But many will have continued to live in small towns and villages, playing their part in local communities in a way that has not been recorded for posterity. They brought capital, people, imperial goodwill, and perhaps initiatives for clearing and draining land, and bringing more under cultivation. They will have had a certain self-sufficiency and know-how which doubtless helped small communities to function, and they provided a nucleus of Roman citizens and a channel of contact between the army and local people. But in the present state of the evidence we cannot say that veterans by their presence necessarily promoted economic development or the Romanization of the empire, still less that this was intended by the government. The following passages can merely outline the role of some veterans in local life (see Brunt 1962; MacMullen 1967: 99–118 (mainly using evidence of the third century and later, and probably exaggerating the veterans' contribution to local life); Keppie 1983: 101–33; 1984b; Mann 1983; also nos 242; 336).

361 Vergil (1st C.BC–1st C.AD), *Eclogues* 1. 70–8

Is a blasphemous soldier to possess these lands which I have cultivated so well, is an outsider to reap these corn fields? See to what depths civil war has reduced our unhappy citizens. We have sown our fields for men like these! Now, Meliboeus, plant your pears, establish your vines in rows. Come on my goats, a flock that once was happy; never again stretched out in a green grotto shall I see you far away, clinging to the bramble-covered hillside. I shall sing no more songs, and, my goats, you will not be led my me to feed upon the flowering clover and the bitter willow.

Cremona was one of the eighteen cities designated to provide land for the settlement of veterans discharged after the battle of Philippi. The land, however, proved inadequate and more was confiscated from the neighbouring territory of Mantua, where Vergil's family property was threatened. The reference to the loss of the goat herd suggests that the settlers took over the animals and chattels of the dispossessed. Cf. *Eclogue* 9 (Keppie 1983: 190–2).

362 *ILS* 6753 = *EJ* 338, inscription, Augusta Praetoria (Aosta), 23/22 BC

To Emperor Caesar Augustus, son of a god, consul for the eleventh time, acclaimed *imperator* eight times, with tribunician power, the Salassi people, residents, who at the outset settled themselves in the colony, to their patron.

This refers to the foundation of Augusta Praetoria Salassorum in 25 BC (see text no. 345), in which some of the displaced inhabitants of the surrounding land were apparently permitted to dwell. Or perhaps they had supported the Roman cause.

363 *CIL* 3. 6825 = *ILS* 2238, inscription, Pisidian Antioch, Lycia, 1st C.AD

Titus Cissonius, son of Quintus, of the tribe Sergia, veteran of Legion V Gallica. While I was alive I drank enthusiastically. Drink therefore, you who are alive! Publius Cissonius, son of Quintus, of the tribe Sergia, his brother, erected (this).

The Legion V Gallica is known from the civil wars and may subsequently be identified with the V Alaudae, which was stationed in Germany from Augustus' reign to AD 69, when it was sent to Moesia; wiped out around AD 86.

364 *CIL* 13. 1906 = *ILS* 7531, inscription, Lugdunum (Lyon), Lugdunensis

To the spirits of the departed and in everlasting memory of Vitalinius Felix, veteran of Legion I M(inervia), a most wise and trustworthy man, seller of pottery ware at Lugdunum, who lived fifty-nine years, five months, ten days, was born on a Tuesday (the day of Mars), enlisted on a Tuesday, received his discharge on a Tuesday, and died on a Tuesday, Vitalinius Felicissimus, son, and Julia Nice, wife, had this set up and dedicated it while under construction.

365 *P. Fayum* 91 = *SP* 17, papyrus, Fayum, Egypt, AD 99 (extract)

18 Phaophi. Agreement of Thenetkouis with Lucius. In year three of Emperor Caesar Nerva Trajan Augustus, Conqueror of the Germans, 18 Phaophi, at Euhemeria in the district of Themistes in the Arsinoite nome. Thenetkouis, daughter of Heron, olive-carrier, Persian, about twenty-six years of age, with a scar on her right shin, with, as her guardian, her kinsman Leontas, son of Hippalus, about fifty-four years of age, with a scar on the right side of his forehead, confirms to Lucius Bellenus Gemellus, discharged legionary veteran, about sixty-seven years of age, with a scar on his left wrist, that she has received from him [directly by] hand from his house sixteen silver drachmas as caution money which may not be disclaimed. Thenetkouis is consequently under obligation to carry at the olive-press which belongs to Lucius Bellenus Gemellus at Euhemeria, from whatever day he gives her orders, the olive crop included in the current third year, performing all the tasks appropriate for a carrier, until the end of the entire process of olive-oil manufacture; and she is to receive from Lucius Bellenus her daily wages at the same amount as the other olive-carriers in the village, and Lucius is to deduct the sum of sixteen silver drachmas in instalments from her wages that are to be paid . . .

Cf. *SP* 109; this veteran owned land in several villages in the Fayum.

366 *CIL* 10. 3903 = *EJ* 329, inscription, Capua, early 1st C.AD

[The Members of the Board of Two] said [_ _ _] that it was appropriate to [dignify with every kind of private] and public [honours] an excellent [man, and asked] what they desired to be done about this matter, [and about this matter] the following decision was taken: since Lucius Antistius [Campanus has completed all his] military service, and during very tough and perilous campaigns [won] the good opinion of [Caesar] the god [and the divine Augustus], and was settled by [the latter in] our [colony _ _ _]; and since he exhibited private and public generosity to such an extent that he [virtually shared] even his own property with the community [by taking upon himself] a large number of different expenses, and indeed always [seemed] happier [to pay out money] which was to be spent for the benefit of everyone, rather than [for the advantage of] his own interests and those of his family, and to grow old [in accumulating] the public offices [offered by the community], so that even now he was [involved in our] most important [affairs], and since he has passed away [in his efforts, which, while beneficial to the community], were nevertheless arduous for a man of his years, the councillors have decided that [the memory of a most distinguished] and helpful citizen [_ _ _] should be glorified by these honours, namely that he be borne from the forum [to his funeral pyre in a funeral arranged] and approved by the Members of the Board of Two, one or both of them, and that legal proceedings on that day should be postponed [so that the people] may not be prevented by such matters from attending in as great numbers as possible the funeral of an excellent and most generous leading (?) citizen, and that a gilt [_ _ _] statue should be errected to him at public expense with this [_ _ _] decree of the town councillors inscribed on it, at the place where Lucius Antistius Campanus, his excellent son and successor to his service and generosity, [should choose _ _ _] and for the other statues, shields, and gifts which he received [_ _ _] up to the time of his death and those which were bestowed [on him after his death], a site should be granted at public expense which Lucius [Antistius Campanus should choose _ _ _] beside the Via Appia [_ _ _

If Mommsen's restorations of this badly damaged inscription are correct, Antistius had served under both Caesar and Augustus and was settled at Capua probably in 41 or 36 BC. His financial generosity to the community was outstanding, and although no office is specifically mentioned, the restoration of the text suggests that he held them all. His son was clearly destined for an important role in Capua and seems to have been Member of the Board of Two in 13 BC (*CIL* 10. 3803).

367 *AE* 1974. 283, inscription, Nuceria Alfaterna

In honour of Marcus Virtius, son of Lucius, of the tribe Menenia, his father, veteran of Legion XIX.

368 *CIL* 10. 1081 = *ILS* 6446, inscription, Nuceria Alfaterna, 1st C.AD

To Marcus Virtius Ceraunus, son of Marcus, of the tribe Menenia, aedile, Member of the Board of Two for conducting legal business, prefect of engineers (a local, not a military post), Member of the Board of Five, on whom the town councillors bestowed, free of cost (i.e. they waived the payment which he should have paid on taking up the magistracy), membership of the Board of Two at Nuceria, because of his generosity, in that he had set up a great equestrian statue and had granted a *denarius* to each citizen on the occasion of its dedication.

Ceraunus' generosity to Nuceria and his elaborate tomb suggest a wealthy man. He is the probably the son of M. Virtius (text no. 367), buried nearby, whose legion, XIX, is likely to have been that recruited by Caesar in 49 BC. Therefore he may have been settled at Nuceria in 41 BC (Keppie 1983: 151–2). Nuceria's badge was a horse, which presumably explains the equestrian statue.

369 *CIL* 8. 14697 = *ILS* 2249, inscription, Thuburnica, Africa

Quintus Annaeus Balbus, son of Quintus, of the tribe Pollia, from Faventia, fifty-three years of age, soldier of the fifth legion, twice decorated, Member of the Board of Two at Thuburnica, lies here. He lived his life honourably. Greetings to you too. On the decision of Quintus Annaeus Scapula.

This inscription cannot be securely dated. Balbus may have served in the fifth Alaudae legion, which had been recruited by Caesar in Transalpine Gaul, and it is possible that he was settled in Africa after the battle of Thapsus in 46 BC. If so, since Balbus came from Faventia in Emilia-Romagna, not Transalpine Gaul, he had presumably been transferred to the V Alaudae from another unit.

370 *ILA* 2201, inscription, Madaura, Africa

Sacred to the spirits of the departed. Lucius Fotidius Absens, son of Lucius, of the tribe Pollia, veteran, priest of the Emperor (*flamen Augusti*) in perpetuity, served twenty-six years and lived ninety years, lies here.

Madaura was a Flavian veteran colony presumably for men discharged from the III Augusta.

371 *CIL* 3. 7979, inscription, Sarmizegetusa, Dacia, 2nd C.AD

To the spirits of the departed, in memory of Gaius Julius Sabinus, soldier of Legion XIII Gemina, clerk of accounts, lived thirty years. Gaius Julius Valens, Member of the Board of Two responsible for legal jurisdiction, and Cominia Florentina, his sorrowing parents, (set this up).

This soldier's father, who was a magistrate at Sarmizegetusa, was possibly a veteran settled in the colony. For veterans in civic life at Sarmizegetusa, where they seem to have a stronger role than in, for example, Carnuntum, Brigetio, or Lambaesis, see Mann 1983: 39. For veterans in the provinces of Dalmatia and Noricum, see Wilkes 1969: 107–15; 134–5; Alföldy 1974: 122–4.

372 *IGR* 3. 1299, inscription, Sahouet-el-Khudr, Arabia, AD 170/1

For the welfare of Marcus Aurelius Antoninus Caesar, sacred to lord Zeus, (set up) by Vaddus Aslamus, Molemus Ananus, and Rufus, veteran, sacred treasurers. Year 66 (of Bostra reckoning).

This inscription was found in the vicinity of Bostra in Arabia, where the III Cyrenaica legion was stationed, and the veteran probably came from that legion. Many ex-soldiers often settled in small villages and communities in the local area.

373 *CIL* 8. 18214 = *ILS* 6847, inscription, Lambaesis, AD 147–50

Sacred to the Fortune of the Emperor, dedicated by Lucius Novius Crispinus, legate of the Emperor with propraetorian power; Gaius Antonius Alexander, son of Gaius, of the tribe Collina, from Antioch, set this up and promised a statue out of an additional sum of 4,000 sesterces, for the fortunate Hadrianic organization of veterans of [Legion III] Augusta, because of the honour of a priesthood in perpetuity which they conferred on him in his absence.

See *Diz. epig.* s.v. *collegia*, p. 369. After they had been settled, some ex-soldiers established organizations where they could associate with fellow veterans. Like other *collegia*, they will have provided a focus of social intercourse for the members, helped to promote their interests, and served as burial clubs (the society in Aquileia had its own burial ground). The *curia veteranorum* in Lambaesis was presumably a similar organization, and the addition of Hadrian's name to it indicates imperial approval.

374 *ILS* 9400, inscription, Uthina (Oudna), Africa, AD 206

To Emperor Caesar Lucius Septimius Severus Pius Pertinax Augustus, Conqueror of the Arabs, Conqueror of the Adiabenici, Greatest Conqueror of the Parthians, son of the divine Marcus Antoninus Pius, Conqueror of the Germans, Conqueror of the Sarmatians, brother of the divine Commodus, grandson of the divine Pius, great-grandson of the divine Hadrian, great-great-grandson of the divine Trajan, Conqueror of the Parthians, great-great-great-grandson of the divine Nerva, chief priest, in the fourth (? error for fourteenth) year of his tribunician power, acclaimed *imperator* eleven times, consul for the third time, proconsul, father of the fatherland, the Roman citizens, veterans residing in the district of Fortunalis whose parents through the generosity of the divine Augustus [_ _ _] received lands in the community of Sutunurca, had this set up at public expense.

Uthina was a colony established by Julius Caesar. The veterans in the vicinity had evidently preserved a common identity and communal spirit which recalled their ancestors' grant of land from Augustus. Or perhaps the tradition of the community's origins had been revived in order to gain some benefit from the emperor.

375 *SP* 85 = *FIRA* 3. 50, papyrus, Fayum, Egypt, AD 189 and 194

col. i   Translation of will

[Gaius Longinus Castor], veteran honourably discharged from [the praetorian fleet] at Misenum, made his will.

[I instruct] that my slave Marcella, aged over [thirty] and my slave [Cleopatra], aged over thirty should be [free], and [each of them is to be my] heir in equal portions. [All others] are to be disinherited. Let them take up their [inheritance], each one taking her own portion, when they recognize it and are able to attest that they are my heirs. It is not permitted to sell or to mortgage it. But if the above-mentioned Marcella sufers the fate of mankind, then I wish her portion of the inheritance to go to Sarapion and Socrates and Longus. Similarly in respect of Cleopatra, I wish her portion to go to Nilus. Whoever becomes my heir shall be required to give, perform, and execute all these provisions which are written down in this my will, and I commit them to the trust imposed by it.

My slave Sarapias, daughter of my freedwoman Cleopatra, is to be freed, and [to her] I give and bequeath five *arourae* (c. 3 acres) of corn land which I have in the vicinity of the village of Karanis in the place called Ostrich, also one and a quarter *arourae* (c. ⅕ of an acre) of a valley, also a third portion of my house, and a third portion of that house which I bought previously from Prapetheus, mother of Thaseus, also a third portion of the palm grove which I have close to the canal which is called (*col. ii*) Old Canal. I wish my body to be borne out and laid out for burial through the care and piety of my heirs. If, after this, I leave anything written in my own hand, written in any manner whatsoever, I wish it to be valid. May malice and fraud be absent from this will.

When this will had been made, Julius Petronianus bought the household effects for one *sestertius*, Gaius Lucretius Saturnilus held the scales. (Confirmed). Marcus Sempronius Heraclianus was summoned to act as witness. (Confirmed).

The will was made in the village of Karanis in the Arsinoite nome, on 17 October(?), in the consulship of the two Silani (AD 189), year 30 of Emperor Caesar Marcus Aurelius Commodus Antoninus Pius Fortunate Augustus, Conqueror of the Armenians, Conqueror of the Medes, Conqueror of the Parthians, Conqueror of the Sarmatians, Conqueror of the Germans, 21 Hathyr.

If I leave any additional document written in my own hand, I wish it to be valid.

The will was opened and read in the metropolis of the Arsinoite nome in the forum of Augustus, at the office of the five per cent tax on inheritances and manumissions on 21 February, in the consulship of the present consuls, in year 2 (194) of Emperor Caesar Lucius Septimius Severus Pertinax Augustus, 27 Mecheir. The remainder who had affixed their seal: Gaius Longinus Acylas. (Confirmed). Julius Volusius, Marcus Antistius Petronianus, Julius Gemellus, veteran.

Translation of the tablets of codicils.

I, Gaius Longinus Castor, veteran, honourably discharged from the praetorian fleet at Misenum, made the codicils. I have appointed Marcus Sempronius Heraclianus, my worthy friend, to act as administrator of my property according to his own good faith. I give and bequeath to my kinsman Julius Serenus four thousand sesterces. I wrote this in my own hand on 7 February. Sealed by: Longinus Acylas and Valerius Priscus. Those who affixed their seals: Gaius Longinus Acylas. (Confirmed). Julius Philoxenus, Gaius Lucretius Saturnilus. (Confirmed). Gaius Longinus Castor, Julius Gemellus, veteran. They were opened and read on the same day on which the will was opened.

(Second hand) I, Gaius Lucius Geminianus, skilled in Roman law, translated the preceding copy, and it tallies with the original will.

(On the back) Of Gaius Longinus Castor.

This will was written in Latin and then translated into Greek after it was opened. Castor, who had settled in Egypt after serving in the fleet at Misenum, owned considerable property around the Arsinoite nome, including two houses, and a number of slaves. It is tempting to speculate that the men with Roman names who acted as witnesses were other veterans living in the vicinity, although only one (Gemellus) is designated as such. It remains obscure why in the first instance Castor left most of his property to two female ex-slaves, even though he had a kinsman.

9 The army in the later empire

The political and military dislocation, and the economic and social upheaval in the fifty years after the murder of Severus Alexander in AD 235 had such an effect on the propertied élite that subsequent writers looked back with nostalgia to the thirteen years of that feeble emperor's inept rule as a kind of golden age. Significantly, one of the fictitious claims in the literary account of Alexander was that he was a strict military disciplinarian. In the face of foreign invasion and internal secession, men recognized the need for an emperor who could command the respect of an army and lead effectively in person. Not only had the balance between the civil and military leader shifted irrevocably towards the military side, but leadership and inspiration were also needed wherever incursions had to be repelled. All these factors contributed to the large number of usurpations which were a feature of this period. However, contemporary writers, doubtless much influenced by the views of their own class which had most to lose from the disruption, perhaps exaggerated the effects, which may have appeared only gradually; moreover the knowledge of writers was probably localized, and the situation may not have been uniformly disastrous. Indeed there is some reason to emphasize the resilience of the empire's economic and social structures in these years (see Whittaker 1976).

Above all, the army remained an essential bulwark of Roman civilization and a vital factor in future recovery; the basic organization of legions and auxilia stationed in the provinces remained intact; territorial loss was confined to Mesopotamia, Dacia, and the *Agri Decumates* between the Rhine and Danube; despite repeated civil wars the army was still able to win battles against outside foes. And presumably the process of recruiting, feeding, equipping, and paying the troops must have continued, although we know little of it. In certain respects the army became stronger, as several emperors, notably Gallienus (AD 253–68) and Aurelian (AD 270–5), attempted to adapt military organization to changing circumstances. Gallienus began regularly to employ men of equestrian rank in legionary commands previously held by senators, and since these equestrians generally had more military experience than senators, it is not surprising that the military responsibilities of senatorial governors were gradually taken over by equestrians, and the old constraint of the senatorial monopoly of high office was at last removed. Moreover, the enhanced role of cavalry and the increased use of detachments of troops for special purposes, fostered the emergence of a kind of central force, containing cavalry and infantry, which was able to move to the support of the troops permanently stationed in individual provinces. Since it attended normally on the person of the emperor and was commanded by him, it might also make him less susceptible to revolt. The appearance of this force, which was a precursor of the later field army, is unlikely to have been the result of a single decision. It was put together originally to deal with an immediate crisis, but in the course of time as its value was appreciated it acquired a more permanent structure. Aurelian brought additional resources to the army by recruiting fighting men from peoples who had fought against Rome, like the Vandals.

Diocletian (AD 284–305) established the tetrarchy, in which the emperor and his co-emperor were supported by two Caesars, each one of the four in practice taking major responsibility for a geographical area of the empire. This more stable military structure allowed Diocletian to make use of the changes in the army made by his predecessors and to introduce further reforms. While preserving the independent field force, he also believed in the maintenance of a strong military presence in the frontier zones of the empire, with legionary and auxiliary troops permanently stationed in the provinces. By AD 305 there were at least sixty-seven legions in service, that is, more than double the number of troops serving in AD 235, if the legions had their usual complement, although the evidence for this is inconclusive. Diocletian also built more forts to ensure good communications by road or river, to provide a base for defence and consolidation, and also a platform for attack or counter-attack. The most notable example is the *Strata Diocletiana* on the eastern frontier, where a chain of forts at twenty-mile intervals garrisoned by infantry cohorts and some cavalry, was linked by a military road; legionary bases were positioned in the vicinity. The object was to guarantee Roman control in the area and also to ensure communications from southern Syria to the Euphrates. Diocletian naturally aimed to preserve Roman territory from outside attack, but his military arrangements did not draw a merely defensive line and did not rule out wars of aggression.

Constantine (AD 307–337), using elements of Diocletian's field
force, developed this part of the army, gave it a formal, permanent
structure, and granted its members (*comitatenses*) special privileges.
However, territorial troops (*limitanei*) remained permanently stationed in provinces on the frontiers, and the essential structure of the
Diocletianic system remained intact; large sections of the frontier
zones, which might include territory from several civil provinces,
were under the control of *duces* who commanded the territorial troops.
Constantine's abolition of the praetorian guard in AD 312 was partly
dictated by political expediency in that it had supported his opponent
Maxentius. But other groups, the *protectores* and the *scholae Pala-
tinae*, had already increasingly taken over responsibility for protecting the emperor's person. Constantine accepted the solutions to
the military problems of the empire which had been arrived at by
experimentation and experience, and with limited innovation provided
the best hope for the maintenance of Roman power in the long term.
Neither Diocletian nor Constantine, however, fundamentally changed
the political set-up in the empire, in which the emperor still depended
on the support and loyalty of his troops, with whom he built up a
personal association, whose emoluments he guaranteed, and to whom
he presented himself as a successful military leader. The soldiers,
recruited from the lower classes, received privileges and status
through military service which set them above other people from the
same class.

There are few reliable literary sources for this period, and in
particular we lack a good narrative historian, since the extant text of
Ammianus Marcellinus only begins in AD 353. The single most
important source is the *Notitia Dignitatum*, an official document
compiled around AD 395, which contains a series of entries for the
eastern and western parts of the empire as it was divided at that time,
listing the main office holders. In the case of the military officers, the
units under their command are set out. From this evidence it is possible
to discover the troops serving in the various arms of the service, and
plot the development and use of certain units from Diocletian's time.
The complexity and scale of the document, however, make it impossible to reproduce in a sourcebook of this nature. Legal texts provide
useful information about the privileged status of the army and concessions granted to individual groups of soldiers. Inscriptions and papyri
are less numerous than in the earlier empire, and so less is known about
the careers of soldiers and their commanders, and the role of the army
in local life. Indeed important aspects of the later army remain obscure,
for example, the number of soldiers, rates of pay and emoluments,

recruitment and settlement (van Berchem 1952; Jones 1964: 52–60; 607–54; 1417–50; Goodburn and Bartholemew 1976; Luttwak 1976: 127–90; Duncan-Jones 1978; Barnes 1982; Johnson 1983; Williams 1985; Isaac 1992: 161–218).

376 Herodian (2nd–3rd C.AD), 7. 2

(Herodian is describing Maximinus' personal bravery in a battle against German tribes in AD 235.) The emperor publicised this battle and his own courageous role in it by means of despatches to the senate and people, but in addition ordered that it should be depicted in huge paintings, which he then erected in front of the senate house so that the Roman people could see as well as hear what he had done. Afterwards, the senate had the painting destroyed along with the rest of the monuments in his honour. There were other battles too where Maximinus intervened personally and performed deeds of prowess in battle and was always congratulated for his bravery.

We can trust this account because all our sources are usually very hostile to Maximinus. He was the first Roman emperor to fight in battle, and in the later third century it became more difficult to isolate emperors from the realities of their role as commander-in-chief. In AD 251 Decius was defeated and killed by the Goths, while in AD 260 Valerian was captured by Shapur I, the Persian king.

377 Aurelius Victor (4th C.AD), *The Caesars* 33. 33

And the senators were disturbed not only by the common misfortune of the Roman world but also by the insult to their own order, because he (Gallienus) was the first, through fear that his own idleness would result in the transfer of power to the best of the nobles, to forbid members of the senate to undertake military service or to go to an army.

Victor's evidence is suspect because of his hostility to Gallienus and his enthusiasm for the cause of the senate, and it is doubtful if the emperor formally decided to exclude senators from military service. Moreover, Victor's attribution of motive is questionable. It is likely that in the first instance Gallienus decided unofficially to employ equestrians to command legions because they had more military experience. There may in any case have been an insufficient number of senators competent and willing to serve. There were precedents dating from the end of the first century AD for the use of equestrians in posts normally held by senators, although usually in exceptional circumstances (Campbell 1984: 404–8; Gallienus – Pflaum 1976; Osier 1977; nos 378–81).

378 *CIL* 3. 3424 = *ILS* 545, inscription, Aquincum (Budapest), Lower Pannonia, AD 267

To the *Genius* of Emperor Publius [Licinius Gall]ienus Unconquered Augustus, Clementius Silvius, most eminent man, acting in place of the governor, and Valerius Marcellinus, prefect of a legion, defender (*protector*) of our emperor, acting in place of the legate, townsmen from the province of Raetia, happily willingly and deservedly fulfilled their vow, in the consulship of Paternus and Archesilaus.

Here two equestrians have taken over positions normally held by senators, but as the wording shows, this was still regarded as a temporary expedient. The *protectores* seem to have been officers or prospective officers attached to the person of the emperor. By the time of Diocletian they constituted a personal bodyguard of which the emperor himself was the commander.

379 *CIL* 8. 2615 = *ILS* 1194, inscription, Lambaesis, Africa, AD 260 (?)

In honour of Jupiter Best and Greatest and the other immortal gods and goddesses, Gaius Macrinius Decianus, most distinguished man, legate of the Emperors with propraetorian power of the provinces of Numidia and Noricum, (set this up) after the slaughter and rout of the Bavares and the capture of their notorious leader, a people who under the united rule of four kings had broken into the province of Numidia, first in the area of Millev, second on the boundary of Mauretania and Numidia, and on a third occasion with the Quinquegentiani peoples of Mauretania Caesariensis, and also the Fraxinenses, who were ravaging the province of Numidia.

Texts nos. 379–81 demonstrate the changing circumstances in the government of the province of Numidia and the command of the III Augusta. Decianus is the last unambiguous example of a senatorial governor exercising military responsibilities; text no. 380 shows that the III Augusta was now commanded by an equestrian prefect (demonstrated by the equestrian title *egregius* – 'outstanding man'), text no. 381 that by Diocletian's time the province was governed by an equestrian with the official title of governor (*praeses*), while another equestrian commanded the legion.

380 *CIL* 8. 2665 = *ILS* 584, inscription, Lambaesis, AD 270–5

In honour of the good god, the boy (Azizos, the 'light-bringer', apparently an attendant of Apollo) for the welfare of our lord Lucius

Domitius Aurelian Pius Fortunate Unconquered Augustus, Marcus Aurelius Fortunatus, outstanding man, prefect of Legion III Augusta Aurelia, and Aelia Optata, most distinguished lady (i.e. of senatorial family), his wife, willingly and enthusiastically fulfilled their vow.

381 *CIL* 8. 2572 = *ILS* 5786, inscription, Lambaesis, AD 286–305

The most unconquered Augusti, Diocletian and Maximian, restorers and extenders of their world, restored to a sound condition and improved the aqueduct of Legion III Augusta of Diocletian and Maximian, our Augusti, which had decayed because of the negligence of many people and had been abandoned for a long span of years, under the supervision of Aurelius Maximianus, most splendid man, governor of the province of Numidia, and Clodius Honoratus, outstanding man, prefect of the same legion.

382 Zosimus (5th–6th C.AD), 2. 34

Constantine also did something else that allowed the barbarians an unimpeded approach into the territory under Roman control. Because of Diocletian's wisdom all the frontier areas of the Roman empire had been protected in the way described above with settlements and strongholds and towers, and all the soldiers were based here. The barbarians, therefore, could not break in, as forces with the capacity to repel incursions would encounter them everywhere. Constantine put an end to this security by withdrawing most of the troops from the frontier areas and stationing them in cities that did not need protection, and therefore deprived of protection the people who were suffering at the hands of the barbarians, and afflicted peaceful cities with the plague of the soldiers. Because of this some have already become desolate and the troops have been enfeebled by indulging themselves in shows and luxurious living. Therefore, to put it bluntly, he himself was the first to sow the seeds of the present disastrous situation.

As a pagan, Zosimus disliked Constantine, the propagator of Christianity, and exaggerated and misrepresented the emperor's innovations in respect of the field army. He also chose to ignore the fact that Diocletian had employed a similar type of independent force, even though it was not necessarily a permanent element of the army at that time. Zosimus was however correct to point out that an essential aspect of Diocletian's policy was the permanent stationing of troops in key provinces.

383 Lactantius (3rd–4th C.AD), *On the Deaths of the Persecutors* **7. 2**

Through his greed and fear he (Diocletian) overturned the entire world. He appointed three men to share his rule, with the result that the world was divided into four parts and the armies multiplied, since each one of the emperors struggled to keep a much larger number of soldiers than any previous emperor had had when he was administering the state alone. The number of people who were recipients began to outnumber contributors, to such an extent that the substance of the farmers was consumed by the enormity of the requisitions, fields were abandoned and arable land was turned into woodland. Furthermore, to ensure that terror permeated everywhere, the provinces too were divided into chunks; many governors and even more officials were set over individual areas, indeed virtually over individual communities; there were also many accountants, and controllers, and deputies of the prefects, among all of whom civil behaviour was a rarity; instead there were only numerous condemnations and confiscations, and exactions of countless resources which were not merely frequent but incessant, and led to insufferable abuse. Moreover, the methods for raising troops were intolerable.

By contrast to Zosimus, Lactantius gives, from the Christian standpoint, a critical opinion of Diocletian's reforms in the army and administration, and in particular the exactions required to finance them. Although he is a hostile witness, he gives us a valuable contemporary reaction to changes which he believed were very painful to many sections of society. It is true that Lactantius cannot be right to suggest that the army was quadrupled, but other evidence indicates the strength of the Severan army was at least doubled (Duncan-Jones 1978; MacMullen 1980).

384 *Act of Maximilianus* **2. 8–9 (Musurillo 1972: 17), AD 295**

Dion (proconsul of Africa) said: 'Think about your youth and serve in the army. This is the right course of action for a young man'.

Maximilian replied: 'My service is for my Lord. I cannot serve the world. I have already stated this, I am a Christian'.

Dion the proconsul said: 'In the sacred retinue (*comitatus*) of our lords Diocletian and Maximian, Constantius and Maximus, there are soldiers who are Christians, and they serve'.

Maximilian said: 'They themselves know what is right for them. I, however, am a Christian and I cannot do evil'.

For the context see text no. 5. The *comitatus* suggests a field force in attendance on the emperor (Jones 1964: 52–4). Cf. *P. Oxy.* 43, recto, col. ii, a papyrus dated to early AD 295, dealing with the collection of chaff for imperial troops on campaign in Egypt, which mentions an officer of the *comites* of the emperor (though it is not certain that Diocletian himself can have been present in Egypt early in 295 – see A. Bowman *JRS* 1976, p. 159; cf. Barnes 1982: 54).

385 *CIL* 6. 2759 = *ILS* 2045, inscription, near Rome

To the spirits of the departed. Valerius Tertius, soldier of the tenth praetorian cohort, who lived thirty-six years, three months, fifteen days, and served in a Moesian legion for five years, in the lancers (*lanciarii*) for eleven years, in the praetorian guard for [_ _ _] years, [_ _ _] century of Salvius [_ _ _

This inscription must be dated before AD 312 when Constantine abolished the praetorian guard. If we may take it that the soldier lists his posts in ascending order of importance, a *lanciarius* ranked above a legionary and below a praetorian, and elsewhere is associated with the imperial *comitatus* (see text no. 386).

386 *CIL* 3. 6194 = *ILS* 2781, inscription, Troesmis, Lower Moesia, late 3rd C. AD

To the spirits of the departed, in honour of Valerius Thiumpus, who served as a soldier in Legion XI Claudia, was chosen as lancer (*lanciarius*) in the sacred retinue (*comitatus*), then served as a guard (*protector*) for five years, was discharged, was prefect of Legion II Herculia, which he commanded for two years, six months, and died, lived forty-five years, three months, eleven days [_ _ _

The legion Herculia was named after Diocletian's co-emperor, Maximian, who was given the honorary name Herculius.

387 *CJ* 7. 64. 9

The same Emperors (Diocletian and Maximian) and two Caesars to Rufinus. To veterans who are serving in a legion or a *vexillatio* and after twenty years' service have received an honourable or medical discharge, we have granted exemption from compulsory personal services and burdens. Furthermore, in order to repay the loyal devotion of our soldiers with this indication of our generosity, we have relieved them from any requirement to appeal (i.e. for exemption).

388 *CJ* 10. 55(54). 3

The same Emperors (Diocletian and Maximian) to Philopator. Exemption from undertaking public office and compulsory public services is legally granted to veterans if they are shown to have received an honourable or medical discharge after twenty years' military service performed in a legion or a *vexillatio*. Therefore, since you say that you served in a cohort, you should realize that it is pointless for you to seek to claim exemption for yourself.

These rescripts grant special privileges only to veterans who served in a legion or cavalry detachment (*vexillatio*), while those serving in auxiliary cohorts are regarded as of lesser status. At this time the field army was not important enough, or perhaps insufficiently firmly established, to qualify for any special recognition. Cf. text no. 394.

389 *CIL* 3. 764 = *ILS* 4103, inscription, Tomi (Constanţa), Lower Moesia, AD 293–305

To the great Mother of the gods, for the welfare and security of our lords the Emperors and Caesars, Aurelius Firminianus, most splendid man, commander (*dux*) of the frontiers in the province of Scythia, dedicated this with good auspices.

In some provinces Diocletian separated civil authority from military responsibilities, the latter being exercised by a *dux*. Several are attested in his reign, some with responsibility for an area covering several civil provinces. This process seems to have begun late in the reign and was a gradual development, perhaps in response to local emergencies, rather than the result of a single decision.

390 *CTh* 7. 22. 1, AD 319

Emperor Constantine Augustus to Octavianus. We order that veterans' sons who are fit for military service, of whom some indolently refuse to perform compulsory military duties while others are so cowardly that they wish to evade the necessity of military service by mutilating their own bodies, if they should be judged incapable of military service because their fingers have been cut off, are to be assigned, without any ambiguity, to perform the compulsory public services and duties of decurions.

Given on 16 February at Sirmium. Received on 7 April at Rhegium in the consulship of Constantine Augustus for the fifth time and Licinius Caesar.

This rescript is probably of a type common in the law codes, where an emperor confirms a previous decision. The insistence that veterans' sons join up would fit in with the tough measures of Diocletian, who laid upon cities or landowners the obligation to ensure sufficient recruits annually from their territory. This should be seen in the context of a general development of hereditary occupational ties. Lactantius (text no. 383) had denounced the oppression associated with the military levy under Diocletian, a burden which from the late third century communities sought to avoid by substituting monetary payments (*aurum tironicum*). One way round the difficulty of finding sufficient numbers of recruits was the absorption into the Roman army of peoples who had fought against Rome and were then settled on Roman territory.

391 *AE* 1981. 777, inscription, near Cotiaeum, Asia, *c.* AD 300

Aurelius Gaius the second, served in Legion I Italica in Moesia, chosen for Legion VIII Augusta in Germany, (served ?) with Legion I Jovia Scythica in Scythia and Pannonia; as a recruit served as novice cavalryman, then as cavalry lance-bearer (*lanciarius*), orderly (*optio*) of a centurion of the third rank, orderly of a senior centurion, orderly of a [chief centurion (?)], orderly of the imperial companions (*comites*) [_ _ _] of Legion I Jovia Scythica, travelled round the empire, to Asia, Caria [_ _ _] Lydia, Lycaonia, Cilicia [_ _ _] Syria Phoenice, Arabia, Palestine, Egypt, Alexandria, India [_ _ _] Mesopotamia, Cappadocia [_ _ _] Galatia, Bithynia, Thrace [_ _ _] Moesia, the territory of the Carpi [_ _ _] Sarmatia on four occasions, Viminacium [_ _ _] the territory of the Goths on two occasions, Germany [_ _ _] Dardania, Dalmatia, Pannonia [_ _ _] Gaul, Spain, Mauretania [_ _ _] then I progressed and after [all] these [troubles (?)] I came to my native community, Pessinus, where I was reared, and am now living in the [village] of Cotiaeum [_ _ _ with (?)] Macedonia (his daughter?); from the proceeds of my labours, I have set up this stone in honour of Julia Arescusa my own dearest wife, as a memorial until the resurrection. Farewell everyone.

Aurelius had served as a cavalryman in the *lanciarii*, who had probably been organized by Diocletian as part of the *comitatus*. In his long military career, in the record of which there are several gaps because of the damaged state of the inscription, he had visited at least twenty-three provinces or dioceses, four towns, and five regions situated outside Roman territory. He served in Legion I Jovia Scythica, which was recruited by Diocletian and based at Noviodunum; moreover the campaigns in which he participated against the Sarmatians, Goths, Germans, and in Mesopotamia, India, and Egypt, suggest a date in the reign of Diocletian, probably around AD 300. Aurelius was apparently a Christian serving in the army, before Christianity had been officially adopted.

392 *CIL* 6. 3637 = *ILS* 2346, inscription, Rome, early 4th C. AD

Sacred to the spirits of the departed. Valerius Genialis, soldier of Legion II Divitensis Italica, standard-bearer, lived fifty years, served twenty-six years; Verina erected this to an estimable man.

The II Divitensis Italica was evidently a detachment of the II Italica stationed in Noricum, which had been sent to Divitia on the right bank of the Rhine. It may be conjectured that Constantine brought it with him to Italy in his campaign against Maxentius, and that Valerius Genialis had died there. The legion then remained as part of the *Comitatenses*, among which it is listed subsequently in the *Notitia Dignitatum*. Constantine considerably strengthened the field army, which now consisted of infantry legions (some may have been only one thousand strong), newly constituted infantry *auxilia*, cavalry regiments, and various other detachments and sections of the field force that had operated under Diocletian. The emperor normally took charge of the *comitatenses* himself, but two new commanders were appointed – the *magister peditum* (commander of the infantry), and the *magister equitum* (cavalry commander), although the earliest known example is in the 340s. In the privileges granted to his troops Constantine eventually distinguished between the soldiers of the field army and territorial troops permanently stationed in the provinces.

393 *FIRA* 1. 93, inscription, Brigetio (Szöny), Upper Pannonia, AD 311

Emperor Caesar Flavius Valerius Constantine Pius Fortunate Un-conquered Augustus, chief priest, in the seventh year of his tribunician power, acclaimed *imperator* six times, consul, father of the fatherland, proconsul, and Emperor Caesar Valerius Licinianus [Licinius] Pius Fortunate Unconquered Augustus, chief priest, in the fourth year of his tribunician power, acclaimed *imperator* three times, consul, father of the fatherland, proconsul.

Copy of the sacred letter.

Greetings, our dearest Dalmatius.

Since we wish always to show consideration in respect of all the benefits and privileges of our soldiers in keeping with their loyalty and toil, we thought it right, dearest Dalmatius, that in this matter also we ought to show consideration for our said soldiers through the providence of our arrangements. Accordingly, since we see the toils of our said soldiers which they undertake through constant expeditions on behalf of the stability and good of the state, we thought it right to make provision and arrangements in order that through our foresight they may happily enjoy during the period of their military service the pleasant fruits of their own toil, and after military service may have peaceful repose and appropriate freedom from care. Therefore we thought it right to indicate to Your Devotion that our said soldiers even during the time of their military service are to be exempt, through our decision, in respect of five tax units, from their property rating and from the normal charges of taxes in kind. Moreover, they are to have the same immunity when they have completed the full legal period of service and acquired honourable discharge (i.e. after twenty-four years). Those men, however, who have acquired honourable discharge but after only twenty years of service, are to be exempt from taxes in kind in respect of two tax units, that is, each man himself and his wife. Any soldier who is made incapable of service because of a wound acquired in battle, even if he has secured release from his duties for that reason within a period of less that twenty years of service, is to be eligible for the benefits of this same indulgence of ours, so that he is to be exempt in respect of his own tax unit and that of his wife. Therefore, the said soldiers may be happy that through our benevolent providence consideration has been given in every way to their peaceful retirement and welfare. Although the previous practice was that a large number of soldiers received their honourable discharge simultaneously from their commander and each man got a copy for himself, while the original copy of the order for discharge remained in the keeping of the clerk, we wish nevertheless that when soldiers have acquired their honourable or medical discharge, as mentioned above, each man should receive from his commander an individual discharge addressed to him in person, so that through this authentic and reliable proof which he has always in his possession, he can enjoy constant and secure peace. Of course Your Sacredness will be aware that those who are discharged because of an offence cannot share in the benefaction of this same law, since it is right to take account of both factors, the practices of a respectable life and honourable discharge. Furthermore, since it is right that they should understand the appropriate rewards granted by us which have been earned through military service, in order that the said soldiers should enjoy in perpetuity the perpetual benefaction of this same indulgence of ours, and that our eternally provident arrangement should become well-established, we wish the content of this indulgence of ours to be inscribed on a bronze tablet and enshrined among the military standards in each military camp, so that both the legionary soldiers as well as the cavalry organized in units (*vexillationes*) in Illyricum may enjoy equal benefits from our foresight, just as they undertake equal toil in their military service.

Added in the divine hand: Farewell, our dearest Dalmatius.

In the consulship of the divine Maximianus for the eighth time and [Maximinus Augustus for the second time, Emperors] on 10 June, at Serdica.

The prescript to this letter was added later. Although in his grant of privileges Constantine specifically mentions the Illyrian troops, the general tone of his letter must mean that all troops in the parts of the empire he then controlled were similarly treated and received an appropriately worded copy of his instructions. The repeated expressions of concern for the welfare of the troops, the generosity of the privileges of exemption, and the special arrangements for the issue of discharge certificates, remind us that in AD 311 Constantine and Licinius had made an agreement against Maximinus Daia and Maxentius, and that with civil war imminent, the absolute loyalty of their soldiers was crucial, whatever the price. Constantine was subsequently to revise these concessions (see below). The organization of the army at this time did not include a formal provision for the field army (*comitatenses*), a designation which is not specifically attested until AD 325 (text no. 394), although Constantine's version of the field army probably originated in the campaign against Maxentius in AD 312.

394 *CTh* 7. 20. 4, AD 325

The same Emperor (Constantine) to Maximus, Prefect of the City (probably an error for Vicar of the East). Soldiers of the field army (*comitatenses*), territorial soldiers (*ripenses*), and imperial bodyguards (*protectores*) may all exempt from tax, themselves, and their father and mother and wife, if they are still alive, and if they have been entered on the tax lists. If, however, the soldiers should lack any one of these people or have none of them, they are to exempt in respect of their own property only so much as they would have been able to exempt for these people, if they had not been lacking. However, they are not to make an agreement with another person so that they gain exemption for property belonging to another by pretending to own it, but they must exempt only that property specifically belonging to them.

{ We sanction that veterans after they have received letters confirming their full completion of service, are to be exempt from taxes in respect of their own person and that of their wives, while the others who receive honourable discharge, shall be exempt only in respect of their own person }. We grant that all veterans from any army whatsoever (i.e. field and territorial troops) along with their wives should enjoy exemption in respect of one person each. A veteran of the territorial troops who in accordance with an earlier law after twenty-four years of service and the award of an honourable discharge, used to enjoy exemption in respect of one person, even if he acquires an honourable discharge after twenty years of service, shall nevertheless have exemption in respect of one person on the precedent of the field army soldiers. {Even if he should be discharged before completion of twenty years of service, he shall have the same munificence since weak and disabled people are not entered on the tax lists.}

Cavalry soldiers and soldiers belonging to infantry cohorts are to be exempt in respect of their own person, as long as they remain on active service; and their veterans are to have the reward of similar exemption, if they should obtain their discharge at any time and in any area. Soldiers discharged from the field army because of old age or disablement are to be exempt in respect of two people, that is, each man and his wife, irrespective of the number of years served. And the territorial troops are to have the same privilege without distinction, if they prove that they were discharged as a result of wounds acquired in war, with the limitation that, if any of them should leave military service after serving fifteen years, before the completion of their twenty-four years, he is to enjoy exemption only in respect of his own person. But it is right to exempt the wife of one of the territorial troops, if he was discharged after twenty-four years' service.

Posted on 17 June at Antioch in the consulship of Paulinus and Julianus.

This law contains a number of obscurities and contradictions, and Mommsen judged the passages marked {} to be interpolations. Moreover, the first paragraph is obscure and seems to contradict the rest of the law. It may have been mistakenly included in garbled form from an earlier law of Constantine on veterans' privileges. On this basis we may distinguish: (1) the field army (*comitatenses*) who earn exemption of two tax units (for the soldier and his wife) after 24 years' service and one tax unit after 20 years' service; (2) territorial troops (*ripenses* – riverbank troops I take to be the equivalent of *limitanei*), who have the same exemptions; (3) soldiers of the *alae* and cohorts who made up the old auxiliary troops and who also constituted part of the territorial troops, who now receive exemption of one tax unit after 24 years' service. In the event of a medical discharge, group (1) received exemption of two tax units in any circumstances, group (2) exemption of two units if they could prove that they had been wounded and had more than 15 years' service; otherwise only one unit; group (3) got no benefits.

Despite the difficulties, this law shows first a reduction in military privileges in relation to the letter of AD 311 (text no. 393); now that he was in full control Constantine was more confident in dealing with the troops, and tax exemptions were costly; and second, a formal distinction between the field army and the territorial troops. Now, although the field army troops are more privileged in respect of medical discharges, in the main the two groups were treated in a broadly similar fashion. Indeed Constantine improved the standing of the territorial troops by allowing them exemption for themselves after twenty rather than twenty-fours years of service. So, on the basis of this evidence we cannot say that Constantine reduced the importance and role of the territorial troops in order to enhance the status of the field army.

395 *CTh* 7. 20. 2, AD 320 (?)

The same Emperor (Constantine). When he had entered the army headquarters and had been greeted by the prefects and tribunes and the most eminent men, an acclamation arose: 'Constantine Augustus, may the gods keep you safe for us. Your welfare is our welfare. We are speaking the truth. We are speaking on oath'.

The assembled veterans shouted out: 'Constantine Augustus, why have we been made veterans, if we have no special privilege?'

Constantine Augustus said: 'I ought more and more to increase not diminish the happiness of my fellow-veterans'.

Victorinus, a veteran, said: 'Do not permit us to be subject to compulsory public services and burdens everywhere'.

Constantine Augustus said: 'Tell me more clearly; what are the most serious burdens, which oppress you most persistently?'

All the veterans said: 'Surely you yourself know'.

Constantine Augustus said: 'Now let it be absolutely clear that through my benevolence all veterans have been granted the right that none of them should be harassed by any compulsory public service, nor by any public labour, nor by any exactions, nor by magistrates, nor by taxes. In whatever markets they do business, they shall not have to pay any taxes on sales. Moreover, tax collectors, who normally make extensive exactions from those in business, are to keep away from these veterans. They are for all time to enjoy repose after their exertions. By means of this same letter we have forbidden our treasury from disturbing any one at all of these men, but they are to be permitted to buy and sell, so that in the peace and repose of our era they may enjoy their privileges unimpaired and enjoy the tranquillity of their old age after their exertions . . .

Given on 1 March, in the community of the Velovoci (?), in the consulship of Constantine Augustus for the sixth time and Constantinus Caesar (AD 320).

It has been suggested that this constitution should be dated to AD 326 in the aftermath of the defeat of Licinius (consuls – Constantine VII and Constantius Caesar; in that case the place will be Heraclea). It would be striking that the soldiers' acclamation mentioned the gods, fourteen years after Constantine had espoused Christianity in AD 312. However Barnes (1982: 69) argues for AD 307. Constantine is notably willing to respond to the direct approach of the soldiers, and associates himself with them by using the flattering term 'fellow-veterans', and by speaking of their deserved peaceful retirement after all the labours of military life. The political relationship of emperor and army had not changed significantly from the first and second centuries. In sum, veterans had a considerable range of exemptions: from the poll and property tax, from compulsory public services and duties on the local council to which they otherwise might have been liable since they owned land, from market taxes, and customs dues.

396 *CTh* 7. 20. 3, AD 325 (?)

The same Emperor (Constantine) to all veterans. In accordance with our instructions, veterans are to receive unoccupied land and they are to hold it tax-free in perpetuity. They are also to receive twenty-five *folles* in cash in order to buy the necessities of rural life, and in addition a pair of oxen and one hundred *modii* of assorted seeds. We grant that any veteran who wishes to engage in business should have a sum amounting to one hundred *folles* tax-free. In addition to these persons, therefore, who are based in farming or business, all you who are without land (?) and have no occupation, should make use of this assistance so that you do not suffer from hardship.

Given on 13 October at Constantinople in the consulship of Constantine Augustus for the sixth time and Constantinus Caesar (AD 320, but on this date Constantine was in Illyricum; Barnes (1982: 76) suggests 325).

As in the early empire, a veteran could receive a plot of land or a cash handout as superannuation. Jones (1964: 636) has calculated, on the basis of the amount of seed, that the allocations would have consisted of about twenty *iugera* of arable land and perhaps as much again for the alternate fallow year. Since the lands used for these distributions were unoccupied, the condition of the soil may have deteriorated, but it was an important concession that the land was tax-exempt.

397 *CTh* 7. 20. 5, AD 328

The same Emperor (Constantine) to Maximus, Praetorian Prefect. Care must be taken that veterans honoured with the status of an imperial bodyguard (*protector*), or who have achieved various distinctions through their merits, should not be subjected to unseemly abuse, and if anyone is caught while committing this crime, it is right that provincial governors should refer the matter to your court and send the above mentioned persons to your office, so that the offence can be most easily punished in accordance with its gravity.

Given on 29 December at Trier in the consulship of Januarinus and Justus.

398 *CJ* 6. 21. 14, AD 294

Emperors Diocletian and Maximian Augusti and the Caesars to the heirs of Maxima. If your mother was appointed heir by her brother while he was in military service and obtained his estate for herself even though the will did not comply with strict legal formulation, it is legally correct that neither the brother of the testator nor his children can recover possession of the estate on the grounds of intestacy.

Given on 3 May, near Sirmium (?) in the consulship of the two Caesars.

399 *CJ* 6. 21. 15, AD 334

Emperor Constantine Augustus to the people. If those soldiers who are engaged on a military expedition, appoint, in an expression of their last wishes, their wives or children or friends or fellow-soldiers or indeed any other person at all as their heirs, they may make a will in whatever way they can, or wish, and neither the merit nor freedom nor rank of their wives or their children are to be challenged, when they have produced the will of their father. Consequently, it is permitted and always will be permitted by the rules of law that, if soldiers have written anything in letters shining red with their own blood on their scabbard or shield, or if they have scratched anything in the dust with their sword at the very moment when they surrender their life in battle, an expression of intent of this kind shall be a valid will.

Given on 11 August (mistaken date – Barnes 1982: 79), at Nicomedia in the consulship of Optatus and Paulinus.

These rescripts show that the privileges enjoyed by soldiers in leaving property, and in making a will that was held to be valid even if it did not adhere to due legal form, continued in the later empire; they were also exempt from certain punishments (*CJ* 9. 41. 8). The emotional language of Constantine, his concern for the welfare of the soldiers and their families, and the fact that this rescript was addressed generally to the people, emphasize the continuing importance of the emperor's personal association with the army.

400 *Historia Augusta, Life of Severus Alexander* 48

(A senator, Ovinius Camillus, plots against Severus Alexander, who welcomes his willingness to share the burdens of ruling.) Then he

(Alexander) gave a banquet for Camillus with all the imperial trappings and indeed on a grander scale than he usually enjoyed himself. When an expedition against the barbarians was proclaimed he invited Camillus to go himself if he wished, or to accompany him. And when the emperor marched on foot, he invited him to share the toil; then, after five miles Alexander told the flagging senator to ride on horseback; and when after two post-houses he was tired even by the horse riding, placed him in a carriage. But this too Camillus could not endure, either genuinely or because he was terrified, and abdicated from the imperial power. Although he was expecting to be executed, Alexander let him go, commending him to the soldiers . . .

The *Historia Augusta* is a series of imperial biographies covering the period AD 117–284 and purports to have been written by six authors in the time of Diocletian and Constantine. However, scholars have been very sceptical, most arguing for single authorship and many for a date in the late fourth century. It is a very unreliable source, containing many inventions and inaccuracies, and in particular most of the supposedly offical documents and letters it quotes are false. It is, therefore, difficult to use the *Historia Augusta* unless it is supported by other source material. This passage is completely fictitious and is presented here (along with text no. 401) as a possible illustration of an upper class view of the role of the emperor with his soldiers in the late fourth century: the threat of conspiracy by ambitious senators, the looming power of the army, the need for an emperor to take personal direction of campaigns, sharing the rigours involved and setting an example, the need to court popularity with the troops.

401 *Historia Augusta, Life of Probus* 22. 4–23. 3

Probus' own words indicate very clearly what he was hoping to be able to achieve, when he said that in a short time soldiers would not be required. Well aware of his own abilities he did not fear either barbarians or tyrants. What kind of happiness would have sprung up if under that emperor soldiers had ceased to exist? No provincial would be providing supplies, no payments would be disbursed in largesse, the Roman state would have an endless supply of money, the emperor would not be spending any money, and nothing would be handed over by owners. Truly he was promising a golden age. There would be no military camps, the trumpet would not need to be heard anywhere, weapons would not have to be made, and that mass of soldiers who now wear out the state in civil wars, would take to the plough, engage in studious pursuits, become familiar with the arts, and sail the seas. Moreover, no one would be killed in war.

This story from the life of Probus (276–82) is also entirely fictitious, but again may indicate disquiet among the articulate about the role of the army in political turmoil and its huge requirements in men, resources, and exactions in kind. Behind the invention and the romantic idealism there may well be genuine ideas about life and government.

Select bibliography

Alföldy, G. (1974) *Noricum*, London.

Baillie Reynolds, P. K. (1926) *The Vigiles of Imperial Rome*, Oxford.

Balty, J. Ch. and Van Rengen, W. (1993) *Apamea in Syria, the Winter Quarters of* Legio II Parthica: *Roman Gravestones from the Military Cemetary*, Brussels.

Barnes, T. D. (1979) 'The date of Vegetius', *Phoenix* 33, 254–7.

—— (1982) *The New Empire of Diocletian and Constantine*, Harvard.

Bingen, J., Bülow-Jacobsen, A., Cockle, W.E.H., Cuvigny, H., Rubinstein, L., and Van Rengen, W. (1992) *Mons Claudianus: Ostraca Graeca et Latina* I (O. Claud. 1 à 190), Cairo.

Birley, A. R. (1981) *The Fasti of Roman Britain*, Oxford.

Birley, E. B. (1965) 'Promotions and transfers in the Roman army II: the Centurionate', *Carnuntum Jahrb.*, 21–33.

—— (1978) 'The religion of the Roman army 1895–1977', *ANRW* II.16.2, 1506–41.

Bishop, M. C. and Coulston, J. C. N. (1993) *Roman Military Equipment*, London.

Blume, F., Lachmann, K., and Rudorff, A., (1848, 1852) *Die Schriften der römischen Feldmesser* (2 vols, reprint 1962), Berlin.

Bosworth, A. B. (1977) 'Arrian and the Alani', *HSCPh* 81, 217–55.

Bowman, A. K. (1970) 'A letter of Avidius Cassius?', *JRS* 60, 20–6.

Bowman, A. K. and Thomas, J. D. (1983) *Vindolanda: The Latin Writing-Tablets*, London.

—— (1986) 'Vindolanda 1985: the new writing-tablets', *JRS* 76, 120–3.

—— (1987) 'New texts from Vindolanda', *Britannia* 18, 125–42.

—— (1991) 'A military strength report from Vindolanda', *JRS* 81, 62–73.

Bowman, A. K., Thomas, J. D. and Adams, J. N. (1990) 'Two letters from Vindolanda', *Britannia* 21, 33–52.

Breeze, D. J. (1969) 'The organization of the legion: the first cohort and the Equites Legionis', *JRS* 59, 50–5.

—— (1971) 'Pay grades and ranks below the centurionate', *JRS* 61, 130–5.

—— (1974) 'The organization of the career structure of the *immunes* and *principales* of the Roman army', *BJ* 174, 245–92.

Bruckner, A. and Marichal, R. (1963) *Chartae Latinae Antiquiores* III, British Museum.

Brunt, P. A. (1950) 'Pay and superannuation in the Roman army', *PBSR* 18, 50–71.

—— (1961) 'Charges of provincial maladministration under the early principate', *Historia* 10, 189–227 (reprinted with additional material in *Roman Imperial Themes*, 53–95; 487–506).

—— (1962) 'The army and the land in the Roman revolution', *JRS* 52, 69–86 (revised version reprinted in *The Fall of the Roman Republic*, 240–80).

—— (1971) *Italian Manpower*, Oxford.

—— (1974a) 'Conscription and volunteering in the Roman imperial army', *SCI* 1, 90–115.

—— (1974b) 'C. Fabricius Tuscus and an Augustan *dilectus*', *ZPE* 13, 161–85.

—— (1975) 'Did imperial Rome disarm her subjects?', *Phoenix* 29, 260–70.

—— (1983) 'Princeps and equites', *JRS* 73, 42–75.

—— (1988) *The Fall of the Roman Republic and Related Essays*, Oxford.

—— (1990) *Roman Imperial Themes*, Oxford.

Campbell, J. B. (1975) 'Who were the "viri militares"?', *JRS* 65, 11–31.

—— (1978) 'The marriage of soldiers under the empire', *JRS* 68, 153–66.

—— (1984) *The Emperor and the Roman Army, 31 BC–AD 235*, Oxford.

—— (1987) 'Teach yourself how to be a general', *JRS* 77, 13–29.

—— (1993) 'War and diplomacy: Rome and Parthia, 31 BC–AD 235', in Rich, J. and Shipley, G. (eds) *War and Society in the Roman World*, 213–40.

Chaumont, M.L. (1987) 'Un document méconnu concernant l'envoi d'un ambassadeur parthe vers Septime Sévère (P. Dura 60 B)', *Historia* 36, 422–47.

Cheesman, G. L. (1914) *The Auxilia of the Roman Imperial Army*, Oxford.

Chevallier, R. (1989) *Roman Roads*, London.

Connolly, P. (1975) *The Roman Army*, London.

—— (1981) *Greece and Rome at War*, London.

Cotton, H. M. and Geiger, J. (1989) *Masada II, The Latin and Greek Documents*, Jerusalem.

Davies, R. W. (1969a) 'Joining the Roman army', *BJ* 169, 208–32.

—— (1969b) 'The *medici* of the Roman armed forces', *Epig. Stud.* 8, 83–99.

—— (1970) 'The Roman military medical service', *Saal. Jahr.* 27, 84–104.

—— (1971) 'The Roman military diet', *Britannia* 2, 122–42.

—— (1972) 'Some more military *medici*', *Epig. Stud.* 9, 1–11.

—— (1974) 'The daily life of the Roman soldier under the principate', *ANRW* II.1, 299–338.

—— (1989) *Service in the Roman Army* (Breeze, D. and Maxfield, V., eds), Edinburgh.

Decker, K.-V. and Selzer, W. (1976) 'Mogontiacum: Mainz von der zeit des Augustus bis zum ende der römischen herrschaft', *ANRW* II.5.1, 457–559.

Dilke, O. A. W. (1971), *The Roman Land Surveyors*, Newton Abbot.

Dixon, K. R. and Southern, P. (1992) *The Roman Cavalry from the First to the Third Century AD*, London.

Dobson, B. (1972) 'Legionary centurion or equestrian officer? A comparison of pay and prospects', *Anc. Soc.* 3, 193–208.

—— (1974) 'The significance of the centurion and "primipilaris" in the Roman army and administration', *ANRW* II.1, 392–434.

—— (1978) *Die Primipilares*, Cologne and Bonn.

Dobson, B. and Breeze, D. J. (1969) 'The Rome cohorts and the legionary centurionate', *Epig. Stud.* 8, 100–24.

Domaszewski, A. von (1895) 'Die Religion des römischen Heeres', *Westdeutsche Zeitschrift für Geschichte und Kunst* 14, 1–124, (Reprinted in *Aufsätze zur römischen Heeresgeschichte*, 81–209, Darmstadt, 1972.)

Duncan-Jones, R. P. (1978) 'Pay and numbers in Diocletian's army', *Chiron* 8 541–60.

Durry, M. (1938) *Les cohortes prétoriennes*, Paris.

Dušanić, S. (1978) 'A military diploma of AD 65', *Germania* 56. 2, 461–75.

Eck, W. and Wolff, H. (eds) (1986) *Heer und Integrationspolitik: Die römischen Militärdiplome als historische Quelle*, Cologne and Vienna.

Feissel, D. and Gascou, J. (1989) 'Documents d'archives romains inédits du moyen Euphrate (IIIe siècle aprés J-C)', *CRAI*, 535–61.

Fink, R. O., Hoey, A. S. and Snyder, W. F. (1940) 'The *Feriale Duranum*', *Yale Classical Studies* 7, 1–222.

Forni, G. (1953) *Il reclutamento delle legioni da Augusto a Diocleziano*, Milan and Rome.

—— (1974) 'Estrazione etnica e sociale dei soldati delle legioni nei primi tre secoli dell'impero', *ANRW* II.1, 339–91.

Freis, H. (1967) *Die Cohortes Urbanae, Epig. Stud.* 2.

Frend, W. H. C. (1956) 'A third century inscription relating to *angareia* in Phrygia', *JRS* 46, 46–56.

Frere, S. S. and St Joseph, J. K. (1983) *Roman Britain from the Air*, Cambridge.

Garnsey, P. and Saller, R. (1987) *The Roman Empire: Economy, Society and Culture*, Berkeley and Los Angeles.

Gilliam, J. F. (1957a) 'Enrolment in the Roman imperial army', *Eos* 48, 207–16 (= *Roman Army Papers*, 163–72).

—— (1957b) 'The appointment of auxiliary centurions', *TAPhA* 88, 155–68 (= *RAP*, 191–205).

—— (1986) *Roman Army Papers*, Amsterdam.

Goodburn, R. and Bartholomew, P. (1976) *Aspects of the 'Notitia Dignitatum'*, *BAR* supplementary series 15, Oxford.

Guéraud, O. (1942) 'Ostraca grecs et latins de l'Wâdi Fawâkhir', *Bulletin de l'Institut français d'Archéologie orientale* 41: 141–196.

Habicht, C. (1969) *Altertümer von Pergamum*, VIII.3.21, Berlin.

Halfmann, H. (1979) *Die Senatoren aus dem östlichen Teil des Imperium Romanum bis zum Ende des 2 Jh. n. Ch., Hypomnemata* 58.

Harmand, J. (1967) *L'Armée et le soldat à Rome de 107 à 50 avant notre ère*, Paris.

Helgeland, J. (1978) 'Roman army religion', *ANRW* 2.16.2, 1470–505.

Hinrichs, F. T. (1974) *Die Geschichte der gromatischen Institutionen*, Wiesbaden.

Holder, P. A. (1980) *Studies in the Auxilia of the Roman Army from Augustus to Trajan*, *BAR* International Series 70, Oxford.

Isaac, B. (1992) *The Limits of Empire, The Roman Army in the East* (revised edition), Oxford.

Jahn, J. (1983) 'Der Sold römischer Soldaten im 3 Jh. n. Chr.: Bemerkungen zu ChLA 446, 473 und 495', *ZPE* 53, 217–27.

Johnson, S. (1983) *Late Roman Fortifications*, London.

Jones, A. H. M. (1964) *The Later Roman Empire 284–602*, Oxford.

Jones, B. and Mattingly, D. (1990) *An Atlas of Roman Britain*, Oxford.

Jones, G. D. B. (1984) '"Becoming different without knowing it". The role and development of *vici*', in Blagg, T. F. C. and King, A. C. (eds) *Military and Civilian in Roman Britain, Cultural Relationships in a Frontier Province*, *BAR* British series 136, 75–91, Oxford.

Kennedy, D. and Riley, D. (1990), *Rome's Desert Frontier from the Air*, London.

Keppie, L. J. F. (1983) *Colonisation and Veteran Settlement in Italy 47–14 BC*, British School at Rome.

—— (1984a) *The Making of the Roman Army, from Republic to Empire*, London.

—— (1984b) 'Colonisation and veteran settlement in Italy in the first century AD', *PBSR* 52, 77–114.

—— (1986) 'Legions in the east from Augustus to Trajan', in Freeman, P. and Kennedy, D. (eds) *The Defence of the Roman and Byzantine East, BAR International series* 297, 411–29, Oxford.

Kraay, C. M. (1960) 'Two new *sestertii* of Domitian', *American Numismatic Society Museum Notes*, 9, 109–16.

Kraft, K. (1951) *Zur Rekrutierung der Alen und Kohorten an Rhein und Donau*, Berne.

Künzl, E. (1988) *Der römische Triumph, Siegesfeiern im antiken Rom*, Munich.

Laporte, J.-P. (1989) *Rapidum, le camp de la cohorte des Sardes en Maurétanie Césarienne*, Sassari.

Le Bohec, Y. (1989a) *L'Armée romaine*, Paris.

—— (1989b) *La IIIe légion Auguste*, Paris.

—— (1989c) *Les unités auxiliaires de l'armée romaine en Afrique Proconsulaire et Numidie sous le haut empire*, Paris.

Lengyel, A. and Radan, G. T. B. (eds) (1980) *The Archaeology of Roman Pannonia*, Lexington, Kentucky and Budapest.

Lenoir, M. (1979) *Pseudo-Hygin: Des fortifications du camp*, Paris.

Lepper, F. A. and Frere, S. (1988) *Trajan's Column*, Gloucester.

Letta, C. (1978) 'Le Imagines Caesarum di un praefectus castrorum Aegypti e l'XI coorte pretoria', *Athenaeum* 56, 3–19.

Levick, B. (1990), *Claudius*, London.

Link, S. (1989) *Konzepte der Privilegierung römischer Veteranen*, Stuttgart.

Luttwak, E. N. (1976) *The Grand Strategy of the Roman Empire from the First Century A.D. to the Third*, Baltimore and London.

MacMullen, R. (1959) 'Roman imperial building in the provinces', *HSCPh* 64, 207–35.

—— (1966) *Enemies of the Roman Order, Treason, Unrest, and Alienation in the Empire*, Harvard.

—— (1967) *Soldier and Civilian in the Later Roman Empire*, Harvard.

—— (1980) 'How big was the Roman imperial army?', *Klio* 62, 451–60.

Mann, J. C. (1963) 'The raising of new legions during the principate', *Hermes* 91, 483–9.

—— (1972) 'The development of auxiliary and fleet diplomas', *Epig. Stud.* 9, 233–41.

—— (1974) 'The frontiers of the principate', *ANRW* II.1, 508–33.

—— (1979) 'Power, force and the frontiers of the empire', review of Luttwak, *The Grand Strategy of the Roman Empire, JRS* 69, 175–83.

—— (1983) *Legionary Recruitment and Veteran Settlement during the Principate*, University of London, Institute of Archaeology Occasional Publication No. 7, London.

—— (1988) 'The organization of *frumentarii*', *ZPE* 74, 149–50.

Mann, J. C. and Roxan, M. M. (1988) 'Discharge certificates of the Roman army', *Britannia* 19, 341–7.

Marichal, R. (1979) 'Les ostraca du Bu Njem', *CRAI*, 436–52.

Marsden, E. W. (1969) *Greek and Roman Artillery, Historical Development,* Oxford.

—— (1971) *Technical Treatises,* Oxford.

Mason, D. J. P. (1987) 'Chester: the *canabae legionis'*, *Britannia* 18, 143–68.

Maxfield, V. A. (1981) *The Military Decorations of the Roman Army,* London.

Maxwell, G. S. and Wilson, D. R. (1987) 'Air reconnaissance in Britain 1977–1984', *Britannia* 18, 1–48.

Meiggs, R. (1973), *Roman Ostia,* 2nd edn, Oxford.

Millar, F. G. B. (1964) *A Study of Cassius Dio,* Oxford.

—— (1981) 'The world of the *Golden Ass'*, *JRS* 71, 63–75.

—— (1982) 'Emperors, frontiers and foreign relations, 31 B.C. to A.D. 378', *Britannia* 13, 1–23.

Mitteis, L. and Wilcken, U. (1912) *Grundzüge und Chrestomathie der Papyruskunde,* 2 vols, Leipzig and Berlin.

Musurillo, H. A. (1972) *The Acts of the Christian Martyrs,* Oxford.

Osier, J. (1977) 'The emergence of third century equestrian military commanders', *Latomus* 36, 674–87.

Parker, H. M. D. (1958) *The Roman Legions* (revised edn), Cambridge.

Passerini, A. (1939) *Le coorti pretorie,* Rome.

Petrikovits, H. von (1958) 'Vetera', *RE* XVI, cols 1801–34.

Pflaum, H.-G. (1976) 'Zur reform des Kaisers Gallienus', *Historia* 25, 109–17.

Pitts, L. F. and St Joseph, J. K. (1985) *Inchtuthil: The Roman Legionary Fortress Excavations 1952–65,* Gloucester.

Rainbird, J. S. (1986) 'The fire stations of imperial Rome', *PBSR* 54, 147–69.

Rea, J. (1977) 'Troops for Mauretania', *ZPE* 26, 223–7.

Reddé, M. (1986) *Mare Nostrum. Les infrastructures, le dispositif et l'histoire de la marine militaire sous l'empire romain,* École française de Rome.

Richmond, I. A. (1935) 'Trajan's army on Trajan's column' *PBSR* 13, 1–40 (reissued with preface and bibliography by M. Hassall, 1982), British School at Rome, London.

Richmond, I. A. and Gillam, J. P. (1951) 'The temple of Mithras at Carrawburgh', *AA,* 4th ser. 29, 1–92.

Roxan, M. M. (1978) *Roman Military Diplomas 1954–1977,* University of London, Institute of Archaeology Occasional Publication No. 2, London.

—— (1981) 'The distribution of Roman military diplomas', *Epig. Stud.* 12, 265–86.

—— (1985) *Roman Military Diplomas 1978–84,* University of London, Institute of Archaeology Occasional Publication No. 9, London.

—— (1986) 'Observations on the reasons for changes in formula in diplomas circa AD 140', in Eck and Wolf, *Heer und Integrationspolitik: Die römischen Militärdiplome als historische Quelle,* Cologne and Vienna, pp. 265–92.

Saddington, D.B. (1975) 'The development of the Roman auxiliary forces from Augustus to Trajan', *ANRW* II.3, 176–201.

—— (1982) *The Development of the Roman Auxiliary Forces from Caesar to Vespasian, 49 BC–AD 79,* Harare.

Saller, R. P. (1980) 'Promotion and patronage in equestrian careers', *JRS* 70, 44–63.

—— (1982) *Personal Patronage under the Early Empire,* Cambridge.

Salway, P. (1965) *The Frontier People of Roman Britain,* Cambridge.

Saxer, R. (1967) *Untersuchungen zu den Vexillationen des römischen Kaiserheeres von Augustus bis Diokletian* (= *Epig. Stud.* 1), Cologne and Graz.

Select bibliography 255

Sherk, R. K. (1974) 'Roman geographical exploration and military maps', *ANRW* II.1, 534–62.
Smith, R. E. (1958) *Service in the post-Marian Roman Army*, Manchester.
Speidel, M. A. (1992) 'Roman army pay scales', *JRS* 82, 87–106.
Speidel, M.P. (1965) *Die Equites Singulares Augusti*, Bonn.
—— (1970) 'The captor of Decebalus', *JRS*, 60, 142–53 (= *Roman Army Studies*, 173–87).
—— (1973) 'The pay of the auxilia', *JRS* 63, 141–7 (= *RAS*, 83–9).
—— (1976a) 'Citizen cohorts in the Roman imperial army', *TAPA*, 106, 339–48 (= *RAS*, 91–100).
—— (1976b) 'Eagle-bearer and trumpeter', *BJ*, 176, 123–63 (= *RAS*, 3–43).
—— (1977) 'The Roman army in Arabia', *ANRW* II.8, 687–730 (= *RAS*, 229–72).
—— (1978a) 'The cult of the Genii in the Roman army and a new military deity', *ANRW* II.16.2, 1542–55 (= *RAS*, 353–68).
—— (1978b) *Guards of the Roman Armies*, Bonn.
—— (1980) 'Legionaries from Asia Minor', *ANRW* II.7.2, 730–46 (= *RAS*, 45–63).
—— (1981a) 'Ala Maurorum? Colloquial names for Roman army units', *Anagennesis* 1, 89–92 (= *RAS*, 109–110).
—— (1981b) 'The prefect's horse-guards and the supply of weapons to the Roman army', Proceedings of the XVI Int. Cong. of Papyr., 405–9 (= *RAS*, 329–32).
—— (1982a) 'The career of a legionary', *TAPA* 112, 209–14 (= *RAS*, 197–202).
—— (1982b) 'Auxiliary units named after their commanders: four new cases from Egypt', *Aegyptus* 62, 165–72 (= *RAS*, 101–8).
—— (1984) *Roman Army Studies* I, Amsterdam.
Starr, C. G. (1960) *The Roman Imperial Navy 31 B.C.–A.D. 324*, 2nd edn, Ithaca, New York and Cambridge.
Syme, R. (1958) 'Imperator Caesar: A study in nomenclature', *Hist.* 7, 172–88 (= *Roman Papers* I (1979), 361–77, Oxford).
Thulin, C. (1913) *Corpus Agrimensorum Romanorum* 1. i, Leipzig.
Van Berchem, D. (1952) *L'Armée de Dioclétien et la réforme constantinienne*, Paris.
—— (1983) 'Une inscription flavienne du musée d'Antioche', *Museum Helveticum* 40, 185–96.
Vendrand-Voyer, J. (1983) *Normes civiques et métier militaire à Rome sous le principat*, Clermont-Ferrand.
Versnel, H.S. (1970) *Triumphus; An Enquiry into the Origin, Development and Meaning of the Roman Triumph*, Leiden.
Watson, G. R. (1969) *The Roman Soldier*, Bristol.
Webster, G. (1985) *The Roman Imperial Army*, 3rd edn, London.
Whittaker, C.R. (1976) '*Agri Deserti*' in Finley, M.I. (ed.) *Studies in Roman Property*, 137–65, Cambridge.
Wilkes, J. J. (1969) *Dalmatia*, London.
Williams, S. (1985) *Diocletian and the Roman Recovery*, London.
Yadin, Y. (1989) *The Documents from the Bar Kokhba Period in the Cave of Letters: Greek Papyri*, (ed. N. Lewis), Jerusalem.
Zanker, P. (1988) *The Power of Images in the Age of Augustus*, Ann Arbor, Michigan.

Index of translated passages

LITERARY SOURCES

Acts of Maximilianus
   1. 1–5: 5
   2. 8–9: 384
Appian, *Civil Wars*
   5. 17: 302
Apuleius, *The Golden Ass*
   9. 39; 42; 10. 1; 13: 291
Arrian, *Ectaxis contra Alanos*
   1–11: 153
   11–31: 159
   Periplous
   6. 1–2: 145
   9. 3–5: 146
   Tactica
   40: 15
Augustus, *Res Gestae*
   3. 3: 320
   4. 1; 3: 135
   4. 2: 128
   15. 3–16: 19
   17: 18
   28: 344
Aurelius Victor, *The Caesars*
   33. 33: 377
Cassius Dio Cocceianus
   40. 14: 151
   40. 18: 213
   49. 30: 160
   53. 11: 303
   53. 25: 345
   55. 23: 143
   56. 42: 120
   60. 15: 306
   60. 24: 255

   64. 9: 309
   65. 14: 221
   68. 23: 131
   68. 32: 116
   69. 9: 122
   71, 3: 26
   71. 3: 163
   74. 11: 311
   75. 2: 312
   76. 15: 313
   77. 3: 23
   77. 13: 124
   80. 2: 316
Codex of Justinian, CJ
   1. 18. 1: 283
   2. 50(51). 2: 274
   3. 37. 2: 28
   3. 44. 5: 281
   4. 32. 6: 29
   4. 51. 1: 27
   5. 16. 2: 280
   5. 65. 1: 332
   6. 21. 2: 266
   6. 21. 5: 267
   6. 21. 7: 268
   6. 21. 14: 398
   6. 21. 15: 399
   7. 64. 9: 387
   9. 9. 15: 261
   9. 23. 5: 282
   10. 53(52). 1: 169
   10. 55(54). 3: 388
   12. 33(34). 1: 277
   12. 35(36). 3: 334

INSCRIPTIONS AND DIPLOMAS

PAPYRI, OSTRACA, AND WRITING TABLETS

COINS

Index of names and subjects

Prominent figures are cited under the names by which they are usually known, others under their gentile names. Auxiliary *alae* and cohorts are cited as they appear in the text, with no attempt to produce a consolidated list.

CPSIA information can be obtained at www.ICGtesting.com
Printed in the USA
BVOW071558170112

280768BV00001B/15/A